AERIAL RECONNAISSANCE FOR ARCHAEOLOGY

Aerial reconnaissance for archaeology

Edited by

D. R. Wilson

1975

Research Report No. 12   **The Council for British Archaeology**

© The Council for British Archaeology 1975
7 Marylebone Road
London NW1 5HA

ISBN 0 900312 29 7

PRINTED BY DERRY AND SONS LIMITED   CANAL STREET   NOTTINGHAM   ENGLAND

Contents

Foreword

The science of geology is often referred to in histories of scientific thought as *the English science*—with some justification when we consider the work of James Hutton, William 'Strata' Smith, and Charles Lyell. In the same way, the scientific study of the ground from the air and the interpretation of air photographs in the service of archaeology could well be called another English science if we recollect the work of Elsdale, Wellcome, Beazeley, Hamshaw Thomas, Crawford, and Allen in the sixty years between 1880 and 1940. This work laid the foundations of archaeological air-photography, and in emphasizing its importance we in no way forget the achievements of Rey, Wiegand, and Poidebard.

It was therefore appropriate and proper that an international conference on Aerial Reconnaissance for Archaeology should be held in London, and I was happy to be its President, to welcome the scholars who attended from Britain, the Continent, and America, to attend with interest its proceedings, and to applaud the decision to hold further conferences of the same kind in future. This volume, edited by Mr David Wilson of the Department of Aerial Photography in the University of Cambridge and amply illustrated with photographs taken in Belgium, Denmark, France, Germany, Great Britain, and Ireland, contains most of the papers and serves as a valuable archive, as well as a true record of the Conference.

It was the 1914–18 War that gave Beazeley, Hamshaw Thomas, and Crawford the opportunity to appreciate the value of air photography. From the First World War until the Second air photography for archaeological purposes was concentrated either on single vertical views, used with great effect in Crawford and Keiller's volume *Wessex from the Air* (Oxford, 1928), or else on oblique photography, exemplified above all by the fine photographs of Major Allen. During the Second World War many scientists—archaeologists, geographers, geologists, such as the late Professors Linton, Wager, Garrod, and Powell, besides those like myself, Professor St Joseph, Professor Stuart Piggott, Professor Emeritus Grahame Clark, and many another, who are still surviving—learnt a new form of air-photographic interpretation, the study of stereoscopic cover of wide areas. This lesson is now being learnt in civil life, and one of the most interesting points made during the Conference was the need for total vertical cover with stereoscopic overlap of large areas, whether they include known sites or not.

The Conference was concerned, among other things, with the future of archaeological air photography. We have in this country several centres dealing with the landscape from the air, notably the Department of Aerial Photography in the University of Cambridge, and (for archaeological aspects) the Air Photographs Unit of the National Monuments Record of the Royal Commission on Historical Monuments (England). Should there in the future be a single central Institute serving and supported by Universities and Government agencies, where all photographic cover of Britain could be kept? This is a problem which the Conference naturally did not resolve: it is a problem which is not restricted to Britain, but affects all other countries where air photographs are used for the location, study, and surveillance of archaeological sites.

Glyn Daniel
Chairman of the Symposium

Preface

This volume contains papers given at a Symposium held at Fortress House, London, on 2, 3, and 4 April 1974.

The Symposium originated as an idea of Arnold Baker in 1972 and was planned by a steering committee (later to become the organizers), under my chairmanship. It was felt at the outset that this should be a joint project involving the Royal Commission on Historical Monuments (England), the Council for British Archaeology, and the Extramural Department of the University of Birmingham, that it should be held in London, and that flyers from other countries should be invited to speak and take part. The committee elected John Hampton as secretary, and we all owe him a deep debt of gratitude for his hard work over a long period and his great patience. The administration of the Symposium was in the capable hands of my administrative assistant, Miss Margaret McLean.

It was decided that attendance was to be by invitation, so that all those present were people who were engaged in taking aerial photographs or using them and, as this was interpreted fairly liberally, there were no protests from anyone who felt he had been overlooked.

The CBA wished to interest town planners, and it was agreed that the first of the three days would be designed as a separate one-day conference for them, although we hoped that some would be with us for the whole time and so it proved to be. The choice of Professor Glyn Daniel as President was a very happy one and added wit and elegance to our proceedings.

We are grateful to all our contributors, to the chairmen of the sessions, and the staff of the National Monuments Record who did such valiant work during the three days, and their friendly help was much appreciated by everyone. To the Commissioners of the RCHM we owe a special debt for arranging a splendid reception at which the Chairman, Lord Adeane, received us; it was graciously attended by Mr. Charles Morris, MP, at that time the Minister of State for Urban Affairs, Department of the Environment, and our most distinguished archaeologist, Sir Mortimer Wheeler. The Committee remained in being after the Symposium to publish the papers and to implement the resolutions passed at the last session; this latter task has now been passed over to the CBA. Finally, this volume could not have been brought into being without the skilful editing of Mr. David Wilson, to whom we are also extremely grateful.

Graham Webster
Chairman of the
Symposium Organizing
Committee

Resolutions of the Symposium

The following motions were put to the Symposium and carried *nemine contradicente*:

1 The Symposium asks the Organizing Committee to arrange for the publication of the papers given to the Symposium.

2 The Symposium asks the Organizing Committee to set up an international committee for the establishment of closer collaboration and to organize meetings and other activities.

3 The Organizing Committee is instructed to press for additional resources to be made available in Britain for greater air cover and improved storage, retrieval, and analysis of photographs and to make them more widely available to government departments and their agencies and to local government bodies and others, so as to enable fuller assessments to be made in problems of conservation, development of rural amenities, and rescue archaeology.

The Organizing Committee

Graham Webster, MA, PhD, FSA, AMA
(Dept. of Extra-Mural Studies, Univ. of Birmingham)
—*Chairman*

W. A. Baker, FSA

Miss B. de Cardi, OBE, BA FSA
(Council for British Archaeology)

C. Farthing, OBE, BA, FSA
(National Monuments Record)

P. J. Fowler, MA, FSA
(Council for British Archaeology)

J. N. Hampton, FSA
(National Monuments Record)—*Secretary*

P. Marchant, BA
(Council for British Archaeology)

J. Pickering, AFC, FGS

Professor J. K. S. St. Joseph, OBE, MA, ScD, LLD,
PhD, FSA
(University of Cambridge)

D. R. Wilson, MA, BLitt, FSA
(University of Cambridge)

Miss M. McLean, MA
(Dept. of Extra-Mural Studies, Univ. of Birmingham)
—*Assistant Secretary*

Soil and crop marks in the recognition of archaeological sites by air photography

R. J. A. Jones and R. Evans

Synopsis

The environmental factors causing soil and crop marks in the British Isles are described. Marks develop best in arable areas of eastern and southern England and eastern Scotland. The major cause of bare soil marks is the occurrence of light-coloured subsoil, particularly that derived from chalk, within plough depth. Crop marks occur mainly in shallow, loamy soils which have rooting depths between 30 and 60 cm, and are caused by soil moisture deficit interacting with nutrient supply and soil depth.

Efficiency in the search for sites of antiquity from the air could be greatly improved by concentrating photography into periods of high potential soil moisture deficit (greater than 50 mm). Good prediction of such periods can be made from short-period rainfall and potential transpiration data.

INTRODUCTION

Soil and crop marks, as recorded by air photography, have been reported in the literature since the end of World War I, notably by a few workers who recognized that the technique would be important in archaeological research (Crawford and Keiller, 1928; Crawford, 1933, 1938). Much has since been written on the occurrence of soil and crop marks of archaeological interest (Bradford, 1957; Crawford, 1939; Riley, 1945, 1946; St. Joseph, 1961, 1965), but, although information on ground conditions is given where available, few attempts have been made to explain systematically either natural or archaeological soil and crop patterns (J. G. Evans, 1972).

In this paper the factors causing the development in the British Isles of soil and crop marks, as they appear on panchromatic (black and white) air photographs, are discussed.

Most natural and archaeological marks are recorded in the arable areas of eastern Britain; they occur sporadically elsewhere depending on local soils and climate. In the cool wet west of Britain pastoral farming predominates and soil and crop marks are uncommon. Rainfall in these areas is usually in excess of plant needs, with the result that arable crops are only grown on light-textured freely drained soils.

Rather than classifying the marks on aerial photographs into bare soil, damp, crop, and parch marks, as defined by Riley (1946), Bradford (1957), and St. Joseph (1965), a primary distinction is made here between bare soil marks and crop marks.

BARE SOIL MARKS

Bare soil marks appear on panchromatic photographs as sharp tonal changes due to differences in surface colour and reflection. They can be photographed from the time of ploughing until crop cover is almost complete, a period which can be of six months' duration.

Soil colours are described using the Munsell Color System (Munsell Color Co., 1954) in terms of hue, value, and chroma (USDA, 1951, 194–203). In the notation, for example 10YR 4/4, the hue, 10YR, denotes the relation to yellow and red; the value, 4/, the relative lightness of a colour, from 0 (black) to 10 (white); and the chroma, /4, the strength or purity of a colour, or departure from a neutral of the same lightness.

Subtle colour changes on the ground are often enhanced on panchromatic air photographs. The colour value is more important than its strength or chroma. For example, there is a greater distinction on a photograph between 10YR 2/1 (black) and 10YR 3/1 (very dark grey) than between 10YR 3/1, 10YR 3/2 (very dark greyish-brown), and 10YR 3/4 (dark yellowish-brown). Colour differences of a single value appear clearly on panchromatic air photographs. The red-sensitive panchromatic films in common use show the redder 10YR colours as lighter tones on photographs than the less red 2·5Y colours of the same value and chroma, provided that the surface reflects light uniformly.

Tonal contrasts on photographs vary with soil moisture content. For example, on shallow soils over chalk they are greater at moisture contents of between 5% and 6% when compared with contrasts in the same soils at moisture contents of 1–2% and 19–22%.

Marks occur on many soil types (R. Evans, 1972), but are most common on soils that are very reflective, for example, chalk soils or Silt Fen soils, in which the underlying subsoil is contrasting enough in colour to appear when ploughed to the surface. Ploughing depths vary from region to region, from 10 to 45 cm, and these differences govern the extent to which subsoils are exposed.

The difference in reflectivity between clay soils and clay infill in ditches is usually very small. Marks are rarely recorded on these soils unless they are brown in colour (Riley, 1946), as, for example, near Warboys, Huntingdonshire, where a Roman villa is clearly discernible on the edge of the fen. Moreover, on many sites with clayey soils buildings were of wood which perished leaving little evidence other than a few stains (Hurst, 1956).

Bare soil marks, revealing ring-ditches, ancient field systems, and settlements, are mainly restricted to shallow soils on chalk and Silt Fen (Riley, 1945), but ploughed-out medieval ridge and furrow is commonly seen on soils developed in many parent materials, for example Keuper Marl, boulder clay, Lias clay, Northampton sands, and Silt Fen. In modern

The authors are with the Soil Survey of England and Wales, at the Rothamsted Experimental Station, Harpenden (Herts.).

ploughing of old ridge and furrow, dark organic-rich surface soil is transferred to the troughs whilst the plough cuts into and exposes the underlying *B* horizon on the ridges. The former troughs appear dark and the former ridges light on aerial photographs. The contrast is faint if the surface and subsoil colours are similar but distinct where the subsoil is light in colour, as on chalky boulder clay.

Some soil marks are caused by variations in surface stoniness. In general a surface cover of more than 25 % with large variations over small distances is necessary. Soils that fulfil these conditions often have rock within 30 or 35 cm of the surface where frost action moves stones to the surface (Corte, 1966). Rainwash and weathering remove soil adhering to the surface of stones, and marks are best developed at the end of the winter or in early spring. Deeper soils appear clearly as dark tones on photographs of stony ground; Bowen and Butler (1960) have recognized dark tones on air photographs as representing old field baulks.

Surface roughness does not usually affect the appearance of soil-marks, which show as well in freshly ploughed fields as on rolled surfaces. More important than roughness is direction of ploughing; if this is east–west, tonal contrast on vertical air photographs is less, as much light is reflected away from the camera. However, soil marks may be obscured on freshly ploughed surfaces if wetter darker clods are exposed.

CROP MARKS

For crop marks to be recorded by air photography, growth differences must be sharply developed within one crop. Growth factors must therefore change suddenly within a field or group of fields so that they become limiting in some places. Crop marks on panchromatic air photographs appear as tonal changes and usually reflect differences in leaf area index,* plant colour and stem height.

Before examining the occurrence and formation of crop marks, it is helpful to examine the factors affecting crop growth in general.

FACTORS AFFECTING CROP GROWTH

Plants grow by converting solar energy, water, and soil nutrients into vegetative matter. Crudely, photosynthesis of carbon dioxide and water produces carbohydrate for the manufacture of plant cells, the absorption of light by the chlorophyll of green plants providing energy for conversion.

Climate

Solar radiation, air and soil temperature, and precipitation are the primary controls on potential crop growth (Hogg, 1971). Topographical and altitudinal modifications of these parameters are significant secondary effects and produce a distinct range of mesoclimate in Britain.

The implications of regional climatic contrast for the growth of plants are evident by comparing the 'growing season' in the north of Britain with that in the south. At Falmouth this period is estimated to be 365 days, whilst along the north Northumberland coast it is 245 days (Miller, 1962); on the summit of Ben Nevis in

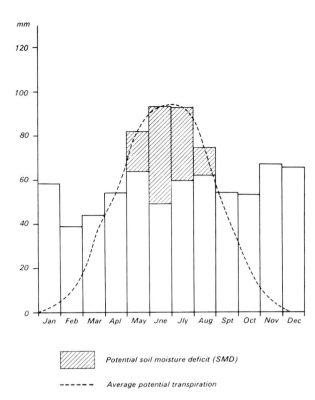

Fig. 1   *Mean monthly rainfall 1959–72 and annual potential transpiration for Newport (Salop.)*

Scotland, which experiences mean monthly temperatures of 0°C or below for almost six months of the year, it is virtually nil (Buchan, 1905).

Regional variation in precipitation is equally significant: Keswick has an annual average rainfall total of 1470 mm whereas Cambridge receives 560 mm (Meteorological Office, 1958). Temperature is the most severe limit on crop growth in the British Isles and accounts for regional differences, but it rarely causes measurable variations on a field scale. These are commonly due to varying supplies of available soil moisture. Rainfall maps do not show effective wetness, and predictions of the soil moisture available for plant growth depend on knowing the precipitation, the water holding capacity of the soil, the availability of ground water, and evaporation and transpiration. Penman (1948) gives a method of using standard weather data to estimate the 'potential transpiration' rate of a crop; it is purely a meteorological concept and has also been called 'potential evaporation' or 'potential evapotranspiration' (Thornthwaite, 1948). It is independent of soil or plant factors and is considered to be the actual rate of water use by an extended area of green crop, actively growing, completely shading the ground, and adequately supplied with water around the roots. It is much less variable than rainfall and, since it is measured in the same units, subtraction of the data from rainfall totals gives the minimum water available for plant growth in any period.

When rainfall exceeds potential transpiration, the difference (Fig. 1) represents a potential soil moisture surplus (SMS). Excess water in the soil causes a lack of oxygen in the rooting zone and consequently

---

*LAI = area of leaf surface (one surface only) in a crop stand covering unit area of soil.

suppresses many of the oxygenated processes essential for plant growth. However, in the study of crop-marks by air photography a deficit of water in the soil is more important as a growth inhibitor than an excess. Detailed consideration is therefore given to soil moisture deficit and its effect on plant growth.

Soil moisture deficit

When potential transpiration exceeds rainfall, the difference (Fig. 1) is called a 'potential soil moisture deficit'—SMD (Green, 1964; Smith, 1967). The actual soil moisture deficit is more variable and can depart from the calculated potential SMD for a number of reasons. When a young crop sprouts it does not completely cover the ground; the water transpired must be added to that evaporated from the surface. If the latter is dry, the sum of the two components will be less than the potential figure, and if the soil is moist, it can be more. Departure of the actual from the potential transpiration rate can also occur when cereal crops reach maturity, lose their greenness, and stop transpiring.

Actual soil moisture deficit is difficult to measure, the procedures necessary being complicated and time-consuming to conduct. However, the size and frequency of potential soil moisture deficits can be easily calculated using mean monthly rainfall data and tabulated mean potential transpiration figures estimated by Penman's method (Smith, 1967). With a knowledge of water requirements of various crops at different stages in their growth, these data can be used as a substitute for actual figures to predict the likelihood of water stress.

The potential soil moisture deficit at the end of a particular month is calculated by accumulating values of the deficits for the previous months. An estimate of the potential deficit obtained in this way should only be regarded as an approximation to the actual deficit because a short period of deficit can be obscured in the water balance data for a month with an overall soil moisture surplus. Similarly, a short period of soil moisture surplus can remain undetected in the data for a month with an overall soil moisture deficit.

As soon as an actual soil moisture deficit develops, a growing plant begins to draw on the available water stored in the soil. The amount of available water per unit volume of soil, usually measured in mm per cm of soil, is calculated as the difference between the volume of water held per cm at field capacity (FC) and at the permanent wilting point (PWP) (Russell, 1961, 404; Salter and Haworth, 1961). When all the available water in a particular depth of soil is exhausted, growth should theoretically cease and the plant should wilt (the PWP has been reached). Several factors, however, affect the validity of this general statement. Firstly, different plant species and varieties vary in their response to severe moisture stress; some simply cease to grow but continue to transpire at a much lower rate, while others rapidly wilt (May and Milthorpe, 1962; Bingham, 1966). Secondly, the effects of moisture stress depend on the stage of growth; the water requirements of cereals are much greater before heading than after. Thirdly, crops may escape drought by drawing on an additional source of available moisture at depths between 60 and 90 cm (a ground-water table) through deep tap roots, or by reaching maturity before the SMD becomes limiting (May and Milthorpe, 1962). Since the major concentrations of roots and nutrients are in the top 30–40 cm, exhaustion of available soil moisture supplies to about 40 cm probably checks the growth of most temperate crops. Deep tap roots, however, often provide minimal supplies insufficient for maintaining maximum growth but adequate for plant survival. Any local barriers to rooting, such as an impenetrable layer (pan) or rock at shallow depth, will thus allow differential exhaustion of available water and hence differential growth.

Clay soils retain more water than sands and loams but, surprisingly, the available water in the top 50 cm of different soil types does not vary greatly and is largest in the surface horizon, which contains the organic matter. More important than any small variations in available water capacity between soils of different particle size (Table I) is the manner in which the water is released. In coarse sand all the water held is readily available and plants make rapid growth until all is transpired; they then suffer a severe and sudden deficit resulting in death if the rooting zone is not soon rewetted. On heavy clay, however, the water is held at progressively increasing tension following the onset of a soil moisture deficit and the reduction in the growth rate occurs more slowly until the permanent wilting point is reached (May and Milthorpe, 1962). Plants therefore continue to accumulate dry matter for a much longer time on clays than on sands, explaining why crop marks develop suddenly in sandy soils and slowly or not at all in clays.

During water stress the growths of plant organs are differently affected—leaves first, then stems, and finally

TABLE I   **Available water in soils of different particle size**

Soil Group	Soil Series	Dominant particle-size class	*Available water for given depths of soil (mm)*		
			0–30 cm	*0–50 cm*	*0–80 cm*
	Bridgnorth	Sandy	47·9	65·7	—
Brown earths	Newport	Sandy	60·0	79·0	101·2
	Wick	Coarse loamy	58·6	79·1	94·1
Gleyed brown earths	Salwick	Fine loamy	62·1	93·3	121·5
	Whimple	Fine silty over clayey	59·9	82·7	114·8
	Clifton	Fine loamy	64·6	92·3	124·3
Surface water gley soils	Salop	Fine loamy over clayey	57·8	76·9	106·6
	Spetchley	Clayey	51·0	77·5	120·8
	Crewe	Clayey	49·9	71·4	105·6
		Mean	56·9	79·8	111·1

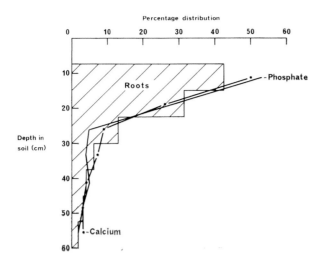

Fig. 2   Distribution of barley roots in the soil, compared with their uptake of phosphate and calcium from different depths (after Russell, 1971)

roots—and with restoration of full water supply this order is reversed (May and Milthorpe, 1962). Orchard (1961, 1964) confirmed that moisture stress first affects the growth of leaves in wheat and barley. Variations of leaf area index are recognized as the cause of most distinct crop marks due mainly to water stress.

The importance of potential soil moisture deficit data for predicting periods when crops will be short of water was shown by Penman (1952), who found that the meteorological estimate of water use by sugar beet was in acceptable agreement with values obtained by soil sampling. In a series of long-term experiments into irrigation need at Woburn (Bedfordshire) Penman (1962, 1970) found that a potential SMD of 50 mm, which corresponds to the available water in the top 30–40 cm of many soils, in practice limits the growth of grass and arable crops. He concluded that this value is probably applicable to a fairly broad range of soils in that it is determined by a combination of rooting depths of plants and depth of soil carrying nutrients.

Although climate determines the potential growth of any crop on a site, actual growth is controlled by soil fertility and is always less than the potential figure.

Soil properties

Soil properties affecting growth include the physical properties of depth, porosity, consistence, degree of compaction, stoniness, structure, and particle size; the chemical properties include the nature of the mineral fraction, the kind and amount of organic matter and macro- and micro-nutrients.

The physical properties of the soil directly affect crop growth through their influence on the nature of the rooting medium and consequently on the development of root systems. Their effects on the water and nutrients available to plants are, however, more important in considerations of differential growth.

Plant growth depends on the availability of nutrients needed for metabolism. Three factors control the absorption of nutrients by plant roots in the soil: firstly, an adequate supply of macro- and micro-nutrients essential for plant growth; secondly, a root system which penetrates and ramifies throughout a moderately deep rooting zone; and thirdly, enough water to allow the transfer of nutrients in the soil to the uptake sites, translocation within the plant itself, and the operation of uptake mechanisms at the root surface.

The macro-nutrients are nitrogen, phosphorus, potassium, calcium, magnesium, and sulphur. Nitrogen has the most important visual effect on crops since it governs dry matter production and greenness. Phosphorus is essential for many metabolic processes and a deficiency can have a striking effect. Calcium plays a major role as a constituent of the cell wall; it controls acidity and consequently the many chemical reactions taking place in the soil–plant system. It affects the microbial population responsible for many important processes such as nitrogen fixation and controls the activity of earthworms, which improve aeration and structure of the root medium generally (Russell, 1961, 442). Magnesium is vital to plants because it is an essential constituent of chlorophyll and is also regarded as a carrier of phosphorus (Salmon, 1963).

Because of weathering and fertilizer application, the macro-nutrients are present mainly in the top 30 cm (Viets, 1972). However, nitrogen and calcium in forms readily available to plants are easily leached from the surface soil and under certain conditions can accumulate at depth. The main root concentrations of cereals are also found in the top 30 cm, related to the availability of nutrients (Cannell and Drew, 1973). Russell (1971) has shown that 90% of roots in a barley crop are found in the top 30 cm of soil, and further investigations showed that the distribution of roots down a soil profile correlates strongly with the uptake of calcium and phosphate (Fig. 2).

The micro-nutrients or trace elements include iron, manganese, zinc, copper, boron, and molybdenum, but their effects on crop growth are usually subtle and not always readily seen on air photographs.

THE OCCURRENCE OF CROP MARKS

Marks occur in grassland, cereals, and rotation crops such as potatoes and sugar beet. They are recorded mainly in eastern and southern England and eastern Scotland.

Soil type and depth in the formation of crop marks

In the British Isles, by far the largest number of crop marks is located on river terraces (Bowen and Butler, 1960, 11; Riley, 1943; Webster and Hobley, 1965). Marks are also frequently reported on chalk, in the silt fens of East Anglia, but rarely on Jurassic limestone, Keuper Marl, or other clayey parent materials.

At 26 localities (Fig. 3) in south–west Scotland, west Wales, East Anglia, the west Midlands, and Lincolnshire natural crop marks have been noted on aerial photographs, and subsequently soil investigations have been made (Soil Survey Officers). At all the sites surface soils are loamy, incorporating drift, and twelve have a sharp subsoil change, either to rock or an impenetrable layer (pan) at 30–40 cm. Gravels underlie 23 of the sites, three being over limestone, or sandstone and shale (Culm Measures). Particle-size class ranges from sandy loam and sandy clay-loam through loam and clay loam to silt loam and silty clay-loam (USDA, 1951, 209); some of the sites are on peaty soils. Soil

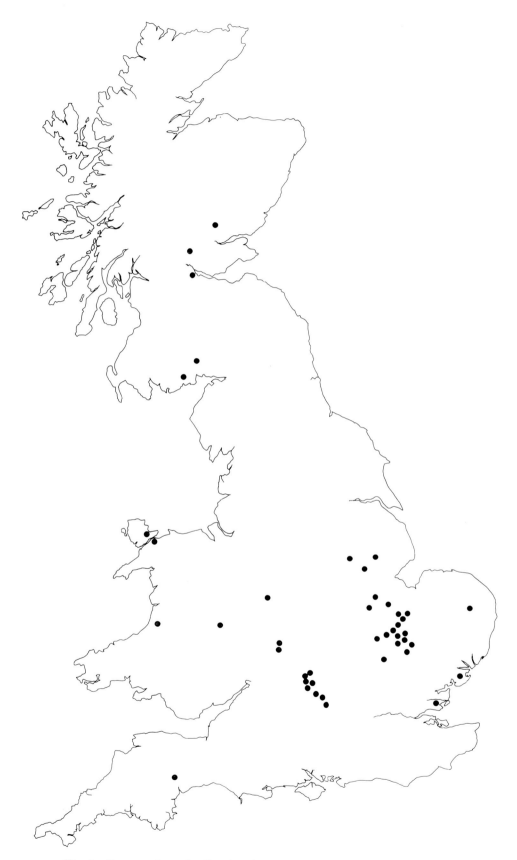

Fig. 3   Crop marks and soils: distribution of sites studied

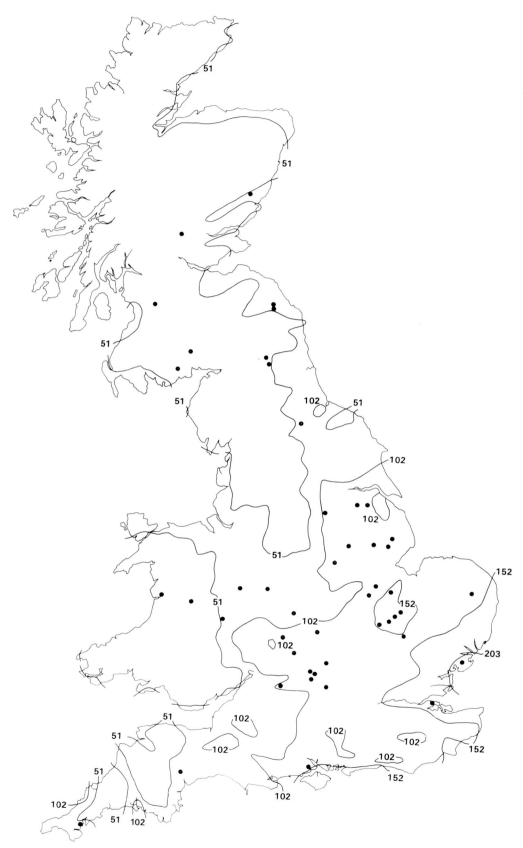

Fig. 4   Soil moisture deficit (SMD), after Green (1966)

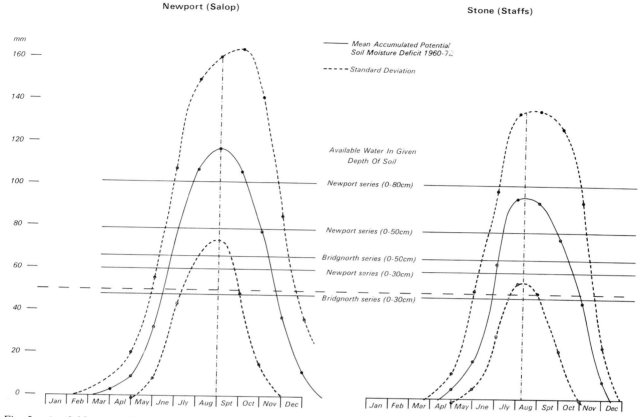

Fig. 5   Available water in two sandy soils in relation to the accumulated soil moisture deficit for two localities in Midland England

depths are between 10 cm and 100 cm, but in seventeen cases are between 30 and 60 cm. At only three sites are soils deeper than 60 cm.

Depths of soil were also measured or estimated for 36 archaeological sites where crop marks have been photographed.* All the sites are on gravels of riverine or glacial origin. At 34 of them soil depth over gravel is less than 76 cm, and at 28 depth is less than 61 cm; no site has less than 15 cm over gravel. These data are in accord with those obtained for the 26 sites described above where natural crop marks have been observed. Soil depth is more important in the formation of crop marks than particle-size class. This was shown from a study of two localities where natural polygonal patterns appear on soils derived from gravel and sown to the same crop. In a field near Chatteris (Cambridgeshire), a pattern is recorded every year on air photographs; sandy or loamy peat overlies gravel to an average depth, from 30 bores, of 56 cm (st. dev. 14 cm) in Fordham soils (Seale, in press). In a nearby field a pattern has only been photographed once in ten years in soils of the Adventurers' series (Hodge and Seale, 1966), which have an average depth of 84 cm (st. dev. 11 cm). Fordham soils cover 23% of the photographed area and Adventurers' soils 32%. In total, the ice-wedge patterns cover 40% of the Fordham soils, but only 7% of the Adventurers' soils.

A pattern in an oat crop was observed from the ground on 11 July 1969, on a river terrace near Colne (Huntingdonshire); it was related to a difference in crop height of 15 cm between different parts of the field.

In adjacent fields sown to wheat and barley the pattern was not visible. On air photographs taken on 4 July 1969, the pattern is clear in the field of oats and faintly visible in the wheat and barley fields. Augering on a grid pattern showed that the average depth of soil over gravel, from 30 bores, in the field of oats is 57 cm (st. dev. 13 cm), whereas in the barley field it is 67 cm (st. dev. 17 cm). Both soils are sandy clay-loams.

Crop marks induced by soil moisture stress

Estimates of potential soil moisture deficit were obtained for 45 localities in England, Wales and Scotland where crop marks have been recorded (Fig. 4). For some of the localities figures were calculated for a number of years. Except at six sites, crop marks did not appear if the potential SMD was less than 40 mm. At sites where marks were recorded every year they began to show when the potential SMD was between 50 mm and 65 mm. The range of potential SMD was wide (40–295 mm) but 32% of all photographs of crop marks were taken when the potential SMD was in the range 50–100 mm, 41% between 100 mm and 150 mm, and 20% in the range 150–200 mm. At some places crop marks were faint at the higher SMD's, presumably because the whole crop, including the plants in areas of deeper soil, over fossil ice-wedges or infilled ditches, was under moisture stress. Generally, where data for available water and potential SMD exist, they are in accord, the shallower and coarser soils showing marks earlier and at lower SMD's. It should be remembered, however, that once

*The original published references to these sites (Fig. 3) are listed in the Appendix following the bibliography.

a crop has ripened or become senescent, transpiration is negligible and SMD of little importance. At Chatteris (Cambridgeshire) the polygonal pattern was recorded in the Fordham series when there was a potential soil moisture deficit of 50 mm, but it did not show well until this figure exceeded 60 mm. Sequential photography has shown that as the season advanced more and more of the pattern became visible. However, the best patterns were photographed when the potential SMD was 150 mm.

The smaller amounts of available water in shallow soils compared with deeper ones, in relation to potential soil moisture deficit, are shown in Fig. 5. The curves give the variation of potential SMD at Newport (Salop) and Stone (Staffordshire) during the period 1960–1972. Crop growth in a soil of the Bridgnorth series, with 67 mm of available water in a 51 cm rooting zone (Hollis and Hodgson, 1974, 89), would be checked earlier than growth in a soil of the Newport series with 101 mm of available water in the top 80 cm. In both soils, available water would be depleted to a depth of 50 cm by the fourth week in June, in an average year, and the 'period of desiccation' to this depth lasts until the SMD begins to decrease from the maximum value. The soils should get wetter once this point has been passed and there should be no restriction on plant growth, whatever the absolute value of the deficit (Penman, 1971). The 'periods of desiccation' last until early August at Stone and the end of August at Newport. On similar soils of the Ross series in Herefordshire, Hodgson and Palmer (1971, 27) noted differential crop growth in dry years where soil depth is variable over Devonian sandstone, resulting in differential exhaustion of available soil moisture.

Further evidence that crop marks are caused by differences in available soil moisture is given by St Joseph (1961), who noted that crop marks do not appear in the Vale of Glamorgan. This is despite the facts that soils are often shallow (Crampton, 1972, 19), an estimated 42% of the Vale having soils less than 60 cm deep over limestone or a pan, and that buried archaeological sites at shallower depth are known to exist in arable land. In an average year, however, the potential SMD reaches a maximum of 40 mm at the end of June.

Crop type, timeliness, and soil moisture deficit

Crop marks are less commonly recorded in grassland than in cereals. This is partly due to the preponderance of grassland in areas of higher rainfall, where potential soil moisture deficit rarely exceeds 50 mm, and in areas with clay soils, rather than to any fundamental differences in rooting (Weaver, 1926, 142, 208, 232, 244; Russell, 1971). An actual SMD greater than 50 mm reduces the growth of grass because of low uptake of nutrients, particularly nitrogen (Garwood and Williams, 1967). However, marks usually occur in grassland only when deficits are 10–20 mm greater than those which cause marks in cereals.

In most cereals, ear emergence takes place by mid-June or early July, depending on sowing date, and the period prior to this is when moisture stress most severely checks growth (Penman, 1970). Late May, June, and early July are therefore the best times for observing crop marks caused by moisture stress in cereal crops.

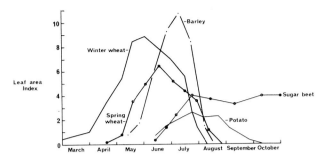

Fig. 6   Change with time in the leaf area index of selected crops (after Watson, 1971)

Barley has a larger leaf area index than wheat (Fig. 6) and the contrast in leaf density between barley plants, under water stress, on shallow soils and adjacent barley plants, adequately supplied with water, on deeper soils is greater than between wheat plants grown in the same conditions. Marks caused by moisture stress therefore show more clearly in barley than in wheat.

In root crops, the leaf area index does not decline markedly in late July or early August (Watson, 1971), as it does in cereals (Fig. 6), and marks therefore show best rather later in the year. Pseudomorph ice-wedges in sugar beet have often been recorded in Essex, for example during September and October 1969, when the potential soil moisture deficit at the end of each month respectively was 280 and 295 mm. The pattern was clearer as moisture stress increased and was probably caused by yellowing of the plants over shallow soils because of manganese deficiency. Such high potential SMD's, however, are not essential for the formation of marks in sugar beet. The potential SMD's calculated from the end of June 1969, when the crop first completely covered the ground, were much less, only 55 and 70 mm on 25 September and 16 October respectively.

Marks rarely appear in fields of potatoes. The leaves of potatoes begin to die after mid-July, resulting in a lowering of the leaf area index, and in many cases this coincides with the period in an average year when the available water in shallow soils would be exhausted. The contrast in leaf density between plants on shallow soils, suffering moisture stress, and those on deeper ones is therefore much reduced.

In cereals the obscuring of crop marks induced by moisture stress is explained by the fact that a heavy shower of rain will stimulate tillering (Rackham, 1972), quickly altering differential growth patterns. This phenomenon was noted by St Joseph (1965), who photographed distinct crop marks on the gravel terrace at Great Shelford, near Cambridge, on 17 June 1960. Tonal contrasts were less marked three days later because 7 mm of rainfall on 19 June removed the restriction on growth and stimulated tillering.

Crop marks and excess soil moisture

Crop marks disappear during the summer when rainfall exceeds evapotranspiration for long enough to bring about a potential soil moisture surplus. However, in soils that are shallow or have an impermeable layer or pan within 60 cm of the surface, crop marks can occur during periods of moisture surplus. Root growth is restricted above the impermeable layer by excess water in the plant-root

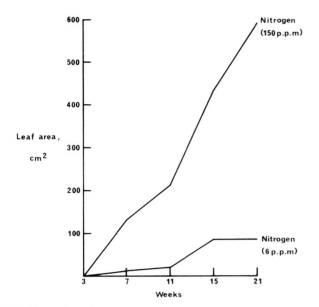

Fig. 7 Effect of available nitrogen on leaf area per plant in timothy (after Langer, 1966)

system which prevents stomatal opening and consequently reduces respiration and photosynthesis (Wright, 1972). Growth of stems and leaves is then checked. Differential growth effects are caused by varying degrees of wetness, which are brought about by the different depths of soil over the impermeable layer. Marks produced by this mechanism usually appear following a wet May and later invasions by weeds often enhance the patterns from the air. Crop marks at six sites in the United Kingdom, photographed when the potential soil moisture deficit was less than 40 mm, were probably caused by excess soil moisture.

Crop marks and plant nutrients

Natural and archaeological crop marks can result from variations in the availability of plant nutrients, particularly nitrogen and calcium. Significant yield responses in cereals are obtained with applications of nitrogen between 0 and 150 kg N per hectare (Cooke, 1967, 227) and hence uneven fertilizer application within this range will have a marked effect. Crop marks on air photographs due to variation in greenness, LAI, and stem height result mainly from differential nitrogen uptake.

Plants growing in deep soil (for example an infilled ditch) have access to larger reserves of soluble nitrogen and soil moisture than plants growing in shallow soil. They are therefore taller, greener, have a larger LAI (Fig. 7, Langer, 1966), a greater number of tillers (Rackham, 1972), and grow for a longer period than those with a shallow rooting zone. It is the dense crop stand viewed against a less dense background which forms the crop mark.

Crop lodging—the collapse of plants because of over-vigorous growth—results from excess nitrogen uptake. It occurs around ditches where nitrate-rich drainage waters are concentrated and it shows clearly on photographs. As well as reducing the greenness of the crop, a nitrogen deficiency inhibits tillering in cereals and reduces stem growth in potatoes (Wallace,

1961, 65). These effects show in the less favoured areas within a field, where a lack of water or a shallow rooting depth suppresses uptake.

On shallow chalk and Silt Fen soils, in Lincolnshire and East Anglia, dark-toned soil marks on air photographs are gradually replaced by dark-toned crop marks in May and June. Growth is earlier and more vigorous on the deep dark-coloured soils, which are less calcareous than the surrounding lighter-coloured soils. In many cases, the dark-coloured soils occur where ditches have been infilled. The differential growth is caused by differential availability of nitrogen related to variations in pH. In calcareous soils, with a pH value greater than 7·5, a build-up of non-available nitrites occurs following heavy applications of ammonium fertilizers because the high pH's severely inhibit the oxidation, by bacteria, of the nitrites to nitrates (Russell, 1961, 301). This effect is accentuated in spring when the highly reflective light-coloured soils radiate more energy back to the sky and stay colder than the dark-coloured soils, because the oxidation of nitrite is slower at lower temperatures.

Correcting calcium deficiency can by itself remove deficiencies of other elements, improving their availability. For example, phosphorus becomes unavailable at low pH and its absorption is optimal at about pH 6·5. The mortar present in a buried wall can supply calcium and encourage differential crop growth. In grassland, increased availability of calcium is occasionally seen from the air as an increase in clover. Crop marks, usually not of archaeological origin, may be caused by differential availability of other nutrients. Variations in the availability of phosphorus are seen as growth and colour differences. Purpling in stems and leaves of wheat and barley and thin growth, with scorch of leaflets in potatoes, are characteristic of areas where deficiencies occur.

Magnesium deficiency has a lesser effect on growth than deficiencies of nitrogen, calcium, or phosphorus. The visual symptoms are again variations in colour in the leaves of cereals and bright-yellow chlorosis in those of root crops (Wallace, 1961, 68, 69); yields are increased by correcting deficiency (Bolton and Slope, 1971).

In arable crops, manganese and copper are the two micro-nutrients which most commonly produce marked visual symptoms when deficient. Manganese deficiency is induced by high pH (above 6·5) and is generally found on organic rich sands, shallow fen peats, or alluvial silts and clays. Wetness is also a contributory factor during early growth of cereals; it causes chlorosis, suppression of tillering, and reduced stem growth (Batey, 1971). These symptoms show clearly on air photographs.

Copper deficiency can appear as dark patches in cereal crops when seen from a distance. These are found on chalkland in central southern and south–east England (Davies *et al.*, 1971); the symptoms appear to be linked with the high pH of the soils.

CONCLUSIONS

Many factors acting individually or in concert cause soil and crop marks. Bare soil marks are more stable than crop marks and are attributed to a number of causes. They occur mainly on light-coloured soils or those with a subsoil markedly different in colour from the surface soil, within plough depth. Areas of deeper surface soil then show as dark tones on photographs. Visibility of soil marks, particularly on chalk, depends to some extent on surface soil moisture, and the period when they can be photographed is long.

Crop marks occur mainly in shallow, loamy soils in which rooting depths are between 30 and 60 cm. Their causes are diverse, though most result from interactions of soil moisture deficit with soil depth, nutrient supply, particle size, and stoniness. Differential exhaustion of available soil moisture in periods of high potential soil moisture deficit accounts for the most distinct marks. Such marks are occasionally obscured when short periods of soil moisture surplus alter differential growth patterns under certain conditions.

In interpreting crop marks of archaeological significance it is important to understand how natural crop patterns develop. The search for sites of antiquity from the air could be made more efficient by concentrating photography into periods of high potential soil moisture deficit (greater than 50 mm). More accurate estimates of periods of potentially high SMD could be made using potential transpiration and rainfall data for periods shorter than one month. Information about soils and crops at sites of archaeological interest can then aid identification of the factors causing differential crop growth.

ACKNOWLEDGMENTS

The authors wish to thank their colleagues in the Soil Survey of Great Britain for the use of unpublished soil information; the Cambridge Committee for Aerial Photography for access to photographs; D. Forsdyke of the Meteorological Office, Bristol, for climatic data used in Figs. 1 and 5; Dr R. Scott Russell of Letcombe Laboratory for permission to reproduce Fig. 2; Dr D. J. Watson (formerly of Rothamsted Experimental Station) for permission to reproduce Fig. 6; Professor R. H. M. Langer of the Department of Plant Science, Lincoln College, University of Canterbury, New Zealand, for permission to reproduce Fig. 7; J. M. Hodgson for much useful advice and for criticism of the manuscript; E. M. Thomson for preparing diagrams; and K. E. Clare, Head of the Soil Survey of England and Wales, for permission to publish this paper.

BIBLIOGRAPHY

Batey, T. (1971). Manganese and boron deficiency. In: *Trace elements in soils and crops*. Technical Bulletin 21, 137–49. Ministry of Agriculture, Fisheries and Food, London.

Bingham, J. (1966). Varietal response in wheat to water supply in the field, and male sterility caused by a period of drought in a glasshouse experiment. *Annals of Applied Biology,* **57,** 365–77.

Bolton, J., and Slope, D. B. (1971). Effects of magnesium on cereals, potatoes and leys grown on the 'continuous cereals' site at Woburn. *Journal of Agricultural Science,* **77,** 253–9.

Bowen, H. C., and Butler, R. M. (1960). *A matter of time.* London, HMSO (RCHM).

Bradford, J. S. P. (1957). *Ancient Landscapes: studies in field archaeology.* London.

Buchan, A. (1905). The interrelations of barometric pressure, temperature, humidity, rainfall, cloud, sunshine, and wind, illustrated by observations made at the Ben Nevis Observatories. *Trans. Roy. Soc. Edinburgh,* **43,** 505–27.

Cannell, R. Q., and Drew, M. C. (1973). Plant root systems and crop growth. *Span* **16,** 38–41.

Cooke, G. W. (1967). *The control of soil fertility.* London.

Corte, A. E. (1966). Particle sorting by repeated freezing and thawing. *Biuletyn Peryglacjalny* **15,** 175–240.

Crampton, C. B. (1972). *Soils of the Vale of Glamorgan.* Memoir of the Soil Survey of Great Britain.

Crawford, O. G. S. (1933). Some recent air discoveries. *Antiquity* **7,** 290–6.

Crawford, O. G. S. (1938). Crop mark at Portchester Castle. *Antiquity* **12,** 478–9.

Crawford, O. G. S. (1939). Air reconnaissance of Roman Scotland. *Antiquity* **13,** 280–92.

Crawford, O. G. S., and Keiller, A. (1928). *Wessex from the air.* Oxford.

Davies, D. B., Hooper, L. J., Charlesworth, R. R., Little, R. C., Evans, C., and Wilkinson, B. (1971). Copper deficiency in crops: III. Copper disorders in cereals grown on chalk soils in South Eastern and Central Southern England. In: *Trace elements in soils and crops.* Technical Bulletin 21, 88–118. Ministry of Agriculture, Fisheries and Food, London.

Evans, J. G. (1972). Ice wedge casts at Broome Heath, Norfolk. *Proc. Prehist. Soc.* **38,** 77–97.

Evans, R. (1972). Air photographs for soil survey in lowland England: soil patterns. *Photogrammetric Record* **7**(39), 302–22.

Garwood, E. A., and Williams, T. E. (1967). Soil water use and growth of grass sward. *Journal of Agricultural Science* **68,** 281–92.

Green, F. H. W. (1964). A map of annual average potential water deficit in the British Isles. *Journal of Applied Ecology* **1,** 151–8.

Hodge, C. A. H., and Seale, R. S. (1966). *The soils of the district around Cambridge.* Memoir of the Soil Survey of Great Britain.

Hodgson, J. M., and Palmer, R. C. (1971). *Soils in Herefordshire I: Sheet SO 53 (Hereford South).* Soil Survey Record No. 2. Harpenden.

Hogg, W. H. (1971). Regional and local environments. Chapter 2 in: *Potential Crop Production* (Ed. Wareing, P. F., and Cooper, J. P.) 6–22. London.

Hollis, J. M., and Hodgson, J. M. (1974). *Soils in Worcestershire I: Sheet SO 87 (Kidderminster).* Soil Survey Record No. 18. Harpenden.

Hurst, J. G. (1956). Deserted Medieval Villages and the excavations at Wharram Percy, Yorks. In: *Recent Archaeological Excavations in Britain.* (Ed. Bruce-Mitford, R. L. S.) 251–73. London.

Langer, R. H. M. (1966). Mineral nutrition of grasses and cereals. In: *The growth of cereals and grasses* (Ed. Milthorpe, F. L., and Ivins, J. D.) 213–26. London.

May, L. H., and Milthorpe, F. L. (1962). Drought resistance of crop plants. *Field Crop Abstracts* **15,** 171–9.

Meteorological Office (1958). *Averages of rainfall for Great Britain and Northern Ireland 1916–50.* Memorandum No. 635. London.

Miller, A. A. (1962). Climate, vegetation and soils. Chapter 2 in: *Great Britain: geographical essays* (Ed. Mitchell, J. B.) 17–32. Cambridge.

Munsell Color Company (1954). Munsell soil color charts. Baltimore, USA.

Orchard, B. (1961). Effects of drought on plant growth. Report Rothamsted Experimental Station for 1960, 95–6.

Orchard, B. (1964). Effect of water supply on growth and yield of wheat. Report Rothamsted Experimental Station for 1963, 83–4.

Penman, H. L. (1948). Natural evaporation from open water, bare soil and grass. *Proc. Roy. Soc. Series A* **193**, 120–45.

Penman, H. L. (1952). Experiments on irrigation of sugar beet. *Journal of Agricultural Science* **42**, 286–92.

Penman, H. L. (1962). Woburn irrigation, 1951–59. I. Purpose, design and weather; II. Results for grass; III. Results for rotation crops. *Journal of Agricultural Science* **58**, 343–8; 349–64; 365–79.

Penman, H. L. (1970). Woburn irrigation, 1960–8. IV. Design and interpretation; V. Results for leys; VI. Results for rotation crops. *Journal of Agricultural Science* **75**, 69–73, 75–88, 89–102.

Penman, H. L. (1971). Water as a factor in productivity. Chapter 6 in: *Potential Crop Production* (Ed. Wareing, P. F., and Cooper, J. P.) 89–99. London.

Rackham, O. (1972). Responses of the barley crop to soil water stress. In: *Crop processes in controlled environments* (Ed. Rees, A. R., Cockshull, K. E., Hand, D. W., and Hurd, R. G.) 127–38. London.

Riley, D. N. (1943). Archaeology from the air in the Upper Thames Valley. *Oxoniensia* **8**, 64–101.

Riley, D. N. (1945). Aerial reconnaissance of the Fen Basin. *Antiquity* **19**, 145–53.

Riley, D. N. (1946). The technique of air archaeology. *Archaeol J.* **101**, 1–16.

Russell, E. W. (1961). *Soil conditions and plant growth.* London.

Russell, R. Scott (1971). Root systems and nutrition. Chapter 7 in: *Potential Crop Production* (ed. Wareing, P. F., and Cooper, J. P.) 100–16. London.

St Joseph, J. K. S. (1961). Aerial reconnaissance in Wales. *Antiquity* **35**, 263–75.

St Joseph, J. K. S. (1965). Air reconnaissance: recent results. *Antiquity* **39**, 60–61, 143–5.

Salmon, R. C. (1963). Magnesium relationships in soils and plants. *Journal of the Science of Food and Agriculture* **9**, 605–10.

Salter, P. J. and Haworth, F. (1961). The available-water capacity of a sandy loam soil. I. A critical comparison of methods of determining the moisture content of soil at field capacity and at the permanent wilting percentage. *J. Soil Sci.* **12**, 326–34.

Seale, R. S. (n.d.). *The soils of the Ely district.* Memoir of the Soil Survey of Great Britain.

Smith, L. P. (1967). *Potential transpiration.* Technical Bulletin 16. Ministry of Agriculture, Fisheries and Food, London.

Thornthwaite, C. W. (1948). An approach towards a rational classification of climate. *Geographical Review* **38**, 55–93.

USDA (1951). *Soil Survey Manual.* Agricultural Handbook No. 18, United States Department of Agriculture.

Viets, F. G. (1972). Water deficits and nutrient availability. In: *Water deficits and plant growth. Volume III: Plant response and control of water balance* (Ed. Kozlowski, T. T.) 217–39. London.

Wallace, T. (1961). *The diagnosis of mineral deficiencies in plants, by visual symptoms: a colour atlas and guide* (Agricultural Research Council). 3rd ed. London.

Watson, D. J. (1971). Size structure and activity of the productive system of crops. Chapter 5 in: *Potential Crop Production* (Ed. Wareing, P. F., and Cooper, J. P.) 76–88. London.

Weaver, J. E. (1926). *Root development of field crops.* New York.

Webster, G., and Hobley, B. (1965). Aerial reconnaissance over the Warwickshire Avon. *Archaeol. J.* **121**, 1–22.

Wright, S. J. C. (1972). Physiological and biological responses to wilting and other stress conditions. In: *Crop processes in controlled environments* (Ed. Rees, A. R., Cockshull, K. E., Hand, D. W., and Hurd, R. E.) 349–59. London.

APPENDIX

Original published references to crop marks at sites recently examined in the field (see above, p. 7)

Atkinson, R. J. C. (1946). A middle Bronze Age barrow at Cassington, Oxon. *Oxoniensia,* **11**, 5–26.

Atkinson, R. J. C. (1953). Excavations in Barrow Hills field, Radley, Berks. 1944–45. *Oxoniensia* **17** and **18**, 14–35.

Bradford, J. S. P., and Morris, J. M. (1941). Archaeological notes. *Oxoniensia* **6**, 84–9.

Catling, H. W. (1959). A Beaker-Culture barrow at North Stoke, Oxon. *Oxoniensia* **24**, 1–8.

Crawford, O. G. S. (1927). Air photographs near Dorchester, Oxon. *Antiquity* **1**, 469–74.

Grimes, W. F. (1944). Excavations at Stanton Harcourt, 1940. *Oxoniensia* **8** and **9**, 19–63.

Harden, D. B. (1942). Excavations in Smith's Pit II, Cassington, Oxon. *Oxoniensia* **7**, 104–7.

Harden, D. B., and Treweeks, R. C. (1945). Excavations at Stanton Harcourt, Oxon. 1940. *Oxoniensia,* **10**, 16–41.

Leeds, E. T. (1936). Round barrows and ring ditches in Berkshire and Oxfordshire. *Oxoniensia* **1**, 7–23.

Myres, J. N. L. (1937). A prehistoric and Roman site on Mount Farm, Dorchester. *Oxoniensia* **2**, 12–40.

Radford, C. A. R. (1936). The Roman Villa at Ditchley, Oxon. *Oxoniensia* **1**, 24–69.

St Joseph, J. K. S. (1945). Air photography and archaeology. *Geogr. J.* **105**, 47–61.

St Joseph, J. K. S. (1951). Air reconnaissance of north Britain. *J. Roman Stud.* **41**, 51–65.

St Joseph, J. K. S. (1953). Air reconnaissance of southern Britain. *J. Roman Stud.* **43**, 81–97.

St Joseph, J. K. S. (1955). Air reconnaissance in Britain, 1951–55. *J. Roman Stud.* **45**, 82–91.

St Joseph, J. K. S. (1962). Air reconnaissance in northern France. *Antiquity* **36**, 279–86.

Thomas, N. (1957). Excavations at Callow Hill, Glympton and Stonesfield, Oxon. *Oxoniensia* **22**, 11–53.

Wheeler, R. E. M. (1929). Caister; and a comment. *Antiquity* **3**, 182–7.

Williams, A. (1947). Excavations at Longford Downs Oxon. (near Lechlade) in 1943. *Oxoniensia* **11** and **12**,, 44–64.

Williams, A. (1948). Excavations at Barrow Hills Field, Radley, Berks, 1944. *Oxoniensia* **13**, 1–17.

Williams, A. (1951). Excavations at Beard Mill, Stanton Harcourt, Oxon., 1944. *Oxoniensia* **16**, 5–22.

Photographic techniques in the air

D. R. Wilson

Synopsis

Techniques of oblique and vertical photography are contrasted and separately described in the two main sections of the paper. In each section a brief discussion of the necessary equipment is followed by a detailed analysis of the photographic procedures involved. Particular attention is paid to determining the correct exposure, to the choice of viewpoint in oblique photography, and to the complex operations of vertical survey. Stress is laid on the value of a good understanding between pilot and photographer. A final note warns the archaeologist not to put too much faith in plans traced from vertical photographs.

The following notes are based on the writer's personal experience. Every photographer will have his own methods, related to his personal preference and to the equipment he has available, but it is believed that the principles set out here will be found to be generally applicable.

An appreciation of the technical considerations involved in taking successful air photographs is of importance to other people than actual and potential air photographers. Many of the same considerations are involved in the detailed interpretation of a photograph as went to its realization; and archaeologists should have some idea of how an air photographer works when making plans to obtain new photographic coverage.

There is a fundamental distinction to be made between oblique and vertical photographs. This is a commonplace of most aspects of air photography, but nowhere is it more evident than at the moment when the photographs are taken. Oblique photographs, at least in archaeological reconnaissance, are normally taken with a camera held in the hand and pointed through one of the window-openings of the aircraft. Exposures are released when an appropriate subject is framed in the camera's viewfinder. The photographs may be taken in rapid succession, but each one is intended as a study of all or part of some archaeological site or its setting. Vertical photographs are taken with a camera fixed in a mounting on the floor, pointing directly downwards through a specially constructed hole in the underside of the aircraft. Exposures are released in a carefully regulated sequence to obtain a series of overlapping photographs, capable of being viewed stereoscopically or assembled in a mosaic. The flight-lines are planned so as to pass over the area of special interest, but the camera itself is not pointed directly at a particular site, nor are exposures necessarily released when there is a site actually in view. Individual frames are simply the constituent parts of a larger block of photography, within which one or more sites will be included. Vertical photography, in short, is a specialized survey technique, involving complex procedures both for the pilot and for the photographer, whereas oblique photography, in spite of some peculiarities of its own, much more closely resembles conventional photography on the ground.

OBLIQUE PHOTOGRAPHY

Equipment

This is not the place for a technical assessment of various makes and models, but the equipment used does directly affect the procedures followed in the air, and we shall need to review in general terms the features which are needed for successful and efficient work. A basic equipment list for oblique photography can be reduced to an aircraft, camera and film, exposure meter, relevant sheets of the Ordnance Survey map at 1 : 63360 or 1 : 50000, and a pencil.

To begin with the aircraft, this should be capable of manoeuvring safely at 120 knots or less and have a good field of view towards the ground. Photographs should not be taken through Perspex panels, so it will be necessary for a conveniently placed window to be capable of being opened for photography during flight, or else removed entirely before the flight begins. If the windows cannot be taken out, the door may have to come off instead, which is certainly cold and draughty, but affords an excellent field of view. It need hardly be observed that in these circumstances the cameraman himself should be strapped in, and all his belongings, including maps and notes as well as camera and meter, should be securely attached to himself or to the aircraft.

Next, the camera. It is obviously desirable that this should be one that has been designed, or at any rate modified, specifically for aerial work. The larger the format, the better will be the chance of recording fine detail, but in practice the choice of camera is sometimes limited by factors such as the availability of spares, or even the availability of suitable film in a particular size in any but the largest quantities. If the lens has been designed for use in the air, it will have the focus fixed on infinity. It must in any case be as free as possible from optical distortion and combine good contrast with a high degree of resolution. The shutter should be reliable and capable of maintaining speeds of 1/300 s or better. If a great deal of work is done in the flying season, it may be necessary to fit a heavy-duty shutter. The film is most easily handled in interchangeable magazines, loaded in the darkroom before take-off and holding not less than 50 exposures each. Changing roll-film or cassettes in the air takes up valuable flying time and occupies the photographer's attention, when both could be more profitably employed on the location and photography of archaeological sites. If cassettes have to be changed, or a new film loaded, every eight or twenty or even thirty-six exposures, the time that is lost becomes considerable. Moreover, the use of cassettes at all cannot at present be considered as satisfactory in sizes larger than 35 mm, since they are too often associated with mechanical difficulties and photographic blemishes.

A useful extra is an electric motor to transport the film and re-cock the shutter automatically after each exposure. The motor can either be connected to the aircraft's own power supply or be powered by a

The author is with the Committee for Aerial Photography, University of Cambridge.

battery. With the aid of a motor, photographs can be taken at intervals of 3 or 4 s, which is quite fast enough to cope with all normal situations, even in the fastest of the aircraft already mentioned. In slower machines there will be less need for such rapid shooting, but the manual transport should be quick and easy to operate. Indeed, it is extremely important that the camera should in general be convenient and easy to handle, even with cold fingers in turbulent conditions.

For map-reading in the air the most useful general-purpose map has long been the Ordnance Survey 1 inch (1 : 63360), now being superseded by the metric replacement at 1 : 50000. Large areas can be covered in relatively few sheets, yet the detail is sufficiently fine to allow most sites to be quickly plotted within 100–200 m, except in the most featureless terrain. Maps at a larger scale may be useful for the study of special areas, but they are too limited in extent to be convenient for actually planning and following a route. Maps, it should be noted, are not only for telling you where you are, but for planning where you should be going next. Their use is not restricted to identifying features already noticed, but includes the prediction of features not yet seen or recognized. And, of course, a personal flying-map will be annotated with the positions of archaeological sites which it is intended to examine from the air.

Procedures

Let us now assume that an air photographer has reached his area of interest and has identified a subject for photography. What settings must he use on the camera, and how does he determine his exposure? The answers to these questions are not so simple as might be supposed.

The question of focus is quickly dealt with. All air photography is carried out at infinity, so if the lens has a variable focus, it must be held permanently at that setting. The only safe course is to use a piece of sticky tape or some similar device to stop the focussing ring on the lens from being inadvertently displaced. The shutter speed, as already implied, should not be any slower than 1/300 s if consistently sharp pictures are to be obtained, and 1/500 s would be better still. This is not something related merely to the ground-speed of the aircraft, but principally to vibrations from the engine transmitted to the airframe. Most of these vibrations are damped out by the body of the photographer himself, but some are passed on to the camera and are capable of producing a fuzzy image if the shutter is too slow.*

There being little scope for changing the speed of the shutter, exposure is normally controlled solely by variation of the aperture. It is obviously important that the aperture-ring on the lens can be easily read, and the setting quickly altered, in the course of actual photography. The exposure required is determined by use of a meter, with important modifications based upon experience. An initial rule of thumb is to stop down one *f* stop on the aperture suggested by the meter reading. This is equally true whether the light is being metered independently or if the camera incorporates through-the-lens metering. (The simplest way to make this correction is to set double the reputed speed of

the film on the dial of the meter.) The application of this rule of thumb should ensure exposures that are of tolerable quality, capable of being refined in the light of experience. There is ultimately no other standard: the exact exposure values have to be determined pragmatically, using the actual camera, emulsion, and developer with which photographs are going to be obtained.

Photographic emulsions are discussed by Rinker below (p. 32). Suffice it to say here that the air photographer has to seek a workable compromise between film speed, grain size, and image contrast. The choice of film speed is controlled by the shutter speed on the camera and the normal range of illumination of the subject, say from 25 to 250 foot-candles in archaeological photography. It should not be forgotten that a 2x yellow (minus-blue) filter is standard in air photography with panchromatic film. The importance of grain size is in proportion to the smallness of the format, but fineness of grain by itself is of little value unless accompanied by adequate contrast in the image. It is a feature of archaeological air photography to require both fineness of detail and a high degree of contrast, if crop marks or shadows are to be recorded with all the clarity that is desired. To reconcile these competing requirements the photographer is led to make use of specialized developers, which often affect the nominal speed of the emulsion with which they are used. Thus the only sure way to determine correct exposure values is to make an experimental flight and to photograph some typical subjects, bracketing the exposure widely and making detailed notes of every camera setting in relation to the conditions at the time. It is assumed in what follows that the effective speed of the film has been established in this way and the meter set accordingly.

In practice it is not convenient to take a meter reading for every photograph. Once the general light level has been determined, the variations of exposure required for particular subjects can usually be judged by eye. A convenient standard is a steep oblique view of a green field. Fields in bare soil may require a greater or less exposure according to the colour of the soil, and this will need to be established by a further meter reading. Buildings in bright sunshine will need at least half a stop narrower than the standard oblique, and as much as a full stop if highly reflective. A view extending into the middle distance will usually need to be half a stop narrower, and if it takes in the horizon, as much as a full stop narrower than the same standard. But rules of this kind are only a guide and have to be regarded as elastic. If the day is overcast, there is little light from the sky, and there need be little adjustment of exposure for a panoramic view. If the conditions are very brilliant, it may be necessary to stop down 1½ stops instead of only one. When photographing a dull subject, such as a hill-fort covered with conifers, on a dull day, it will do no harm to open up half a stop beyond what the meter strictly suggests. Similarly, when photographing a reflective subject such as sand dunes on a brilliant day, it will be wise to stop down even more than the reading of the meter actually demands. With snowscapes the reflected light is so intense that a special filter may well be needed to reduce exposure to an acceptable or convenient level.

---

*Techniques for reducing image movement and vibration are described by Chevallier (1964, 106–7) and Agache (1970, 19, note 1). Mr H. Wingham informs me that photographs may be taken from an airship with a shutter-speed as slow as 1/25 s.

a

b

In variable conditions the selection of the correct aperture becomes more complex. On a day of broken cloud, readings should be taken both in bright sunshine and in deep shadow to establish the range within which individual exposures will have to be interpolated. On a cumulus-type day in mid-summer this range may amount to at least two *f* stops. Less easy to cope with is the rather dull day on which several layers of strato-cumulus and stratus vary in thickness, combining to produce every condition from weak sunshine to complete gloom. Variation within this range can be rapid but unobtrusive, and constant monitoring with the exposure meter will be needed to exclude inadvertent error, as well as to train the inexpert eye.

The presence of haze is another complication, reducing the contrast of the photographic image (Fig. 14). When haze becomes really noticeable to the eye, but is not so obtrusive as to exclude photography altogether, exposure should be reduced by up to half a stop on what the meter says. A slight degree of haze must be regarded as normal in modern Britain, so that completely clear conditions, with visibilities of 50 km or more, will also call for special measures. This time it will be wise to open up a little and, if possible, to reduce contrast in development.

Corrections of this kind, although desirable, are not completely essential when using panchromatic film, in view of the latitude that such emulsions usually offer. In colour films, however, the latitude is normally much reduced and, when working with colour, the correct level of exposure becomes a matter of high importance.

Under- or over-exposure affects the quality of the photograph in a number of ways. Insufficient colour saturation results in a wan picture in which the colours looked washed out. Over-saturation turns the colours dark and muddy. Incorrect exposure, in addition, distorts the colour balance. These defects are particularly distressing with reversal film, since they cannot be detected until the transparency is fully processed. With negative film faults in the negative can to some extent be corrected in the print, but it is always better to expose a good negative in the first place, since there can certainly be no question of going back to compare a trial print with the original subject. Quite apart from the level of exposure, incorrect colour balance may be caused by industrial haze, which is liable to give a brownish cast to the photograph. It is therefore prudent to restrict the use of colour emulsions to conditions of even lighting and good visibility, depending solely on monochrome in difficult conditions. A strong haze filter will, in any case, be needed with colour film for all but the closest views, to eliminate excessive blue in distant parts of the subject.

The use of infrared-sensitive 'false-colour' film is described by Rinker below (p. 42). This emulsion is much slower than conventional colour and correct exposure is very critical; nevertheless, it has the advantage of good haze penetration in difficult conditions (Agache, 1970, 19, note 1).

With his aperture adjusted to give the appropriate exposure, our photographer is now ready to take photographs. With most aircraft he will find that, as long as the machine is held in level flight, he cannot take views of anything except the middle distance and horizon. To gain a clear field of view for the camera, the wing must be lowered on his side, putting the aircraft into a bank. This manoeuvre takes him round the site in a circle, allowing him to study it from all sides and to take photographs from whatever angles appear the most rewarding.

The direction of view is in fact a consideration of first importance in oblique photography, in whatever form the site itself is seen. For someone who has never engaged in archaeological air photography it is difficult to appreciate the dramatic increase in tonal contrast to be seen in a field of soil or crop marks, when they are viewed from one particular direction. For a moment or two they appear almost to be written in black and white (Fig. 1). When crop marks are poorly developed, they may not be visible at all except from a single, narrowly defined, direction, which may be restricted to as little as 15° out of the full circle. In these conditions it is only by constantly changing the direction of view that crop-mark sites can be recognized at all. Effects of this sort depend upon the position of the sun, but account will also need to be taken of wind direction, the presence of haze, and the composition of the subject matter. These are all topics to which we shall return.

In selecting the best viewpoint, the final judge is the eye of the photographer himself. What he is normally seeking is the best possible definition of the visible traces of a particular site. Earthworks and crop marks alike are capable of giving a vague and confused impression, yielding little precise information, especially on first inspection. It can be seen that something of an archaeological character is present, perhaps, but not of what it actually consists. Faced with such an enigmatic site, possibly of little significance but possibly concealing important details, the photographer needs to take particular care in selecting the most rewarding viewpoints, either to obtain the maximum contrast in the photographic image (Fig. 2), or to draw attention to suspected and hypothetical features. Each photograph should be taken with an appreciation of what features it is intended to show: a general view of a hill-fort in its setting, for example, will involve different technical considerations from a close-up of one of the entrances, quite apart from the pictorial quality and composition of the photographs.

Considered as subjects for air photography, archaeological sites fall into four main categories. These are (1) upstanding buildings and substantial ruins, (2) earthworks, (3) soil marks, and (4) crop marks. Each one of these has its own requirements, and these may conflict when different parts of the same site belong to different categories. In a castle, for example, different lighting may be required for the most telling photography of the keep and curtain-wall, of the great

Fig. 1   Crop marks of ring ditches on the south bank of the River Stour north of Lawford (Essex) (TM 086327), 16 June 1970: a. looking south, into sun; b. looking north–north–east, with the sun. The two photographs were taken within a minute of one another; the difference in tonal contrast is entirely due to the different direction of view
Photos: University of Cambridge; copyright reserved

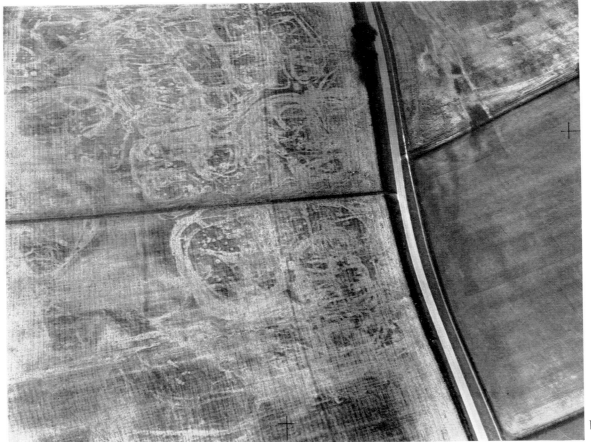

Fig. 2   Crop marks of a prehistoric settlement on the Yorkshire Wolds at Butterwick, south–west of Foxholes (Humberside) (SE 988710), 28 July 1970. a. Looking north–east: marks in the ripe crop are low in contrast and make a confused impression. b. Looking south–west: increased contrast results in better definition and allows more confident interpretation. The pattern resolves itself into a number of oval enclosures, each with a perimeter-ditch many times renewed, clustered closely together. It may even be possible to recognize the positions of circular timber houses
Photos: University of Cambridge; copyright reserved

Fig. 3   Brough Castle (Cumbria) (NY 792141), looking north. a. In diffuse lighting, 9 July 1949: the absence of strong shadows permits nearly all the visible stonework to be studied in detail. Lines of parching in the grass (west of the house in the foreground) may be caused by the street system of the underlying Roman fort. b. In bright afternoon sunlight, 6 July 1971: oblique lighting picks out the earthworks of the Roman fort and medieval castle.
Photos: (a) Crown Copyright reserved, (b) University of Cambridge; copyright reserved

a

b

Fig. 4   Romano-British agriculture in the Fens, south–south–west of Fleet (Lincs.) (TF 320103), 4 June 1965. The visible pattern is made up partly of surviving earthworks, partly of crop and soil marks. a. A view looking south–west, across sun, picks out the earthworks. b. Looking east–south–east: the crop and soil marks are emphasized, but the earthworks almost disappear from view
Photos: University of Cambridge; copyright reserved

Fig. 5   Byland Abbey (N. Yorks.) (SE 550789), 10 August 1953. The photograph was taken in the late morning, with the sun slightly east of south. The shadows fall along the north–south walls and behind the east–west ones, encroaching only slightly on the main open spaces. Note that the shadows are not suppressed completely, as this would tend to produce a flat and lifeless picture

moat outside, and of the slight traces of ruined subsidiary buildings within the bailey (Fig. 3). In a deserted medieval village, or an area of Romano-British agriculture, partly surviving as earthworks and partly revealed by crop and soil marks where it has been ploughed, the crop and soil marks and the earthworks will call for photographs from opposite directions. A view looking one way will emphasize crop marks and soil marks, while one looking the other way will underline the earthworks: both views will be needed to complete the photographic record (Fig. 4). For the photography of buildings in Britain the light needs to be diffuse and not too bright. British architecture is not designed for the dramatic lighting of Mediterranean lands; glare and strong shadows produced by bright sunshine simply obscure the architectural details. Even in strictly utilitarian architecture like that of a castle wall, soft lighting will yield the best rendering of the structural details on which archaeological interpretation is liable to depend (Fig. 3a). Similarly, in major ruins such as abbeys, strong shadows can be obtrusive and distracting, especially at certain times of day; the effect can be much reduced by careful or fortunate timing (Fig. 5). It is nevertheless true that there are occasions when shadows thrown on the ground can illustrate aspects of the structure not readily appreciated from a given point of view in any other way (Fig. 6).

With earthworks it is the shadows which make them visible. The slighter the relief, the longer in proportion the shadows need to be to be readily seen. Oblique lighting is therefore called for, involving photography when the sun is low in the sky. For minor earthworks, such as 'Celtic' fields, prehistoric farmsteads, and deserted medieval villages, the best photographic conditions are when the sun is within 20° of the horizon. In winter this happens even at midday, but in June the same conditions are found only before 7 in the morning or after 7 in the evening (British Summer Time). With larger earthworks, such as hill-forts and castles, such emphatic lighting is less desirable, too much of the site being lost within the shadows.

Special mention should be made of photography in wintry conditions, when the ground is covered with hoar-frost or a light covering of snow. Earthworks then appear with brilliant clarity, picked out by bright highlights and crisp shadows against the smooth background of the snow surface (Fig. 7). A heavier filter will almost certainly be needed on the camera to cope with the intensity of the light reflected. Even when the snow does not lie as a continuous blanket, earthworks may be picked out by a variety of special effects, so as to yield a distinctive photogenic pattern. White lines of snow may lie in the shade of banks or

Fig. 6   Stonehenge, near Amesbury (Wilts.) (SU 123422), 22 April 1954. Here shadows are exploited to give extra information about the structure of the sarsen circle, otherwise not easily appreciated from this viewpoint
Photo: University of Cambridge; Crown Copyright reserved

Fig. 7   Deserted medieval village, Eastburn (Humberside) (SE 991555), 1 January 1971. A continuous blanket of snow covers the ruined cottages, tofts, and hollow ways of a small deserted village on the Yorkshire Wolds, with part of a field in ridge and furrow
Photo: University of Cambridge; copyright reserved

Fig. 8   Deserted medieval village, Preston le Skerne (Durham) (NZ 307240), 11 January 1967. Snow lying in the shelter of banks and in hollows picks out details of the village plan which would otherwise be scarcely visible in the weak sunlight of a winter afternoon
Photo: University of Cambridge; copyright reserved

walls or in hollows (Fig. 8). Dark bands of bare earth may reveal where snow or frost has melted first above the filling of buried ditches (Fig. 9). This effect is extremely transient, but it has obvious relevance to the possibilities of recording archaeological sites by thermal imagery, as described by Baker below (p. 46). A similar effect is seen where the lines of buried foundations (or perhaps more probably of their robber-trenches) are picked out by early melting of hoar-frost on grass (Fig. 10).

Another aspect of winter photography relates to the seasonal behaviour of vegetation. There are many hill-forts and other earthworks which in summer are smothered in bracken or virtually concealed by trees. These can only be satisfactorily photographed in winter, when the bracken has withered and the trees are bare (Fig. 11). Even if the trees are not in fact deciduous, a tolerable record can be obtained as long as there is an unbroken carpet of snow to pick out the surface of the ground beneath the trees. In these conditions bright sunlight should as far as possible be avoided, since the shadows of the trees are distracting to the eye and break up the outlines of the earthworks themselves.

We may note here, in passing, the opportunities offered by summer photography in time of drought, when earthworks are revealed not so often by the shadows

they cast as by the parching of grass over the tumbled stonework which they contain (Fig. 12). While many examples show equally clearly in winter lighting, there are others where little surface relief now survives to be detected by other means.

Ideally the photography of earthworks should be repeated at different times of day and in different seasons of the year, to obtain views in which the shadows fall in a variety of directions. On any site it is the earthwork features lying across the line of the sun's rays that are most in evidence; those lying along them may be virtually invisible (Fig. 13). Photography with the sun at different relative positions ensures that all visible earthworks are adequately recorded.

Earthworks on sloping sites present particular problems. Those on a steep slope facing east of north may only be seen in oblique lighting in the height of summer, when the sun sets well to north of west. In general, earthworks on a slope facing towards the sun throw little shadows, whereas those on the opposite slope, if in sun at all, have shadows that are especially long. Where there are changes of slope within the area of a given site, each part may need to be photographed separately, at its own appropriate time.

Fig. 9 Henge monument, Hutton Moor (N. Yorks.) (SE 353735), 27 November 1969. A thin powdering of snow has melted first over the ditches and has lasted longest on the inner and outer banks. The two opposed entrances are clearly seen
Photo: University of Cambridge; copyright reserved

Fig. 10 Kirkham Priory (N. Yorks.) (NZ 736657), 6 February 1970. Differential melting of hoar-frost has revealed the plan of buildings north of the priory church, normally quite invisible beneath a well-mown sward
Photo: University of Cambridge; copyright reserved

Fig. 11 *The hill-fort at Coed y Bwnydd, Llanarth Fawr (Gwent) (SO 365068), 3 February 1969. The snow-covered earthworks of the defences are visible beneath bare trees. The viewpoint is chosen to minimize tonal contrast in the very bright conditions*
Photo: University of Cambridge; copyright reserved

Fig. 12 *Deserted medieval village, Walworth, Durham (NZ 232191), 31 May 1957. The medieval cottages of Walworth were ranged on at least three sides of a rectangular green, now partly occupied by farm buildings. The grass-covered ruins of the houses and their croft-boundaries, although surviving in low relief, are here picked out principally by lines of parching in the grass.*
Photo: University of Cambridge; Crown Copyright reserved

Fig. 13   Deserted medieval village, North Marefield, Leics. (SK 751089). a. With the sun a little south of west, 30 March 1965: streets and buildings on an east–west alignment are difficult to see. b. With the sun only slightly west of south, 28 November 1972: the east–west features are now strongly emphasized, but some north–south features are beginning to disappear. Certain buildings near the centre of the village actually appear to have changed shape between the two photographs
Photo: University of Cambridge; copyright reserved

The effect of shadow is emphasized in pictures taken looking directly into sun. Provided the view is steeply oblique, any normal lens hood will protect the lens itself from direct sunlight, though care should be taken to avoid unwanted flaring reflections from pools or other pieces of water on the site. (Naturally, there will be occasions when such reflections are part of the photographic effect intended.)

The converse effect is equally true: shadows can be minimized by taking photographs looking down or across sun.

These observations are valid as far as they go, but the situation is considerably complicated by the effects of atmospheric haze. The presence of haze is made more noticeable by just those conditions of lighting which are best for photography of earthworks, and it is further emphasized by taking the pictures looking into sun. Amounts of haze which do not seriously affect photography in the middle of the day rapidly become significant as the sun approaches the horizon. The remedy is to take photographs looking across the sun, balancing the resulting loss of emphasis with the still increasing length of shadow (Fig. 14). Once again, the trained eye of the photographer is the best guide to the choice of viewpoint, and questions of photographic composition in relation to the layout of the remains may sometimes outweigh purely technical considerations.

The photography of soil marks needs only a brief comment. Soil marks usually appear with greatest clarity and contrast when seen and photographed looking down sun. Special care needs to be taken with the exposure when working over chalk downland, where marks are seen to such good advantage. A field of chalky soil can be very highly reflective, and unless the aperture is stopped down sufficiently far, the marks of ring-ditches and enclosures may disappear completely in a sea of white.

Crop marks give rise to more complicated questions. The marks themselves are produced in a variety of ways: by differences of tone or hue, by sparse or luxuriant growth, and (especially in cereals) by the length of stalk. On the whole, the same rule applies to crop marks as to soil marks: tonal contrast is greatest when the marks are seen by someone looking with the sun (Fig. 1, but cf. Figs. 2 and 15). Although published photographs are often striking in their clarity, the majority of crop marks do not look like this at all. They are frequently difficult to discern and awkward to photograph, and everything must be done to gain maximum contrast in the image, if they are to be visible on the photograph at all.

When crop marks are poorly defined, it is a mistake to pass them by and wait for better marks to develop with the passage of time. Frequently a poor crop mark will develop into something beautifully clear and photogenic. But just as frequently it will disappear altogether (Fig. 16). Nor can anyone be completely certain that he will be able to return to a given site at the appropriate time, supposing the marks do develop as he hopes. A line of showers, or a military exercise, or a long run of settled hazy summer weather, may intervene at the crucial time and thus prevent a second chance.

The general rule of photography looking with the sun has to be modified in the light of special circumstances. When crop marks are made visible not by any change in tone or colour, but by differences in the height of the plants themselves, they then constitute a special sort of shadow-site. What is being photographed is differences of relief in the surface of the crop, and this needs to be seen (indeed can only be seen) when looking into sun (Fig. 17). Another complication occurs when the crops are rippled by a summer breeze. Clarity of definition is immediately lost: fine detail cannot be detected at all, and even the clearest of marks become blurred in outline. Really satisfactory photographs cannot be achieved in windy conditions, but the effect can be reduced by seeking a viewpoint that is directly up or directly down wind (Fig. 18). The rippling effect is then foreshortened, and passable photographs can be obtained, especially of features aligned on the wind direction. It will be seen that, if the sun is in the south and the wind is from east or west, results are likely to be disappointing, since there is no direction of photography that can alleviate all the unfavourable factors.

Apart from the question of wind, the photographic conditions demanded for the photography of crop marks are less stringent than those for earthworks. Work can proceed in the middle of the day when the sun is high, even in summer, and the amount of haze that can be tolerated is therefore not so critically small. Visibility of 10 km, although far from being as good as would be desirable, will still serve for the acquisition of a working record. Good visibility and plenty of sunshine are always valuable, since they make the sites easier to find and the photographs themselves more pleasing; but neither is essential. Provided that the general light level is sufficient for the speed of film in use, crop marks can perfectly well be photographed in total shadow.

Something should be said of the more practical side of taking photographs from the air. Communication between photographer and pilot is most easily achieved by an 'intercom' system, if the aircraft has one. A throat microphone will be required, in place of the conventional hand microphone, which cannot be operated at the same time as taking photographs. Failing an intercom, communication must be by direct word of mouth or by hand signals. Whatever the arrangements, the effectiveness of reconnaissance is greatly enhanced if the photographer and pilot are used to working together as a team. It is important that an air photographer should understand the limitations imposed by the design of the aircraft, meteorological conditions, air-traffic regulations, and an aviator's concept of civilized behaviour in the air. It is equally desirable that the pilot should be able to recognize an archaeological site, at least when it is pointed out to him, so that he can place the aircraft correctly for photography. One of the most difficult things to do in the air is to describe to somebody else the exact position of a site which he is simply unable to recognize because of its novelty.

While taking photographs it is most important not to rest the camera, hand, or arm against the window-frame, since this is certain to produce an unsharp picture. The camera should be held as steadily as possible, and all temptation resisted to pan it while the photograph is being taken. Rapid turning of the camera may well be called for between exposures, but it must be avoided at the actual moment of photography.

Fig. 14   The ruins of Bradgate House (Leics.) (SK 534102), 30 January 1966: a. looking south-west, directly into sun; b. looking west. Quite a small change in the direction of view makes an enormous difference to the contrast of the subject, when photographs are taken in hazy conditions
Photos: University of Cambridge; copyright reserved

Fig. 15 Crop marks of the Barrow Hills, Radley (Oxon.) (SU 517984), 18 June 1966. a. Steep oblique view, looking down sun. Double rings are visible at the foot of the photograph and right of centre. A number of other ring ditches can only be discerned with considerable difficulty. b. A view looking up sun, from greater height. Seven ring ditches (either single or double) are now clearly visible. Both photographs were taken on the same occasion, within a few minutes of each other Photos: University of Cambridge; copyright reserved

Fig. 16   Crop marks of a probable Iron-Age settlement south of Steventon (Hants.) (SU 543451), 13 June 1973. Crop marks were only just beginning to appear in spring-sown cereals in north Hampshire at that date and were still very faint. The best definition was obtained by taking photographs looking into sun, so as to emphasize height differences in the crop. Most crop marks in this area disappeared later in the month and had not re-appeared in early July
Photo: University of Cambridge; copyright reserved

Fig. 17   Crop marks in the Welland valley north–east of West Deeping (Lincs.) (TF 116093), 21 June 1966. A variety of pits and ditches, including a double ring ditch and a 'pit-alignment', is made visible by differences in the length of stalk among the plants of a cereal crop. The archaeological features appear solely in terms of highlight and shadow, produced by slanting sunlight on the surface of the crop
Photo: University of Cambridge; copyright reserved

Fig. 18 Crop marks on the Cotswolds east of Temple Guiting, Glos. (SP 112279), 4 August 1969. a. Vertical view: a squarish enclosure can be seen in the bottom left-hand corner, but crop marks in the main field are almost entirely obscured by rippling of the crop in a fresh breeze. b. Oblique view, looking nearly into wind: a second enclosure is now visible, as well as other marks, in spite of rippling in most parts of the field. The increased contrast of an oblique view helps the marks to stand out even against a mottled background

Photos: University of Cambridge; copyright reserved

This description of the procedures of oblique photography possibly gives an over-elaborate account of a relatively simple task. For an air photographer, taking the photographs is only a beginning. His other tasks include planning the course of the flight, giving directions to his pilot, searching for archaeological sites, keeping track of what he has photographed and where, and making a full and detailed record of the flight at the earliest opportunity. It is only when he has learnt to co-ordinate these activities and perform them as a matter of routine that he will have enough attention to spare to pursue his work with the imagination that leads to really exciting results.

VERTICAL PHOTOGRAPHY

The techniques of vertical survey are more complex than those of oblique photography, but they need not take so long to describe. This is partly because some of the ground has already been covered; partly because some topics, such as the direction of view, scarcely need discussion; and partly because procedures which are complex to put into practice are nevertheless quite simple to describe.

Equipment

For vertical photography the equipment list is more impressive than for obliques, and few people are likely to undertake this kind of work except in a professional capacity. The aircraft, first of all, has to be specially modified, by cutting a hole in the underside through which the photographs can be taken. It is useful to fit some kind of a hatch or camera-door over the hole, capable of being wound back out of the way when photography is to begin. The purpose of the hatch is to protect the camera lens from stones flying up during taxi-ing, take-off, and landing, and from spots of engine-oil possibly collecting on the lens surface during a protracted flight. The camera itself does now have to be one designed for the purposes of air-survey, and a special mount has to be obtained or manufactured to hold it firmly, though not too tight, in the vertical position. Also essential are an intervalometer and electric motor, to allow a particular time-interval between exposures to be set and automatically realized. For most cameras a form of suction has to be supplied, to keep the film flat at the moment of photography, either by means of a special pump, or else by a device such as a Venturi tube.

Some other pieces of equipment are so desirable as to be a virtual necessity, though it is possible to muddle through without them. These are a vertical sight, with which to follow the aircraft's track over the photographic area, and an exposure meter mounted in the underside, with a field of view similar to that of the camera lens.

Procedures

Successful survey photography involves the close co-operation of the flying crew, which normally comprises pilot, navigator, and cameraman. The duties of the navigator may, however, be distributed between the other two, if two-man working is more convenient. The pilot's task is to fly the aircraft along prearranged flight-lines, holding it steady and level at the altitude required. The photographer's primary duty is to operate the camera, but in the absence of a navigator he will also monitor the track of the aircraft in relation to the intended line, issuing corrections as required, and check that the photographic area has been covered.

In summary, the photographic tasks consist of the following: to level the camera; to set the intervalometer, exposure, suction, and drift; to switch on when the correct area is reached; to maintain the correct exposure over different parts of the subject; to maintain the correct suction and keep the camera level; and to switch off at the end of the run. It should not be necessary to mention preliminaries such as removing the dark slide from the film magazine and opening the camera-door, but few practising photographers can say that they have never forgotten to take these important steps.

Most of these tasks require some further comment. The camera is levelled by centring a bubble. The normal tolerances for vertical survey are that no exposure should be more than $3°$ out of vertical, and that no two successive exposures should differ by more than $5°$. If the conditions are too bumpy for the camera to be kept level, because the aircraft itself is continually changing attitude, the conditions are not suitable for survey photography at all.

The intervalometer is a timing device connected to the camera and motor, which enables exposures to be released at a selected constant interval. This interval is calculated so as to yield a certain degree of overlap, normally 60%, between the areas recorded on each successive frame. The interval chosen is related to the focal length and format of the camera, the scale of photography, and the ground-speed of the aircraft. The focal length and the format are constant for any given survey camera. The scale of photography is itself a simple function of the flying height and the focal length of the lens. Most modern wide-angle survey cameras have a focal length of 6 in on a 9-in format. As 6 in amount to half of 1 ft, the scale of photography is equal to twice the height of the aircraft above the ground, measured in feet. To take a very simple example by way of illustration: if the average ground height of the photographic area is 350 ft above Ordnance Datum, and the desired scale is 1 : 2500, the aircraft will have to fly at an altitude of 350 ft + 1250 ft = 1600 ft. The ground-speed is the final factor in the computation and is estimated by the pilot. The length of the interval in seconds can then be read off from a prepared table appropriate to the camera, and the intervalometer is set accordingly.

The scale of photography that can be achieved with a fixed-wing aircraft is limited by the speed of the aircraft itself. Safe and level flight cannot be maintained below a certain critical speed; and the lower the aircraft is flying, the more important it is to preserve adequate safety margins. This means that, although the area covered by each photograph is reduced as scale increases, the speed at which the ground is traversed cannot be reduced beyond a certain minimum. Now the camera takes a certain minimum time to wind over (usually a little over 3 s) and at large scales the aircraft will have sped on during that time beyond the point at which the next photograph ought to have been taken. The 60% overlap cannot be maintained, and at very large scales it may prove impossible to achieve any overlap at all.

At the same time the apparent image-movement of the subject in relation to the camera frame has also increased, so that very high shutter-speeds are required if critical definition is to be retained. Using a normal shutter-speed of 1/300 s at 90 miles/h, the minimum height for critical definition is 660 ft, giving a maximum scale of 1 : 1320. At 120 miles/h, the figures would be 880 ft and 1 : 1760 respectively. Vertical photography at very large scales (for example of archaeological excavations) is therefore one of the few photographic tasks for which a helicopter is better suited, in spite of the difficulties caused by its typically high vibration. An airship, if obtainable, would possibly be ideal.

To return to the tasks of the cameraman, exposure is calculated according to the same elastic rules as are used in oblique photography. If there is a vertical light meter installed, the light reading is first of all corrected as previously described, and then the exposure is set in the usual way. If there is no vertical meter, the vertical reading may be assumed to be equivalent to half a stop wider than a steep oblique. The principal advantage of a vertical meter is that the light reading can be monitored throughout the duration of photography, and appropriate changes of exposure made to allow for variations in the subject and the lighting. The alternative is to gather this information, as far as possible, in advance, by taking selected readings over typical portions of the subject.

Drift is principally the problem of the pilot. It is the angle made between his heading and his actual track when he is being blown off course by the wind. His solution is to turn the aircraft into wind by a similar amount, so that his actual track follows the flight-line planned. It is evident that if the aircraft is no longer pointing in the direction in which it is really going, the camera will have to be turned to bring it back into alignment with the line of flight. Thus, if the drift is found to be 10° to starboard, the pilot corrects approximately 10° to port, while the camera is turned 10° to the right to bring it once again into the correct line. This drift correction is a very important step in successful vertical photography. If drift is ignored, there is 'crabbing' in the photographs and the effective width of the strip is reduced. The normal side overlap between strips of photography is 30%, but crabbing can reduce this overlap to negligible proportions. Forward overlap is also affected. The degree of drift is determined by direct observation, but can be predicted from an estimate of the strength and direction of the wind at the altitude concerned.

During photography then, observation of the ground is maintained, as it were, with one eye, while the other follows the line on the map, monitors suction and exposure, and checks that the camera is level and that the film is still turning. When necessary, the exposure is adjusted to take account of cloud shadow and changes of tone in the subject, and the levelling screws on the camera are turned to bring the bubble back to the centre of its run. Adjustments to the camera should not be made when a photograph is actually being taken, but only in the interval between exposures. Vertical photography requires considerable concentration and co-ordination, as well as a good understanding between photographer and pilot. The camera operator who gets into a muddle in the middle of photography cannot pause to gather his wits. If he does not get it right, he must go back to the beginning and start again.

A note on the use of vertical photographs

The value of vertical photography is as a means of survey yielding stereoscopic imagery. Earthworks and topographical detail may be studied in three dimensions under the stereoscope, and accurate contoured plans may be produced by photogrammetry A typical example might involve photography at a scale of 1 : 3000 from a height of 1500 ft. From this an experienced operator could draw out a plan at a scale of 1 : 600 with contour intervals 1 ft (300 mm) apart.

It is worth emphasizing for the archaeological reader the limitations of the *single* vertical photograph (as opposed to the stereo-pair) as a means of survey. The normal tolerances for so-called 'vertical' photography have already been described. But even supposing that the camera were precisely level, and that the ground were both level and flat (which it very seldom is), there would still be only one point on the ground lying directly beneath the camera. The view in every other part of the photograph is always in some degree oblique, quite apart from effects caused by unevenness in the terrain. It simply is not true that a vertical photograph has a constant scale. The upshot is that a plan obtained by tracing from a single vertical photograph will not be precisely accurate, either in scale or perspective, except by good fortune. It is only necessary to compare the outline of a field on the photograph with that on a large-scale Ordnance Survey plan to confirm that this is so. When used on its own, the vertical photograph should be thought of as a special sort of oblique, in which distortions are kept to a minimum but are not completely eliminated.

ACKNOWLEDGMENT

The writer's experience of air-photography has been gained during nine years' work at Cambridge under the auspices of the University's Committee for Aerial Photography. Figures 1–18 are all photographs from the University's Collection.

REFERENCES

Agache, R. (1970). *Détection aérienne de vestiges proto-historiques, gallo-romains et médiévaux dans le bassin de la Somme et ses abords.* Numéro spécial du *Bull. Soc. Préhist. du Nord*, 7. Amiens.

Chevallier, R. (1964). Détections aériennes dans le Sud du département de l'Aisne. *Colloque International d'Archéologie Aérienne 31 aout–3 septembre 1962*, 95–108. Paris.

Some technical aspects of film emulsions in relation to the analysis and interpretation of aerial photographs

Jack N. Rinker

Synopsis

Cameras, films, and filters have improved greatly over the years, and performance characteristics that, at one time, were a problem, are of much less concern now, unless one is working near the design limits of the system. However, general information about aberrations, resolution, acutance (or edge sharpness), film sensitivities, characteristic curves, etc., does provide a background understanding that can be of help in applying photographic techniques to any given problem, whether it be laboratory, field, or airborne oriented.

INTRODUCTION

The workhorse of the remote sensor family is, and has been from the beginning, the aerial camera, and rightfully so, for a photograph, particularly in the stereo form, contains more information per unit area than does any other form of imaging device. The analysis and interpretation of aerial photography provides a rapid and economical method for obtaining a variety of regional and local information about any given environment, such as soil and rock types, drainage, vegetation, resources inventory, land use, site selection and location of engineering materials, crop monitoring, detection of archaeological sites, etc. Comparatively speaking, aerial photography is economical, relatively easy to acquire, requires a minimum of training for some uses, and can be had in a variety of forms with reference to film, filter, scale, and format.

Aside from the well known mapping uses, there are two fundamentally different methods for exploiting aerial photography: that of detection and that of analysis and interpretation. In detection procedures, the burden of the effort is on the system. Whatever the target—old ruins, fire damage, crop damage, pollution, vegetation types, etc.—one relies on the fact that the target differs from its background in some parameter such as colour, brightness, texture, size, or shape and that some combination of film/filter/scale/processing/time of day/etc. will make the target of interest easier to discern in the imagery. In analysis and interpretation procedures the burden of the work is not on the system but on the individual. The image is a pattern of grey tones that have meaning only in the eyes of the analyst. For example, a photograph does not give geological information, but a person with knowledge and experience in geology can extract much of such information from stereo photos, and the quantity and quality of this information are based more on his limitations than on those of the photography. To him, the three-dimensional structure of the land that is revealed in the stereo image provides clues about the nature of the materials, their origin, and their physical properties. By such a procedure, the geologist, the forester, the soil scientist, etc., working jointly with the imagery, can produce a tremendous amount of environmental information, and in a relatively short time. Common to either procedure, however, is the aerial photograph, which represents the combined knowledge of other specialities, principally chemistry and physics. Although detailed knowledge of these may be of little practical concern to the photo user, a general knowledge does grant him more familiarity with the principles, procedures, and limitations of photography as it is used to record various aspects of the colour world.

THE COLOUR DOMAIN, VISION, AND PHOTOGRAPHY

All matter reflects, absorbs, transmits, and emits electromagnetic energy. The extent to which any of these actions occur is a function of the electrical properties of the material in question, its temperature, and of the frequency or wavelength of the electromagnetic energy involved. When the wavelengths of the energy fall within the visual portion of the electromagnetic spectrum, the characteristics of the reflections, transmissions, and absorptions define what is called the *colour world*. Figure 1 is a diagram of the electromagnetic spectrum that shows the relation between the visual and photographic bands.

It is difficult to determine the number of colours that exist in the colour world. Judd (1952, 171) suggests that it might be as high as ten million. Of this colour world, how much can be matched with colour chips? How much of it can be seen by the eye? How much of it does a panchromatic emulsion or a colour film record? *The Dictionary of Color* by Maerz and Paul (1951) uses some 7056 colour chips to represent the colour world. The *Book of Color* (Matte Finish) of Munsell (1967) uses about 1185 samples for the same purpose. The human eye is sensitive to electromagnetic energy that has wavelengths of 400–700 nm. It is not uniformly sensitive, being least sensitive to violet and red and most sensitive to yellow. The wavelength discrimination of the eye is rather remarkable, being about 1 nm for a 2° field of view and about 0·2 nm for a wide field of view, and for each wavelength increment the eye can perceive a number of different brightnesses. Summing up these possibilities leads to a figure of 600 or more as representative of the total number of colours that the eye can differentiate.

Without doubt, a trained eye can do better, but whether it can approach the figure of 200,000 as reported in some literature is a moot point. Under normal viewing conditions, a black-and-white transparency represents the colour world with perhaps 30–40 shades of grey, with a paper print being

The author is with the Photographic Interpretation Research Division, US Army Engineer Topographic Laboratories, Fort Belvoir, Va., USA.

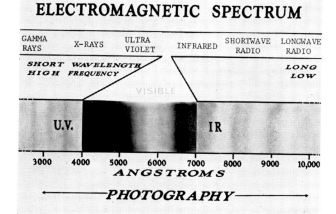

ELECTROMAGNETIC SPECTRUM

Fig. 1   A representation of the electromagnetic spectrum, showing the relative locations of the major regions. The sensation of violet is at the short-wavelength end of the visible band. As the wavelength increases, the eye perceives this as a change in colour, as indicated in the diagram

restricted to some lesser value, perhaps 15–20. For a colour transparency, using various assumptions for the response of the eye and the capabilities of the three dye layers, the colour world is portrayed with perhaps 200–500 colours. This is certainly an increase over the limits of a black-and-white emulsion and, aside from aesthetics, this fact probably accounts for the preference of many for colour films over panchromatic emulsions. Colour systems do thus have the basis for a higher information content. However, this is by no means the only factor that must be considered in selecting a film. Other factors must be considered, such as cost, speed, contrast range, lighting conditions, intended use (such as mosaicking needs versus strip photography), etc.

PHOTOGRAPHIC EMULSIONS

Any photographic material is made up of one or more thin layers of a colloidal suspension of silver halide microcrystals. The suspending medium is usually gelatin, and the suspended silver halide salts are silver chloride, silver bromide, silver iodide, or mixtures of these. This combination is called the emulsion, and it is usually less than 0·03 mm in thickness. The suspended silver halide crystals, which range in size from less than 1 μm to several microns in diameter, are the light-sensitive elements. The size distribution of these grains, plus the types of halide, determine the characteristics of such properties as film speed, acutance, resolution, image spread, etc. The emulsion is coated on some type of supporting material such as acetate or polyester when flexibility is needed, or glass or paper for other purposes. Light-sensitive emulsions can also be placed on other surfaces such as cloth, wood, textured materials, etc., to satisfy artistic or decorative desires. Emulsions for coating papers have a much lower proportion of silver halide, as compared with the gelatin, than do emulsions intended for negative or transparency use. Emulsions designed for x-radiation have an even greater proportion of silver halide than negative stock, and nuclear track emulsions have the highest proportion of all.

The latent image

The details of image formation within an emulsion are exceedingly complex. In a general way, the term *light-sensitivity* means that, when the material is exposed to radiation, some of the silver halide grains are changed to a different but relatively stable condition. This condition is called the *latent image*. During the developing process, the altered grains are reduced to metallic silver at a faster rate than the unaltered or unexposed grains. In a quantum physics sense, when light strikes a photo-sensitive surface, certain of the light quanta are absorbed by the silver halide crystals with a consequent release of electrons into conduction bands where they are free to wander through the crystal lattice in a manner similar to electrons moving through a metal. Some of the electrons become trapped in what are called *sensitivity centres*, producing in each one a net negative charge. Silver ions, which also wander through the crystal lattice, enter the sensitivity centres and combine with the electrons to form neutral atoms of silver. After a sufficient number of silver atoms have been accumulated, a stable image forms within the emulsion. The sensitivity centres, which are scattered throughout a crystal, are located at sites of structural weakness caused by the presence of impurities in the lattice structure of the silver halide. Since the number of sensitivity centres is in direct proportion to the size of the grain, the overall sensitivity of an emulsion increases with the size of the grain.

On an idealized basis one would suppose that the response of an emulsion (i.e. the amount of free silver formed) would be directly proportional to the intensity of the radiation multiplied by the length of time that the radiation was incident on the emulsion. In a practical sense, and for a certain range of conditions, this is true. Although, on a total energy basis, an exposure of intensity N acting for 0·001 s is equivalent to an exposure of intensity $N/100,000$ acting for 100 s, the response of the film to these two situations is not the same. This departure from what one would expect is called *reciprocity failure*. Experiments have shown that when an emulsion absorbs large amounts of energy in a short period of time, a surplus of electrons is produced—an electron avalanche. The effect of this is an excess negative charge at each sensitivity centre, which prevents further trapping of electrons from the over-abundant supply. By the time the silver ions have migrated to the centres and neutralized the charge by forming metallic silver, which would allow more electrons to be trapped, etc., the surplus of electrons has been dissipated. Thus, there is less silver deposited than would be expected on the basis of the exposure. This is *high-intensity reciprocity failure*. To a certain extent, one can compensate for this apparent loss of sensitivity by increasing the developing time. However, the payment for this is an increase in background density.

When radiation of very low intensity falls on an emulsion for a long period of time, other events prevent the formation of large aggregates of silver at the sensitivity centres. As silver atoms are formed, thermal motion causes some of them to break apart. In order for a latent image centre or speck to be stable, it must contain a certain number of silver atoms. If the intensity of the incoming energy is below a given value, the thermal breakup rate of silver exceeds the formation rate, and consequently the latent image never attains stability; since there are too few silver

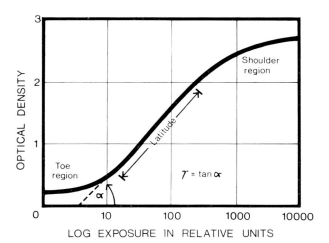

Fig. 2   A characteristic curve representative of a negative material processed under some set of standard conditions. The latitude is that region where there is a linear relationship between exposure and optical density. The slope of this straight-line portion of the curve is called the gamma *of the film, and it is indicative of contrast properties of the emulsion for a given set of processing conditions*

atoms in some of the centres, some of the grains cannot be developed. This apparent loss of sensitivity is called *low-intensity reciprocity failure.* Emulsions can be designed for short exposures, or for long exposures, to offset to some extent the effects of reciprocity failure.

Development

If an emulsion is exposed to enough radiant energy, the latent image will become visible as a darkened area of accumulated metallic silver. The developing process is basically an amplifier, for it reduces by several orders of magnitude the amount of radiant energy required to produce an equivalent darkening.

A photographic developer acts by reducing the silver halides to free metallic silver, which forms the shades of grey that can be seen in a black-and-white print or film transparency. Eventually, the chemicals within a developer will reduce all the grains to silver, including those that have not been exposed to radiation. Of necessity, the developer must be of such a nature that it reduces exposed grains at a greater rate than unexposed ones. Any development system is a rate-dependent phenomenon that discriminates to some extent between exposed and unexposed parts of the emulsion. However, unless something interferes, the developer will eventually reduce all of the unexposed silver halide as well, resulting in a uniformly dark piece of film or paper. Usually, development is terminated by removing the emulsion from the developer before there is any serious reduction of unexposed grains. The reduction reaction is most active in an alkaline pH and slows down as the pH is lowered. This is the basis for the common practice of immersing emulsions in an acid stop-bath, normally dilute acetic acid, after the required developing time has expired. Next, the emulsion is put into a silver halide solvent which removes the remaining silver halide grains, leaving behind only the visible silver image which may now be examined in the light. This solvent is called the *fixing agent.* The emulsion must

be thoroughly washed, otherwise the dissolved chemicals, distributed throughout the gelatin, will eventually destroy the silver image.

There are two types of development processes. One is called *physical development* and the other *chemical development,* the latter being the more common of the two. Physical development is probably present to some extent in the chemical procedure. In physical development, the emulsion is immersed in a solution that contains silver salts and silver ions. Silver atoms from this solution are deposited on the silver atoms in the latent image centres. A chemical developer contains a silver halide solvent, and silver dissolved in the developer solution is deposited on grains that have already been partially reduced to free silver. Both processes are intensification procedures that increase the sizes of the original silver aggregates of the latent image. As development proceeds, a variety of by-products are formed that eventually diffuse through the gelatin to the surface of the emulsion, where they accumulate to form a barrier to incoming fresh developer. Agitation of the emulsion prevents the surface barrier from forming and thus fresh developer can diffuse into the gelatin. As by-products accumulate in the developer, its reducing action becomes exhausted and fresh chemicals must be used.

The characteristic curve

The way in which an emulsion responds to variations in exposure can be expressed by a graph that plots along the ordinate the amount of silver deposited within the emulsion, and along the abscissa the amount of energy incident on the emulsion. The amount of silver deposited, or degree of blackening, is expressed in terms of optical density. For a transparency, the optical density is the negative of the logarithm, to the base 10, of the ratio of the light incident on the film to the amount of light transmitted through the film. For example, if the film transmitted all the light incident on it, the ratio would be 1 : 1, or 1; the log is zero and the optical density would be zero. If the film transmitted 10% of the light, the ratio would be 1 : 10 or 0·1. The log of this is − 1, and the optical density would be 1. If the ratio were 1/100, the optical density would be 2. The exposure, which expresses one way or another the amount of energy incident on the emulsion, is usually expressed in logarithmic form also.

Figure 2 is a generalized graph representing the response of a negative material exposed to different amounts of radiant energy and developed under some fixed set of processing conditions. Such a graph is called an *H and D curve* (after Hurter and Driffield), a *characteristic* curve, or a *D-log E* curve. At the very left of the graph in Fig. 2, the curve indicates a measurable level of film density even at zero exposure. This value, which is called *background density* or *fog density,* represents the cumulative effects of discolourations and base density levels of the emulsion and its support. From this threshold value, the film density gradually increases in response to greater exposure levels. This general region is called the *toe* of the curve.

Beyond the toe portion, the curve enters a straight-line region where film density increases uniformly with increasing exposure. This area of response is called the *latitude* of the film. Beyond this region there is a reduction in the response of the film to increasing exposure and this part of the curve is called the *shoulder.* Eventually a point is reached where all of the

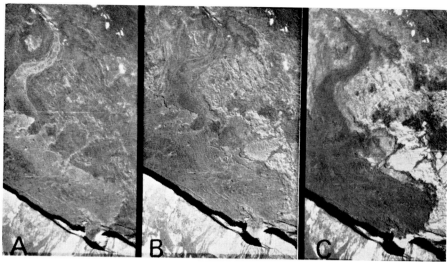

Fig. 3   Portions of three consecutive frames from an air-photo strip over the volcanic region on the island of Hawaii. Two types of lava flow are present (AA and Paneohoe), each with a different surface structure. As shown in this series, the tones can be reversed as the sun angle changes. In one image the ground site shows up on the edge of the image, towards the sun; in the middle photograph the same ground site is essentially below the camera; and in the other photograph the same ground site is near the image edge away from the sun. These photographs are from the collection of Professor Robert Decker of Dartmouth College, Hanover, NH

silver halide grains have been exposed and no increase in film density is possible. In fact, excessive exposure can reduce the optical density, and even destroy the latent image. This effect is called *solarization*. The slope of the straight-line portion of the curve is called *gamma* and its value, for any given film type, is influenced by the make-up of the developer, its temperature, and the time allotted for the developing process. As the development time is increased, gamma increases to some limiting value. Development beyond this will reduce the value of gamma because background density (unexposed grains, shadow detail, etc.) continue to increase, whereas areas of maximum exposure have already reached a maximum density and cannot increase further.

A high gamma (or steep slope) means that the exposure range over which the film responds with any degree of uniformity is greatly compressed, i.e. the film has a narrow latitude. For line copy work, or where higher contrast is desired, a high gamma film/developer combination is useful. For pictorial work, or where the negative will be used to prepare a positive image on photosensitive papers, a lower gamma value is needed. Gamma values between 0·6 and 1·0 cover most pictorial and scientific needs. With a gamma of 1, tone reproduction of the scene will be normal in the sense that image tonal contrast will equal object tonal contrast within the latitude range of the film. A higher gamma means that the scene will be reproduced at a higher contrast. In aerial photography, one sometimes chooses a gamma value suitable to a given type of mission. For example, in high-altitude work, the intervening atmosphere greatly reduces the apparent contrasts at the image plane, as compared with the tone contrasts that can be seen on the ground. High-altitude image contrast is sometimes no greater than 2 to 1. The quality of aerial photographs taken under such conditions can be improved by using

high-gamma films, some of which produce gammas of 2 or more when processed normally. Since gamma is defined by the straight-line portion of the characteristic curve, it has use only with those materials that give a reasonably straight-line response over some reasonable exposure range. Such a response is more typical of black and white emulsions coated on transparent supports. Photographic papers have a characteristic curve that is sigmoidal in shape, with little or no straight-line portion.

In a practical sense, no emulsion can simultaneously record black and white. If one has a 22-step wedge (i.e. a series of 22 levels of brightness ranging from near white to near black) there is no exposure that will reproduce the 22 separate steps in the negative with the same tone relations that exist in the original. One can increase the exposure and separate the darker tones, but the tones at the other end of the step wedge will be merged into a single density value, and vice versa. Thus, the proper exposure is a function of whether the photographer wants to record information in the highlights or in the shadows. This situation is of much less concern in aerial photography than it is in photography where the camera is relatively close to the subject.

Exposure variations

As indicated in the preceding section, variations in exposure and processing alter the structure of the final image. This is the basis of the characteristic curve. There is a variation in exposure across the field of view of an aerial camera that can be equivalent to a change of two *f* stops or more. This variation can be caused by changes in viewing angle of a given surface with respect to the sun, or by differences in the amount of energy reaching the camera from off-axis areas as compared with on-axis areas. As an example of the

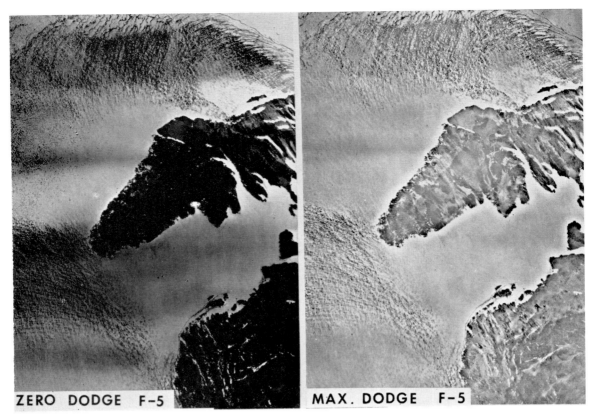

ZERO DODGE   F-5   MAX. DODGE   F-5

Fig. 4   A comparison of a standard contact print and a 'dodged' print. The left photograph is a standard contact print and the exposure deficiencies are obvious. The right-hand photograph is an automatically dodged print made by a Logetronic printer (Logetronics Inc., Springfield, Va.). Note the gain in pattern detail in both highlight and dark areas

first, consider an area with a uniform grass cover over a very gently rolling terrain, so gentle that under normal midday sun conditions none of the slopes are in shadow. Nevertheless, for a camera station above any one hill, the slope tilted towards the sun will reflect more light to the camera than will the slope tilted away from the sun. This is a variation in exposure, and two different density values will develop in the image, even though they both represent the same material under the same physical conditions. For the second case, consider a large flat area of uniform surface material and the photo plane flying in the direction of the sun. In that part of the field of view towards the sun, the surface material will reflect a different amount of energy to the camera station (diffuse plus specular) than that same material when it is part of the image away from the sun (diffuse minus specular). Figure 3 shows a reversal of tone values for two types of lava surfaces as a function of the angle between the camera, the surface, and the sun. A third type of exposure variation, called *vignetting,* comes about because the amount of energy per unit area that reaches the camera from the edge of the field of view is less than that from the centre, and a print from such a negative will have a darker border around the periphery. The corners, representing the most distant scene in the field of view, will be the darkest. The amount of vignetting is a function of the focal length of the camera lens, being greater for a wide-angle lens and least, or non-existent, for a telephoto lens. Whether a lens is wide-angle or telephoto depends on the relation

between the focal length of the lens and the longest dimension in the format. A normal lens, for any given camera, is one whose focal length is equal to the longest dimension of the format. A lens with a focal length shorter than this distance is a wide-angle lens. If the focal length is longer than this distance, it is a telephoto lens. For an aerial camera with a 9 × 9 in format, the diagonal is almost 13 in, and the 12in lens cone is considered to be the normal lens. This type of camera, however, is most frequently used with a 6in lens and the resulting photographs are vignetted. This effect is more noticeable in colour emulsions than in black and white.

With black-and-white film, exposure variations cause a change in the optical density—i.e. the film gets darker, or lighter. In colour emulsions, the effects are more complex. A colour emulsion consists of three silver halide layers, each responsible for sensitivity to one of the three primary colours. Each silver halide layer is coupled to a dye so that the various colours of the final image are formed by a sandwich of three coloured (dyed) layers. The final colour of any given portion of the image is a function of the ratio of the intensities of the dyes in the three layers. However, the three silver halide layers do not have identical sensitivity characteristics. Consequently, as the exposure changes, the three coloured layers do not get equally darker or lighter, and the colour characteristics of the image are changed. This is why vignetting is more pronounced in a colour emulsion; the borders are not only darker, they have a different colour.

In some instances, excessive exposure variation within an image can be partially corrected by a technique known as *dodging*. In this procedure one selectively retards, or passes light through the negative to offset any imbalance. Where the negative is dense, more light is allowed to pass through than where the negative is thin. For manual techniques, this is accompanied by the use of masks or stiff paper shields. The procedure can also be done automatically, as shown in Fig. 4. The air photograph was taken over a portion of Greenland, which contained dark bare ground and bright snow in the same scene. This combination is such that no single exposure can clearly portray the detail at both ends of the contrast range. The print at the left is a standard contact print. Since exposure tended to favour the snow surface, the negative has but little density in land areas, and the contact print portrays the land as nearly black and without detail. At the right is an automatically dodged print made on a Logetronic printer. For this print, the scanning beam was reduced in intensity when passing through thin parts of the negative, and increased in intensity when passing through denser parts of the negative. The result is a gain in detail contrast in both light and dark areas of the scene.

Speed

For identical exposure and processing conditions, different emulsions will generate different characteristic curves. Therefore, some sort of index is needed that tells how to expose a particular type of film to obtain a satisfactory picture. Although there are several ways of determining this factor, it is basically a number derived from the characteristic curve of a given film, which describes the sensitivity of that film for specific exposure and processing conditions. The number is usually computed from the reciprocal of the exposure (in meter-candle-seconds) multiplied by a constant, to give some specified optical density. Results of many early experiments showed that the best prints came from negatives that had been exposed so that the darkest part of the scene was reproduced at a definite location on the toe of the characteristic curve. In earlier years, the method adopted by the American Standards Association (ASA) specified this location as the point where the gradient was $0 \cdot 3$ of the average gradient over a log exposure of $1 \cdot 5$ (James and Higgens, 1960, 213). Current ASA procedure still computes speed as the reciprocal of the exposure multiplied by a constant, $0 \cdot 8$ in this case. The exposure used corresponds to a certain point on the curve that is $0 \cdot 1$ of a density unit above fog-plus-base density. A second point is located $1 \cdot 3$ log exposure units from the first, and in the direction of increasing exposure. Processing conditions for the given negative material are fixed so that the density of the second point is $0 \cdot 8$ of a unit above the density of the first point. The exposure corresponding to the first point is the value from which the film speed is calculated (Derr, 1972, 150). Whatever the method—ASA, DIN, Exposure Value, etc.—the attempt is to provide an index that will tell the user the minimum exposure that will produce a good print or picture. A rule of thumb that is sometimes helpful is that for a scene of normal brightness, not snow or sand, under a clear sunny sky, the ASA number is the shutter speed at *f* 16.

When the ratio of blue skylight to sunlight is great (i.e. a high colour temperature, which occurs at high latitudes) exposure meters can give misleading

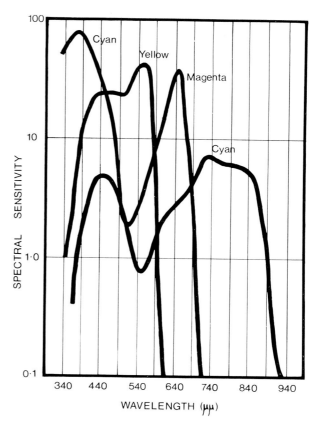

Fig. 5 A spectral sensitivity curve for Kodak Ektachrome Infrared film. The cyan layer, which is the infrared monitoring layer, is also sensitive to blue light. (From data kindly supplied by Eastman Kodak)

information, for they are usually calibrated for lower colour temperature light sources. The film data sheet supplied by the manufacturer is the best source of information about exposure and processing.

Spectral sensitivity

Photographic emulsions vary in their sensitivity to different wavelengths of light, particularly for the longer wavelengths of the visible spectrum and the near infrared. However, all emulsions, including infrared, are sensitive to radiation from the blue, violet, ultraviolet, x-ray, and gamma-ray portions of the spectrum, as well as to charged masses such as beta rays and alpha particles. This sensitivity is an inherent property of silver halide. Emulsions that have only this sensitivity are called *blue-sensitive*. If the sensitivity of the emulsion is extended to include green light, it is called *orthochromatic*; emulsions sensitive to the red part of the spectrum as well are called *panchromatic*; and emulsions that have been treated to extend their sensitivity out to the wavelength regions of $0 \cdot 9$ μm and beyond are called *infrared films*.

The sensitivity of a silver halide emulsion can be extended by the use of special organic dyes that can be absorbed by the silver halide and which can absorb energy in the spectral region of interest. Light quanta absorbed by the dye cause a transfer of electrons to the conductance band of the crystal and initiate the process of latent image formation previously described. Most aerial films have an extended sensitivity to just beyond the visible red (about $0 \cdot 72$ μm).

The spectral sensitivity of a film is measured on a qualitative basis by means of a wedge spectrograph, and on an absolute basis by means of a spectral sensitometer. The latter instrument produces a plot of the energy required to produce a specific density against the wavelength of the radiation. Figure 5 shows a spectral sensitivity curve for Ektachrome Infrared film. Being a colour film, it has three silver halide layers, each of which is coupled to a dye (cyan, magenta, or yellow) during processing to produce the colours in the image. Each curve represents the spectral sensitivity of the silver halide layer coupled to the specified dye. Note that the cyan layer, which has the infrared sensitivity, is also sensitive to energy throughout the spectrum, being even more sensitive to blue light than to infrared radiation. In order to ensure that the modulation of the cyan layer is caused by infrared energy, it is necessary to use a filter over the lens that prevents blue light from entering. A yellow filter, such as a Wratten 12 or 15, is frequently used for this purpose. It transmits red and green (the combination of which is yellow) and infrared, and rejects the blue, cutting off wavelengths shorter than 0·5 μm. The resultant image represents about equal contributions of visible and infrared energy. Since this film is also sensitive to ultraviolet energy, it can be used with a Wratten 18A filter for ultraviolet photography. First, the lens of the camera must be exchanged for a quartz lens which is transparent to such wavelengths, because the normal glass lens cannot transmit energy with wavelengths shorter than 0·38 μm.

Black-and-white infrared film is also sensitive throughout the spectrum and must be used with a special filter for infrared photography. With a Wratten 87C filter, the image is totally infrared since the 87C does not transmit any of the visible spectrum. With a Wratten 25A filter (deep red) the image represents about one-third visible and two-thirds infrared.

Resolution and sharpness

In addition to information about speed and spectral sensitivity, one frequently needs to know something about the ability of a film to record fine detail. The oldest procedure for evaluating this characteristic is to measure what is called the *resolving power* of the film. A lens has a similar parameter and the detail recorded in a photographic image is a function of both sets of properties. To measure the resolving power, a photograph is taken of a graded size series of a pattern of equal lines and spaces. Each set of parallel lines (three lines and two spaces per set) differs from its neighbours by several lines per millimetre, and the reduction in size goes down virtually to the microscopic scale. The film is processed under some set of standard conditions, and viewed under a microscope. The resolving power is defined in terms of the highest number of lines per millimetre that can be discerned. In order to reduce the effect of the lens to a minimum, its resolving power should be at least three times better than the emulsion being tested.

Resolving power, and the ability to record fine detail, is a function of the brightness contrast of the target, whether it be terrain or the parallel bar pattern. It is easier to see a small white spot against a black background than a grey spot against a darker grey background. In general terms, the resolving power of an emulsion is about halved if the contrast ratio is reduced from 1,000 : 1 to 2 : 1.

With terrain scenes, the ability to record fine pattern detail is also a function of the shape of the particular element. For example, in aerial photography of 1 : 15,000 scale, one can frequently detect individual cables of a power line. The width of this element would be considered below the resolving power of the system, and if it were only a few times longer than its width, it would not be discernible in the image.

One physical property of an emulsion that influences the resolving power is its turbidity. An emulsion consists of silver halide particles, which have a high index of refraction, dispersed in a medium with a lower index of refraction, a combination that causes the scattering, or reflection, of incoming light, back and forth among the grains. Thus, when a point of light is focussed on the emulsion, the light is scattered as it passes through, and produces a darkened area much larger than the original point size. The distribution of light in such an image is called a *point spread function*. In general, emulsions with small grain size have less turbidity and a higher resolution. The resolving power is also a function of exposure, increasing with exposure to some peak value, and then decreasing as exposure continues.

Resolving power is not the only criterion of image quality, and sometimes it is not an important one. The resolving power of the eye is about 10 lines/mm at the normal reading distance and one might ask what difference does it make if the resolving power of the film is 50 or 150 lines/mm? A good picture is frequently defined as one in which the details are produced with clarity or sharpness. Thus, edge sharpness can be more important than resolving power, and the focal properties for edge sharpness differ from those associated with resolution. Nevertheless, there are advantages to the use of resolution as an index of performance. For one, it has an historical tradition and its meaning is understood throughout the photographic community. It is also easier to measure than the sine-wave response or the modulation transfer function, since only a microscope is required, as compared with the need of a scanning microdensitometer for the other methods. More important, resolving power summarizes the effects of all the links in the system; lens, emulsion, processing, image motion, etc.

This all-encompassing ability is also a drawback, for it is difficult to determine the exact cause of image degradation by a consideration of resolving power. Neither is it a consistent indicator of image quality. Even so, it is a useful and widely used index of performance, particularly when combined with modulation transfer function factors.

The modulation transfer function (MTF) is another way of evaluating the performance of a lens, an emulsion, or a complete system. In the case of an emulsion, it describes the behaviour as influenced by exposure, edge sharpness or acutance, and resolving power. A special target is used, which consists of a series of straight parallel lines that decrease arithmetically in width and spacing from one end of the display to the other. This pattern results in a sine-wave type of density distribution when it is scanned and recorded with a microdensitometer. In use, the test pattern serves as a negative to print an image on the emulsion to be evaluated. A microdensitometer trace is made across the lines of the test pattern and across the lines of the image in the emulsion. With the exception of opposite values of density (one for the negative target and one for the positive image), the density trace of an ideal response would duplicate the trace of the original test pattern. However, in the real case there is always some deviation in the values of the minimum and maximum densities as the spatial frequency increases, i.e. as the lines get narrower and closer together. This deviation represents the modulation change of the film caused by emulsion turbidity. At low spatial frequency, where the lines are rather far apart, the emulsion pattern does duplicate the original. As spatial frequency increases, the deviation increases, as low-density spaces begin to fill in. At the limits, in the high-frequency end, both the test pattern and the film pattern attain some intermediate but uniform density value. A graph of these results can be made by plotting along the ordinate the ratio of the modulation in the image to the modulation of the target as a function of frequency, which is plotted along the abscissa.

An advantage of the procedure is that the MTF of a complete system can be calculated from the MTF's of the individual elements (lens, negative, positive) by multiplying the curves together, ordinate by ordinate at each abscissa value. Thus, the designer can predict not only total system response, but can also assign weighting values to the amount of image degradation caused by each element of the system.

OPTICS

As with factors considered in the previous section, some of the items discussed here become important only at the limits of the system, and are not particularly noteworthy in the everyday sphere of photographic work. Furthermore, both lenses and emulsions have so improved over the years that many previously important relations no longer have practical significance. Lens design and manufacture are complicated fields in themselves and detailed information about such items can be found in texts of physics and optics, or in manuals published by professional societies associated with such matters. Discussion in this section will be confined to general remarks about some of the fundamental properties of any lens system, simple or compound.

Aberrations

A wide beam of light rays incident on a convergent lens will not be brought to focus at a unique point, i.e. light passing through the periphery of the lens will not focus in the same plane as light passing through the centre. This departure from expected performance is called *spherical aberration*. A lens that has been corrected for this condition is called *aplanatic*.

Chromatic aberration describes the fact that light of different colours, or wavelengths, does not focus in the same plane. The amount of bending of a light ray, for a given lens curvature, depends on the change in speed that the light undergoes as it crosses the interface between two media (air to glass and then glass to air for a simple lens). This, in turn, is determined by the difference between the indices of refraction of the two media. The index of refraction of optical glass increases as the wavelength of the energy decreases, and thus there is a different focal point for each colour. The lens designer combines elements of different glasses (different indices of refraction) in an attempt to bring two or more specified colours to the same focal plane.

The resultant lens is called an *achromatic lens*. Note that although the two or three colours may fall into common focus, colours outside of those specific wavelengths will be focussed in different planes. The nature of the chromatic correction depends on the intended use of the lens. For example, a projection or enlarger lens must be corrected with reference to wavelengths of maximum output of the light sources as well as to wavelengths of maximum sensitivity to the eye. These do not match the corrections needed for a camera lens designed to photograph bright sunlit objects, and neither of these lenses makes a good substitute for the other. If the lens is to be used for infrared photography as well (i.e. a universal lens), some critical wavelength in that band must be taken into the design consideration. Although many aerial cameras have achromatic lenses, they give fuzzy-looking infrared photographs, because the infrared rays do not focus in the same plane as the visible light. Most aerial cameras have a lens cone that rigidly fixes the lens-to-emulsion distance, a distance which, though satisfactory for visible light, is too short for infrared energy. In order to bring the infrared focal plane into coincidence with the emulsion plane, shims are added between the camera body and the magazine, or the camera body and lens cone, to extend the distance to its proper value. With the development of the universal lens, corrected for both the visible and infrared portions of the spectrum, such a procedure is not necessary.

Lens diaphragm

Camera lenses are usually equipped with some form of an adjustable opening or diaphragm, which controls the amount of light that can pass through the lens. In order to indicate the relative amount of light that can pass through a lens, for any given diaphragm opening the diaphragm scale is marked with a series of numbers called *f* numbers or *f* stops. Each *f* number is a value obtained by dividing the focal length of that lens by the diameter of the diaphragm opening. The smaller the number, the more light will pass through the lens. The *f* number series 1·4, 2, 2·8, 4, 5·6, 8, 11, 16, 22, 32, and 45 indicate successive reductions in light passing through the lens, each reduction being one-half of the previous value. With shutter speed held constant, an aperture of *f*8 will give twice the exposure of *f*11 and one-half the exposure of *f*5·6.

When a lens is focused for a given distance, presumably only objects at that specific distance from the camera will be in sharp focus. For all other distances, objects within the scene will be more or less out of focus. The *depth of field* of a lens/aperture system denotes the range of distances before and behind the object plane, for which details will be imaged on the emulsion with acceptable clarity. This does not say they are all equally in focus, but only that the clarity of object detail within that range of distances is acceptable. Depth of field increases with increasing lens–object distances, decreasing focal length, and increasing *f* numbers, or smaller apertures. However, an increased depth of field is not the only effect of smaller apertures; there is also a loss of resolution. Most lenses have relatively poor resolution when the diaphragm is wide open and, as the diameter of the aperture is decreased, the resolution improves to some maximum value and then falls off. The best resolution is usually achieved when the diaphragm is stopped down two or three *f* numbers below the largest opening.

Resolution and focus

Although the human eye has a wide field of view, something over 180°, it can form a good-quality image over only a small part of that field, about 4° in the forward direction. A photographic lens, on the other hand, has a much narrower field of view, but with relatively uniform resolution throughout the field. As indicated in a previous section, resolution is not the only criterion for judging an image; there is also the aspect of sharpness. For any given scene, at some specified distance from the lens there is a lens–image distance (focus setting) that will provide maximum resolution, and another lens–image distance that will provide maximum edge sharpness. The difference between these two focal distances can be greater than the thickness of the emulsion.

Most aerial cameras have a cone of fixed focal length for each lens. This fixed distance is such that detail from some specific near range (perhaps 1000 m) out to infinity is in acceptable focus. However, there is only one lens–object distance that satisfies any selected lens–image distance, and in an absolute sense there is only one altitude above the terrain that a fixed lens cone will be in focus for maximum resolution or for maximum sharpness. For any camera, as the lens–object distance becomes large, the adjustment needed in the lens–image distance to correct the focus becomes exceedingly small, so small that it is impractical to make the correction, whence the necessity of using a fixed focal distance. Complicating the issue is the fact that, in many areas, the landscape is so rugged that some surfaces are several, sometimes hundreds of, metres closer to the camera lens than are other surfaces, and consequently there is no single lens–image setting that will bring all of the scene into equal focus. Some portions of the scene may be at just the right distance from the lens to be focussed for maximum resolution, while others will be at a distance that coincides with the focal setting for edge sharpness. In early photography, such variations could be found in a single frame. For the most part, lenses are now so improved that, though these effects can still be observed at the limits of the system, they are of little practical importance to most photographic applications.

FILM/FILTER COMBINATIONS

Each emulsion or film/filter combination has certain advantages and disadvantages which, under certain conditions, can be of aid in acquiring specific types of photographic information. The questions arise as to what these conditions are and how they are evaluated to select a given filter and emulsion.

Any photograph is a summation of the optical properties of the light source, the surface in question, the intervening atmosphere, the filter, the lens, and the emulsion. These considerations are more important for detection-oriented studies than they are for general-purpose photography, but even in the latter case they can become important, when one must use a filter to offset the effects of haze or to correct the colour-balance of a scene for a given colour emulsion, etc. The light sources normally used for aerial photography are the sun and the sky. Sunlight is the richer of the two for it contains all of the colours of the visible spectrum, plus ultraviolet and infrared components. Skylight, on the other hand, is composed essentially of blue light. Variations in the ratio of these two lights,

as the sun rises to its height and again settles to low elevations in the evening, cause apparent changes of colours within a scene. The landscape photographer is aware of this, for he patiently awaits the right moment for the lighting to create the mood he is seeking to capture. The aerial photographer is not as interested in mood as he is in recording a given set of details, but, since he cannot control the light sources, in either intensity or position, he must on occasion exercise the patience of the landscape photographer and wait for the right conditions to present themselves. Sometimes subtle relief variations are easier to record with the low sun angles of morning and evening than when the sun is high in the sky. Other patterns, such as linear features, can be more apparent when illuminated by the sun from a given direction.

Shadow detail can be an aid in interpretation and detection, and it can also be a nuisance. The contrasty and complex shadow pattern of temperate-region deciduous woods during the autumn, when the leaves are gone from the trees, can mask any other ground pattern that might be present. If such shadow patterns will be a bother, the photographs must be taken with the diffuse light of a high overcast, when shadows are not formed. However, an overcast greatly alters the spectral composition of the light, which can render it useless for other tasks. If one is involved in a study where infrared reflectance properties are important, such as vegetation typing, mapping of wetlands, detection of altered vegetation, etc., it is necessary to use not only the proper filter and emulsion but also to take the photography with the proper light sources— i.e. sunlight, which contains infrared radiation. An overcast prevents infrared energy from reaching the ground, and under such conditions it is not possible to take an infrared photograph.

Shadows, which are formed by blocking the sun's rays, are backfilled with skylight, which is blue in colour. Therefore, if one wants to record detail within a shadow region, it is necessary to use the blue light, since it is this band that is carrying whatever information is there. An example of this is shown in Fig. 6, which is a comparison between two types of photograph: an unfiltered panchromatic and an infrared taken with a filter that excludes all energy within the visible part of the spectrum. In the panchromatic photograph, which includes the blue light, detail within the building shadows is relatively clear, as evidenced by the ease with which one can discern the various automobiles and the sidewalk. In the infrared photograph, the shadows are black and contain little evidence of their contents, for the blue light which carries such information has been excluded from the image.

A material surface usually modifies the light that strikes it so that the reflected energy differs in several properties from the incident illumination. The optical characteristics of a material determine how much of which wavelengths are reflected, transmitted, or absorbed, and the surface structure of the material determines to what extent the light is reflected specularly or diffusely. An example of this latter effect is shown in Fig. 3. The true colour, or physical colour, of a substance is a measurable property that exists independent of how we see it or how we photograph it. The instrument for making such measurements is called a spectrophotometer. In it, a sample of the material in question is sequentially illuminated by different wavelengths of electromagnetic energy, and the amount that is transmitted or reflected at each wavelength increment is recorded. Various optical arrangements allow one to measure and record total hemispherical reflectance, and to separate and record the specular and diffuse components. Sample preparation can greatly influence the results of such measurements. Sometimes an author is not specific as to how the sample was mounted (with or without light-trap, backed or unbacked, etc.) and whether he measured total hemispherical reflectance, diffuse reflectance, diffuse minus specular, or specular reflectance. One can come to erroneous conclusions from such data. Another problem arises when one attempts to apply laboratory measurements to the natural scene as an aerial camera views it. For example, one can measure the diffuse reflectance of a leaf from a tree. However, the aerial camera views not a single leaf, but a scene that contains a tree, or a grove of trees, each with a surface composed of leaves oriented at all possible directions, with reference to the sun and to the camera—some tilted to cause a specular reflection, and others tilted to cause a shadow. Furthermore, the tree may be back-illuminated with light reflected from the surrounds (bare soil, dry grass, etc.). Nevertheless, reflectance data can be helpful in evaluating proposed film/filter combinations for detection problems.

Figure 6 also shows one effect of colour variances in different parts of the spectrum. In the left-hand panchromatic photograph, note in the upper centre,

above the middle building, that the sidewalks are lighter than the grass. These cement walks are reflecting more energy to the camera than the adjacent grass. In the infrared photograph to the right, these same walks are slightly darker than the grass and much less apparent. The grass itself is much lighter than in the panchromatic photograph, which one would expect, since most vegetation is quite bright in the infrared region, reflecting 40–60% of the incident energy.

If the atmosphere were truly clear, an impossible condition for many places at the present time, its influence on radiant energy would be insignificant at the path-lengths associated with conventional aerial photography. However, even without man's activities, the atmosphere takes on a variety of additives such as dust, water vapour, volcanic material, and the metabolic by-products of plant respiration. To this, man adds his portion in the form of particulates, gases, and organic molecules, and the resultant mixture acts on transient electromagnetic energy by selectively transmitting, scattering, or absorbing the various wavelength components. Even with a clear atmosphere, there is a fall-off of ground contrast with altitude, and any contaminants simply cause further deterioration, the limit being the loss of pattern detail, even at low altitudes, typical of a dense fog or haze. More often than not, the photographer's problem is how to eliminate or reduce the effect of a marginal amount of haze. The haze itself is the result of the scattering of light from particles and molecules in the air. In general terms, the wavelength of the scattered light is

Fig. 6   Comparison of an unfiltered panchromatic (Tri-X) photograph and an infrared (Wratten 87C filter) photograph. In the panchromatic photograph (left), the arrows indicate two shadow areas in which automobiles and sidewalks can be seen. These details were recorded because the blue skylight, which illuminates all surfaces, including shadows, was incorporated into the image. In the infrared photograph (right), a filter prevented any visible light from reaching the film, and consequently pattern detail within the shadows was not recorded

proportional to the size of the particle causing the scattering. Very frequently, the particle sizes are such that the scattering is associated with the short wavelength (i.e. blue) end of the visible spectrum. The longer wavelengths (i.e. red) pass through with little deviation. In a colour emulsion, haze causes an overall bluish cast to the picture, and its presence is more evident than in a black-and-white image, where there is an alteration only of grey tones. If, by using a filter, the blue scattered light is prevented from reaching the emulsion, there is a gain in pattern clarity with any film. Film/filter combinations favoured for this purpose include panchromatic/Wratten 12, Ektachrome Infrared/Wratten 12 or 15, and Infrared Aerographic/Wratten 25A or 87C. The chemical composition and particle-size distributions are different for different sorts of haze and the same film/filter combination is not equally applicable. For example, the haze found over a heavily wooded region, such as the Smokey Mountains in the USA, contains a variety of metabolic by-products of plant respiration that causes a different spectral distribution of the scattered light, extending it into longer wavelengths. Note also that shadow detail relies on blue light and haze is a carrier of blue light; thus, one cannot simultaneously record pattern detail in shadow regions and eliminate haze light.

Photographic filters are usually made of dye compounds distributed in a gelatin layer and sealed between glass sheets. The choice of dye determines which wavelengths will be transmitted and which absorbed. The variety is such that one can find a ready-made filter for transmitting any reasonable narrow band of energy ranging from the ultraviolet, through the visible, and into the infrared portions of the spectrum. At the short wavelength end is the Wratten 18A, or its equivalent, which transmits a band of energy in the ultraviolet (wavelengths of approximately 0·3–0·38 μm) plus a small amount of infrared energy at the long wavelength end of the visible part of the spectrum. As stated previously, such a filter must be used with a quartz lens, which is transparent to ultraviolet, since the normal camera lens does not transmit energy with wavelengths shorter than about 0·39 or 0·38 μm. Next are the three standard primary colour filters, Wrattens 47B (primary blue), 58 (primary green), and 25A (primary red). In addition to special purposes, these filters are frequently used in multi-band photography with panchromatic emulsions to study grey tone shifts or to provide images for additive colour procedures. The 25A is also used for modified infrared photography, since it is transparent to red and infrared energy. The Wratten 87C is a commonly used infrared filter that does not transmit any visible light. Figure 7 shows the spectral transmission for the 47B, the 58, and the 87C. Note that both the 47B and the 58 are also transparent to infrared. They are basically infrared pass filters with added small transparencies in the visible region. When used with infrared aerographic film they provide not only a typical infrared capability, but also allow some blue or green light to be added to the image, so that the shadows are not quite as dense and consequently contain some shadow information. This is more of a help with large-scale photography than with small. The common minus-blue filters (Wrattens 12 and 15) reject the blue and transmit green and red (plus infrared). These are used with panchromatic film for haze penetration, and with Ektachrome infrared film

to provide its standard response. The infrared sensitive layer in this film is also sensitive to blue light (cp. Fig. 5) and, in order to make certain that the desired effect is caused by infrared energy and not the blue, a filter must be used to block entrance of blue light. Figure 8 is one example of the use of a film/filter combination to enhance a given pattern element. The photographs are from the comparative photography collection of Professor Harp at Dartmouth College. At the left is an unfiltered panchromatic image and at the right is an infrared image. In general, water boundaries are more obvious in infrared photographs than in panchromatic. In the panchromatic photograph, the dense vegetation and enclosed ponds have similar brightness values. This is particularly evident to the left of the river. In the infrared band, bare rocks appear somewhat darker, vegetation lighter, and water as dark grey or black, a set of tone conditions that makes it easier to detect and identify isolated ponds. If the water contains a suspended load of silt or clay, it might be easier to detect the boundaries in the visual band than in the infrared, or in a normal colour image versus a panchromatic, depending on the colour and brightness of the suspended material.

Figure 9 is of interest, not because of any technical aspects of films and filters, but because it portrays the detection of a pattern element that, at first thought, would seem impossible to photograph. The pictures are of a padi/dike area in Thailand, specifically, a portion of the floodplain of the Chao Phraya River, north of the ancient capital city of Ayutthaya. They were taken during the dry season when the rice harvest

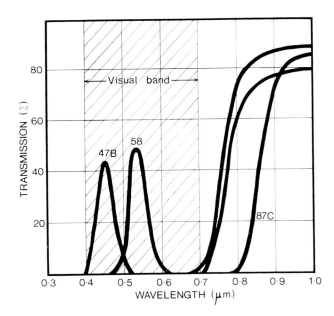

Fig. 7   Transmission characteristics of three commonly used Wratten filters. The 87C transmits only infrared wavelengths and is used with black-and-white infrared films. The 47B (primary blue) and 58 (primary green) are frequently used in conjunction with a Wratten 25A (primary red) to obtain three separate exposures that can be used for additive colour studies or multi-band photography. The 47B, 58, and 25A are also transparent to infrared and can be used for black-and-white infrared photography.

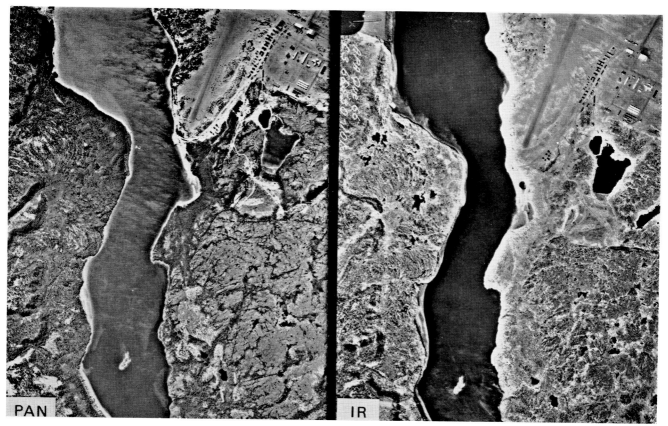

Fig. 8 *A comparison of panchromatic and infrared imagery over a site at Great Whale, Que., Canada. In the infrared band the contrasts between water and rock and between water and vegetation are much greater than in the panchromatic band and consequently isolated ponds of water are easier to detect and identify. These photographs are from the collection of Professor Elmer Harp Jr. of Dartmouth College, Hanover, NH*

Fig. 9 *Aerial photographs of a padi/dike area in Thailand*

was almost complete. In many of the fields the rice has been cut and the stubble burned, exposing the soil to the drying effects of sun and wind. Near the middle of each photograph, the pattern of an old river channel extends diagonally up to the right. Adjacent to this is a waffle-like or cross-hatch pattern superimposed on the present padi/dike complex. This pattern traces the location of an old dike system that existed many years ago. The old system was destroyed and a new padi/dike system built, with larger fields oriented to a river channel to the north. Since then, these fields have been ploughed and flooded twice a year; and yet,

when the surface cover is reduced so that the soil can dry, the old pattern re-establishes itself. That it shows is due to differential drying rates between the field soil and the denser soil beneath the old dikes; denser, because it was compacted over the years by the weight of the dike structure. This pattern showed equally well in all of the photography: panchromatic, black-and-white infrared, and colour infrared. The two photographs in this illustration were taken a few days apart. The infrared image also shows a pattern of white lines or streaks. Some look like ticks, some form a series of equally spaced dashes, and others resemble

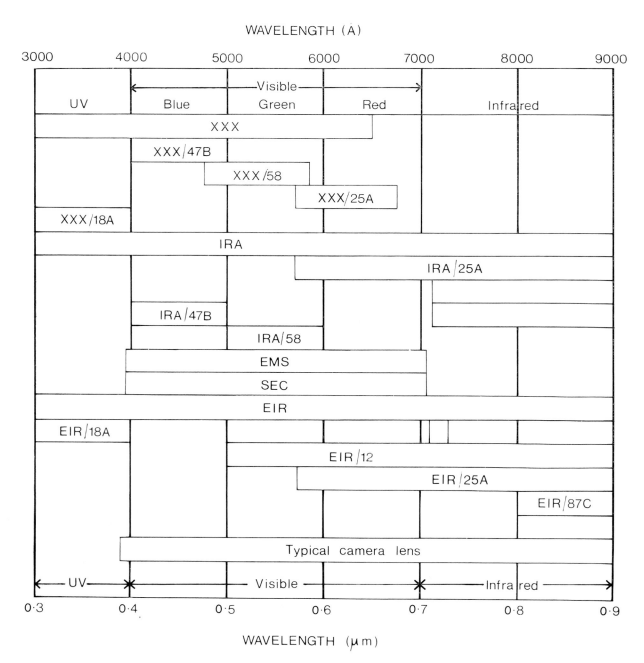

Fig. 10   *A schematic presentation of the bandpass and sensitivity limits of some common filters and films. This does not give information about relative sensitivities of the emulsions or relative transparencies of the filters.*

XXX = Tri-X   IRA = Infrared Aerographic   EMS = Ektachrome MS   EIR = Ektachrome Infrared   SEC = Special Ektachrome

Numbers refer to Wratten filters

TABLE I **Ranking of the application of some films and film/filter combinations to specific tasks**

The preferred order decreases from left to right. In most instances, for the columns marked *Preferred* and *Acceptable,* the film/filter to the right is only slightly less desirable than that to the left of it.

Factor	Preferred	Acceptable	Poor
Multiplicity of tones	EMS, XXX	47B, 58, 25A	EIR, 87C
Shadow sharpness	25A, EIR	87C, 58, EMS, XXX	47B
Detail within shadows	XXX, 47B	EMS, 58	25A, EIR, 87C
Materials separation	EMS, XXX	58, 47B	25A, EIR, 87C
Soil and rock tones	EMS, XXX	47B, 58	25A, EIR, 87C
Water/shore boundaries	87C, EIR	25A, 47B	EMS, 58, XXX
Surface moisture	EIR, EMS	XXX, 25A	47B, 58, 87C
Vegetation typing	EIR, 87C	EMS, 25A, 47B	58
Species (within a type)	EMS, 25A	58, 47B	EIR, 87C
Turf conditions	EIR, EMS	87C, 25A	47B, 58, XXX
Urban vegetation studies	EMS, EIR, XXX	47B, 25A, 58	87C
Structures	EMS, XXX	58, 47B, 25A	EIR, 87C
Functional aspects	EMS, XXX	58, 47B, 25A	EIR, 87C
Small-site detection	XXX, EMS, EIR	47B	58, 25A, 87C

EMS = Ektachrome MS
EIR = Ektachrome Infrared
XXX = Unfiltered Tri-X
47B = Tri-X and Wratten 47B filter

58 = Tri-X and Wratten 58 filter
25A = Tri-X and Wratten 25A filter
87C = Infrared Aerographic and Wratten 87C filter

small lightning flashes. This pattern is caused by static electricity which builds up and discharges as the film moves across the platen, a characteristic common to infrared emulsions, particularly when used in dry conditions.

If one has the required colour information about the item of interest and its background, then selecting the best film or film/filter combination for enhancing contrast between the two is a straightforward procedure. Usually such information is not to be had, and resort must be made to trial and error procedures. Such tests can sometimes be initiated with ground photography before committing funds and efforts to the airborne phase. One fortunate aspect is the fact that seldom does a colour/brightness contrast exist that allows an object to be portrayed in only one spectral band. Usually, an object can be detected against its background in any part of the photograph spectrum, though frequently with greater clarity or contrast in one band than in another. Figure 10 shows the wavelength limits of some common Wratten filters and Kodak emulsions. It does not show the relative sensitivity or transparency from wavelength to wavelength, only the limits of response.

For general-purpose stereo aerial photography that will be used in the form of regional photographic mosaics, unfiltered (except for haze requirements) panchromatic photographs are the best choice. For strip photography or detection of specific items, colour or certain film/filter combinations can provide better results. Table I lists some film and film/filter combinations preferred for certain tasks. For many of the factors listed, it was difficult to decide which of the preferred two or three films or film/filter combinations was better. A repeat of these various experiments might exchange some portions of the order of merit, but it is not likely that exchanges would occur between columns, particularly between the data in the 'Preferred' and 'Acceptable' columns, and in the 'Poor' column.

SCALE

The scale of a photograph is the ratio of the focal length of the lens to the altitude above the terrain. A 6in lens (0·5 ft) at an altitude of 10,000 ft gives an image with a scale of 1 : 20,000, i.e. one unit in the image is equal to 20,000 units on the ground. A 12in lens at the same 10,000ft altitude yields an image with a scale of 1 : 10,000. As with film and filter, the choice of scale is not always an easy one. The size of the object that one needs to detect is certainly an important consideration, and the smaller the size, the larger the scale needed in the image. If one is dealing with only a few sites, then as low a scale as the terrain allows can be used. However, if one must study a relatively large region and must have full coverage, large scales such as 1 : 5000 or more become impossible from the standpoints of expense and of handling the large number of photographs involved. For general terrain information such as geology, hydrology, vegetation, land use, etc., scales of 1 : 15,000 to 1 : 20,000 represent the best compromise. From the standpoint of archaeological investigations, Harp (1968, in press) agrees in general with these findings, with the reservation that if small-site detection within a relatively large area is the primary goal, a scale of 1 : 10,000 is best for compromising the various needs of detection, cost, aerial coverage, number of photographs, etc.

BIBLIOGRAPHY

Derr, A. J. (1972). *Photography Equipment and Techniques. A Survey of NASA Developments* (NASA SP-5099). Technology Utilization Office, National Aeronautics and Space Administration, Washington, DC, USA.

Harp, E., Jr. (1968). Optimum Scales and Emulsions in Air Photo Archaeology. *Proc. 8th International Congress of Anthropological and Ethnological Sciences,* **3**, 163–165. Tokyo.

Harp, E., Jr. In Press. *Basic Considerations in the Use of Aerial Photography in Archaeological Research.* School of American Research, Santa Fe, New Mexico.

James, T. H., & Higgins, G. C. (1960). *Fundamentals of Photographic Theory* (2nd edition). New York and London.

Judd, D. B. (1952). *Color in Business, Science and Industry.* New York and London.

Maerz, A., & Paul, M. R. (1951). *A Dictionary of Color* (2nd edition). New York and London.

Munsell (1967). *Munsell Book of Color. Matte Finish Collection.* Baltimore, Md., USA.

Infra-red techniques

W. A. Baker

The object of this paper in the context of archaeology is to consider the possibilities of airborne sensor techniques in the infra-red spectrum which do not depend upon reflection derived from visible light in the conventional sense.

In a natural environment, energy from the sun is absorbed by vegetation and objects on the ground, which in turn emit energy in the form of infra-red radiation (Fig. 1). This constitutes electromagnetic energy, with comparable characteristics to those of radio waves and visible light. Although commonly referred to as 'radiant heat', it is not transferred by convection or conduction in a physical medium. Self-radiation from surface features at ambient temperatures only takes place at wavelengths longer than $3\mu m$ and cannot be detected by photographic techniques, using infra-red film.

The energy emitted from natural objects increases with wavelength, approaching a maximum in the region of $10 \mu m$, after which it slowly decreases. Within this spectrum there are constraints in the transmission of radiation because of its attenuation in the atmosphere, arising mainly from the presence of water vapour and carbon dioxide. There are other constituents in the environment which influence the loss of energy, but these are relatively unimportant in the context of aerial reconnaissance in archaeology.

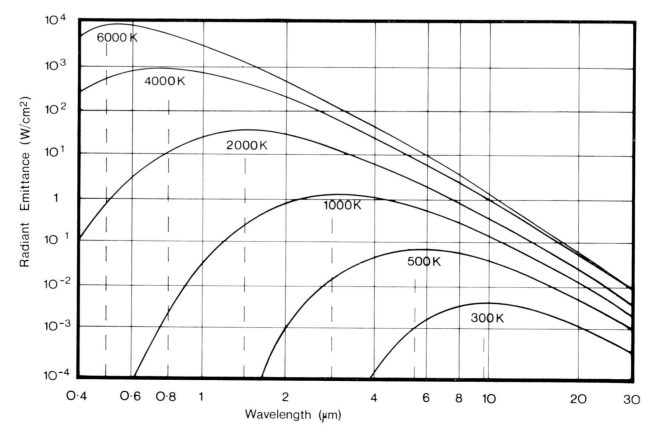

Fig. 1   Wein's Law: effect of temperature on radiation

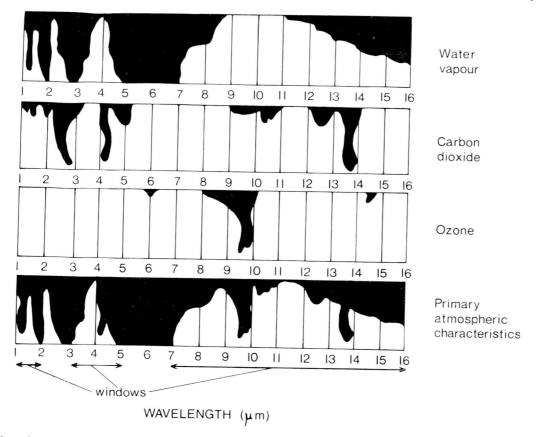

Fig. 2   The infra-red spectrum, showing absorption of infra-red energy by various constituents of the atmosphere

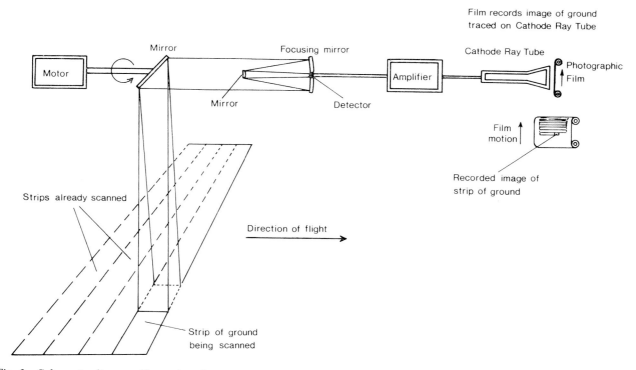

Fig. 3   Schematic diagram illustrating the operation of an infra-red linescan system

Fig. 4   Ridge-and-furrow by conventional photography

Between 5·5 and 7·5 μm the atmosphere is almost completely opaque, and this condition persists beyond 14 μm, leaving two atmospheric 'windows' through which the airborne sensor can function; these lie between wavelengths of 3–5·5 μm and 7·5–14 μm, with most of the available energy contained in the latter bandwidth (Fig. 2).

Within these limitations a thermal picture of the landscape can be achieved, the clarity or contrast being dependent upon the relative emissivity or radiation efficiency of adjacent surface features. The amount of infra-red radiation emitted will be determined by factors such as absolute temperature, surface texture, thermal capacity, composition, and colour. Thermal imagery, as in conventional photography, is also subject to variations in environmental conditions as given by time of day, air temperature, wind velocity,

precipitation, and seasonal variations, all of which have a profound effect on its use in landscape interpretation.

Before considering the possibilities of this medium for the detection of archaeological features in the landscape, some technical matters require further elaboration. A brief outline of the technique involved in obtaining thermal imagery will be followed by a consideration of the nature of the imagery itself.

The conversion of infra-red radiation into a visual record may be achieved by a linescan system (Fig. 3). In this method a thermal image of the landscape over which the aircraft is flying is built up by the successive scanning of parallel lines across the aircraft track.

The size of the scanning spot directly below the aircraft determines the linear resolution, which is the

Fig. 5   Ridge-and-furrow recorded using infra-red linescan

product of angular resolution and height. The angular resolution is the field of view of the detector through a focusing mirror. Obviously, to achieve a coherent picture the scanned lines must be contiguous. It follows that the spacing between the line centres is proportional to aircraft speed, while the line width is determined by the spot size, which will vary according to aircraft height. The minimum scan rate is therefore directly related to V/H, that is, *velocity* over *height*.

Essentially linescan comprises an optical system using a rotating mirror from which energy is focused on a detector device: this is generally mercury-doped germanium, maintained at a low temperature by a cryogenic system using liquid helium. The resultant signal, corresponding to changes of thermal input produced by the scanner, is electronically processed and used to modulate the beam of a cathode ray tube, which in turn is exposed to photographic film (Fig. 3). Since each recurring line on the cathode ray tube is synchronized with the optical scanner and stays in the same place on the tube face, the image is produced by moving the film across the modulated time base at a rate proportional to the aircraft V/H. In this way the line spacing on the film is consistent with that on the ground given by the forward motion of the aircraft. The final product is a continuous thermal picture of the terrain along the aircraft track in which hot objects appear white and cold objects black on the photographic print. Imagery derived in this way is subject to inherent geometric distortion in the absence of correction between the scanning and recording processes.

Fig. 6   Bronze Age barrows by conventional photography

Before an interpretation of some typical thermal photographs is attempted, it may be as well to consider the significance of the term *emissivity*. This is defined as the ability of a substance to absorb and subsequently emit energy in proportion to the total amount of energy incident upon it. To arrive at a numerical value, a theoretical object known as a *black body* is used. By definition such an object absorbs all incident radiation and emits the same amount; its emissivity factor can therefore be regarded as unity. On this basis, assuming the same absolute temperature, the emissivity factor of sand approximates to 0·95 and that of masonry and dry grass to 0·87. From this it is apparent that parching effects in pasture, for example, would register extremely well.

A further important factor is the total radiation emitted by an object and is known as *radiometric temperature*. Total radiation equals the emissivity times the absolute temperature to the 4th power, $R_T = ET^4(c)$, that is to say, doubling the temperature will increase total radiation 16 times. It is possible, however, to postulate a situation where adjacent features having different temperatures and emissivity factors could produce the same radiant emittance values at the detector with no signal contrast as a consequence. Two natural objects at the same physical temperature could not be resolved unless they exhibit different emissivity factors. In general terms, provided that there is a significant change in absolute temperature between two objects, with a 4th-power law they will stand out in marked contrast.

If these factors are now related to archaeological features, extant remains illuminated by the sun at low angles of incidence should produce strong thermal shadows with contrasting highlights arising from the difference in temperature.

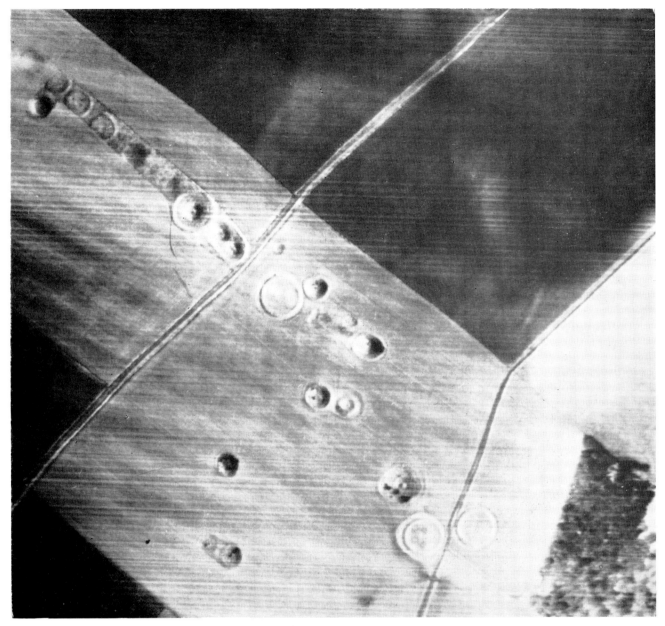

Fig. 7   Bronze Age barrows recorded using infra-red linescan

Height, or the distance between the radiating object and infra-red detector, is also of significance in that, if height is increased by a multiple R, the intensity of radiation received would be decreased by I/R^2. In other words, increasing height by a factor of 2 would result in only one-quarter of the radiation being received at the detector. Taking this into consideration, together with limitations in sensor resolution and sensitivity, implies survey at low altitudes if crop-mark features are to be resolved and small differences of radiometric temperature recorded.

In conclusion, from the illustrations there is no doubt that the technique of recording emitted infra-red offers advantages in air archaeology. It is particularly able to record variations in landscape profile, whether presented by substantial structures such as hill forts, or by the detailed patterns of banks, tracks, and field systems.

These effects are enhanced by direct sunlight, although the conditions are not so critical as those required for shadow sites through conventional photography. Obscuration of surface features by the effects of shadow is also considerably less, when the level of illumination does not rise far above the minimum required. There are disadvantages in that rainfall will reduce variations in the surface temperature of natural objects to a more constant level, resulting in a loss of contrast, particularly under overcast conditions. Interpretation, of course, presents specific problems and the technique of infra-red merits continued study and experiment before it can be applied to good effect in an archaeological context.

Transformation of extreme oblique aerial photographs to maps or plans by conventional means or by computer

Irwin Scollar

Synopsis

Three methods are given for transferring coordinate information from extreme oblique air photographs to maps. The first two require simple graphical constructions and give modest accuracy when used on pictures taken over flat terrain. They require little equipment or expenditure. The third method uses an interactive computer program which solves for camera position and angle with multiple oblique images taken from arbitrary viewpoints. It produces high accuracy along with error estimates, regardless of terrain, but requires access to a computer and to a monocomparator for film measurement. The first two methods are useful for rough sketches with a small number of points. The third method is useful when precise maps of complex sites are needed. All require knowledge of a number of ground control points which must be visible in at least one image.

INTRODUCTION

The most important information contained in an archaeological air photograph is the geometric form of the visible site and its position on the ground. The location of the main features of the site should be achieved with an accuracy which is sufficient so that, if necessary, an excavation can be carried out without moving too much earth. Vertical mapping pictures taken with the appropriate equipment pose no problem. There is an arsenal of photogrammetric techniques which has been developed over the last half-century to deal with this case. The map-making services of almost any country can provide appropriate information and help. The situation is quite different if, as is frequent, the air photograph is an extreme oblique made with a hand-held camera of unknown type, and in which the horizon is not visible. Although a number of special optical devices have been produced from time to time to deal with this kind of image, they are not commonly available, nor are they easy to use. If the obliquity exceeds about 30° from the vertical, most purely optical devices are incapable of creating a vertical image from an arbitrary oblique negative in one step. In this paper, attention will be directed to several methods which are readily utilized without any sophisticated equipment, and which appear to be unknown to many archaeologists. A mathematical method will also be described which can be run on almost any computer, when precise results are required.

The simple methods require only pencil, tracing paper, and ruler, and make use of some properties of the projective transformation which governs the relationship between the image on the film and the points of interest on the ground. One very useful property of the projective transformation is that for reasonably flat terrain straight lines in the picture also represent straight lines on the map, no matter how oblique the image is. Therefore this is also true of a line drawn between any two points visible in both the image and the map.

THE PAPER STRIP METHOD

In many cases, the user of an archaeological air photograph merely wants to know where the centre of the site lies. A simple technique for this is shown in Fig. 1. Suppose that we want to know the position on the ground of point *g* in the photograph. To use the paper strip method, we must be able to identify at least four points, *a*, *b*, *c*, and *d* in the picture as being the same as four points *A*, *B*, *C*, and *D* on the map. The lines connecting point *a* with all the other points in the picture are drawn, including a line to point *g*. This gives four lines, *ad*, *ac*, *ag*, and *ab*, reading clockwise around *a*. These lines can then be drawn on the map, giving *AD*, *AC*, and *AB*, but not *AG* as yet. *AD*, *AC*, and *AB* must, by the properties of the projective transformation, be identical with those in the image. The problem is to find *AG*. A strip of paper is carefully folded, in order to obtain a good straight edge. It is placed over the image so that it cuts all four lines radiating from point *a* as shown in Fig. 1. Marks are made carefully with a sharp pencil at each point where the ray from *a* crosses the folded edge of the strip. The strip is then placed on the map and moved about until the pencil marks coincide with rays *AD*, *AC*, and *AB*. The mark corresponding to line *ag* in the photograph now defines the direction of line *AG* on the map and it can be drawn. Similarly, using the other side of the strip and working from point *b*, the line *BG* can be obtained. Point *G* must lie at the intersection of *AG* and *BG* as required.

The paper strip technique, if carefully drawn, is surprisingly accurate. It is readily seen that the map must be a fairly detailed one for, if the map and the image differ too much in size, considerable errors are possible in positioning the strip. There is also an error introduced if the altitudes of the control points differ substantially from that of the desired image point. In practice this is not likely to be much greater than the errors of drawing or control point determination. The tedious point-by-point transfer, with a graphical construction required at each step, makes this method suitable only when a few points need be considered.

THE MÖBIUS NETWORK METHOD

If one wishes to transfer a considerable amount of information from picture to plan, another simple method based on projective transformation properties may be useful. In the centre of the air photograph shown in Fig. 2 there is a large Roman marching camp lying near a modern road which follows the course of

The author is with the Laboratory for Field Archaeology of the Rheinisches Landesmuseum, Bonn, Federal Republic of Germany.

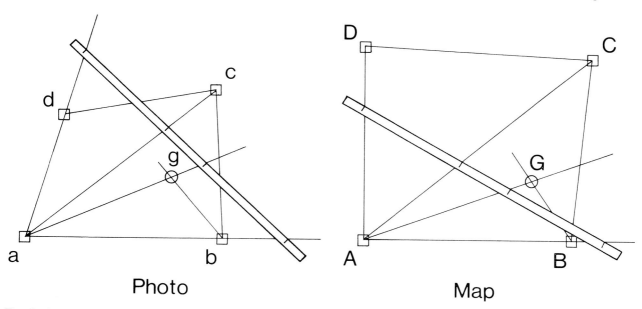

Fig. 1   Diagram to illustrate the paper strip method

the Rhine *Limes* south of Xanten in Germany. The site lies on the lower Rhine terrace, which is quite flat. A pre-Roman Rhine arm is also visible as the long wide dark strip running diagonally through the picture. The features of this camp had to be drawn on the 1 : 5000 base map for the Monuments Protection Service. In the highly built-up area it was quite easy to find an adequate number of fixed points which were also visible on the map (Fig. 3). For the Möbius network method, a minimum of five identifiable points is required, and six were used. These are circled and numbered in the photograph. The corners of houses, field boundary-road junctions, or street corners are readily identified to within a few metres. As shown in Fig. 4*a*, a tracing was made with all possible lines joining the six fixed points visible in photograph and map. From the projective transformation properties, the same lines were drawn on a tracing placed over the map, as shown in Fig. 4*b*. If at least five points are present, additional intersections in this network of lines become available. It is a property of networks of this kind that the intersections of the lines in the image correspond to the same intersections on the map. Therefore new lines can be drawn between the inter-section points and/or the fixed points. Thus the network may be made as fine as is desired, since new intersections are created every time a line is drawn. When the network is fine enough, the features of the site can be sketched in on the map relative to it with adequate accuracy. This method has the advantage that a large number of features can be drawn by hand with considerable speed, once the networks on map and image have been constructed. Again, as with the paper strip method, the heights of the points of interest in the image must not differ too drastically from those of the fixed points, especially when the picture is made at low altitude. In the example shown, with a photograph made at a height of 505 m, errors due to ground height were negligible, since the terrain was quite flat. Overall accuracy is about that of the line thickness used in making the tracings, referred to the base map scale, or about ± 2 m in the example.

A COMPUTER METHOD

The techniques described above are simple, but they are not highly accurate if there is a considerable difference between the actual ground heights at the known control points and those at points of interest at the site. The error will be important when the picture is taken at low altitude with extreme obliquity. Furthermore, at least four points per image must be visible. This is not always the case in open country. Frequently, a series of pictures has been made from decreasing altitudes while circling around the site. The high-altitude pictures show suitable control points but not the features of the site, while the low-altitude pictures show the site but not the control points. If one has access to a computer, the technique to be described below is preferable and relatively painless once the program is working. The method is completely general and produces estimates of the errors in the results in certain cases. It is based upon a well known derivation of the basic equations of photo-grammetry (Tewinkel *et al.*, 1966). Accuracy is limited mainly by the ability one has to measure the position of the ground control points on the film and on the ground, and by the geometric distortion produced by the camera lens.

The mathematical method has several steps. If the positions of three or more ground control points visible in a given picture are known, it is possible by an iterative technique to find the ground coordinates of the position from which the picture was taken, the altitude of the aircraft, and the angles of pitch, swing, and tilt. If more than three image points corresponding to ground control points are available, one can calculate probable errors referred to the film plane. When the position of the camera and its angles are determined, the projective transform equations can be solved for the ground position of any other image point, if the ground height of that point is known. For some purposes, the ground height can be estimated, giving a sufficiently accurate result. If two pictures are at hand showing the same area from a

Fig. 2   Crop marks of a Roman marching-camp, Alpen-Veen

different point of view, it is not necessary to know the ground height at all. If, better still, a series of pictures is available, the redundant information makes it possible to calculate the probable error in the ground height. Usually it is assumed that the focal length of the lens used for taking the picture is known very accurately. This is seldom the case for archaeological pictures. It is possible to compute the focal length from the redundant information in several images, or from one image if at least four control points are known. Using the mathematical technique, points from a site visible in one or more pictures may serve as ground control points for further pictures in the sequence after their ground coordinates have been computed. Errors increase in this way, of course, but not alarmingly so. In effect, any pair of pictures containing a sufficient amount of control information serves as a sort of stereo pair, allowing all photogrammetric relationships to be worked out.

The mathematical details of the method are described in the Appendix. Here discussion is limited to a brief description of our program, which is a modified version of the method described in the reference. It has been written for an interactive time-sharing computer and it allows format-free input of data from a remote terminal. The heart of the scheme, the calculation of camera position, is shown in the flow diagram of Fig. 5. The numerous coefficients required for a least-squares technique are computed. Then the program library's least-squares sub-routine is called. This produces a set of solutions which are estimates of the departure from initially assumed angles and positions required for best fit to the data. A fraction of this difference is subtracted from the initially assumed positions and angles, the coefficients are recalculated, and the least-squares routine is repeated. This process is continued, with rising fractional differences, until the departures calculated are less than pre-set tolerances. Usually,

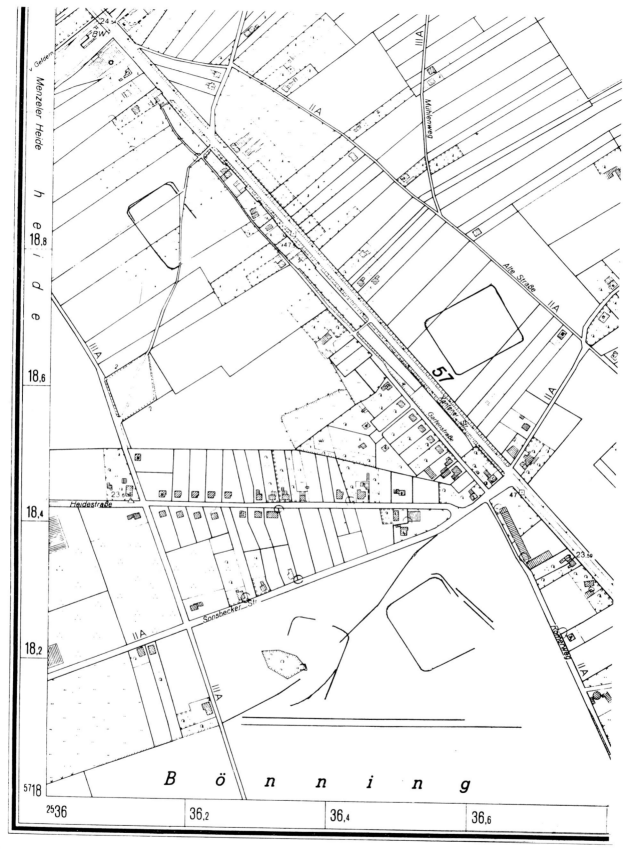

Fig. 3 Extract from map at 1 : 5000 (reproduced here at 1 : 5400), with the outlines of Roman camps and other features revealed by crop marks drawn on (cf. Fig. 2)

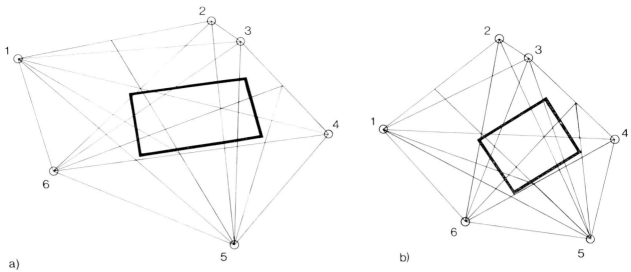

Fig. 4   Diagram to illustrate the Möbius network method: (a) *construction on photograph,* (b) *construction on map*

even from a very incorrect starting position, the process terminates with positions accurate to within 1 m on the ground and angles to within 0·001 radian in less than ten iterations. On the machine used, this process returns the camera position to the terminal with no perceptible delay. The program stores the position and angle, as well as the projective transformation coefficients for the image. If only one image is available, or if the terrain height of the site is known or can be estimated, the ground coordinates for unknown image points can be obtained immediately. Naturally, unless the terrain is quite flat or the height of the site is well known, this method is less accurate than when using multiple images.

If desired, some features of the first image can be used as ground control points for further images. If multiple images are available, the program returns to that part which asks for information about a new image. The camera position for the second image is then computed in the same way as that for the first one.

Typical input and output from the computer terminal in dialogue with the machine can be briefly described. The program asks for the camera type and focal length, the map numbers, and ground and image coordinates of a series of control points in an image. At least three are required or an error message is produced. A check is made to see that the coordinates really correspond to the maps in question and that the values are reasonable. A check is also made to see that the focal length specified is reasonably correct for the named camera; if the camera is unknown, this must be explicitly stated, in which case at least four control points will be required. The user is then asked if he wants to see how the computations proceed, and if he wants to specify initial camera positions and angles, and the tolerances on the results. If he specifies nothing, default options are used. For these, the camera is assumed to be vertically over the centre of the control point system and pointing downwards. If a rough camera position is specified—north of the centre, for example—a rough calculation of a possible starting angle is made. The iteration for camera position is carried out and, if so specified, the user can follow the progress of the movement of the camera as

the program adjusts it to fit the data. At the end of iteration, the position and the projective transform is available. This is applied to the stated image positions of the ground control points one after the other. If all has gone well, the ground coordinates of the control points will be returned within the calculation tolerances of camera position, otherwise an erroneous position has been arrived at. One erroneous position which causes much amusement gives the aircraft height as a negative number: flying in this way is to be deplored! Actually, ground values computed from such a position may be quite correct, since one is looking up at the image from underneath the Earth's surface. A more unpleasant possibility sometimes arises, when the camera position is obtained in such a way as to satisfy the control tolerances but with high error referred to the film plane. This sometimes happens when the default option is used on starting, the image is very oblique, along a map diagonal, and the picture is taken from a steep bank, so that it is skewed as well. The remedy is to specify an approximate starting position which can readily be judged by eye by looking at the map and the picture. At least, one can guess whether one was north, south, east, or west of the ground control point centre, and this is usually enough.

When the camera position is satisfactory, the program politely enquires if the picture is one of a series. If it is, it goes on to ask the user about further images, and computes their positions and projective transforms. When all images of interest are in store, the user is asked to supply film coordinates for identical points of interest on several images. The projective transform of these points is computed, and the equation of ground position is applied. Then the ground coordinates and an estimate of error are returned. Further points in the image series are examined for as long as desired. A return to a new set of images may then be made or the computation ended.

The principal source of inaccuracy in this technique is attributable to errors in measurement of the coordinates of control points on the film plane. If the control points are taken from maps, these points are rarely known to better than 2 m on a 1 : 5000 base

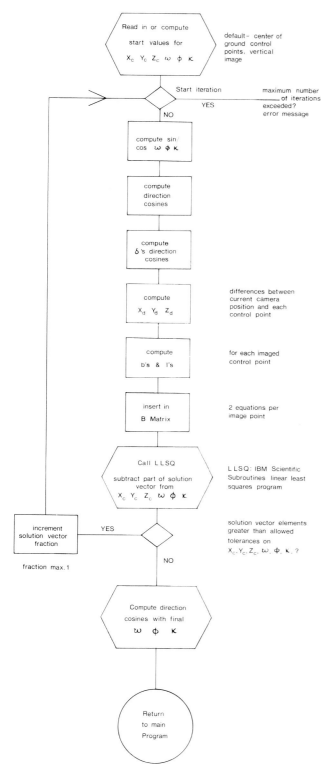

Fig. 5   Flow diagram for computer program

which can expand up to 3% in one direction and a smaller amount in another during development. On the larger hand-held aerial camera films (13×13cm image), measurements to about one part in a thousand are possible with relatively cheap equipment. One uses a contact film positive on a polyester base rather than the original negative. On smaller films, such as 6×6cm roll film or, even worse, on 35mm colour material, accuracy is greatly reduced. For the latter size, unfortunately much in favour among some practitioners, a great deal of trouble will have to be gone to if any precision at all is to be achieved. A discussion of suitable measuring instruments is beyond the scope of this paper. With the larger images, the errors in measurement are likely to be of the same order of magnitude as those in the determination of the coordinates of the ground control points, using good large-scale maps. There is little need for ground survey of the control points unless decent map cover is not available. If, for some reason, highest accuracy is required, the camera will have to be calibrated by photographing a known reseau to determine geometric distortion and centring of the lens. A table can then be provided for in the program to interpolate correct values when entering image points from film–plane measurements. Account will have to be taken of dimensional changes in film-base materials, and other precautions which need not be mentioned are also required. In practice, these niceties have not as yet proven themselves necessary when a 2m ground error is acceptable.

The relative accuracy of the points in the image with respect to each other (i.e. the fidelity of geometric reproduction of the shape of the site) is a function of the precision of film–plane measurement only. Hence accurate readings are really a must if good plans are to be obtained.

APPENDIX

In the mathematical discussion the treatment in Tewinkel *et al.* (1966) is followed, with some modification. It is assumed that the reader has sufficient background to understand this presentation, which is made to enable an experienced scientific programmer to duplicate the program mentioned in the main body of the text.

From elementary geometric considerations, as shown in Figures 2–14 and 2–15 of Tewinkel *et al.* (1966), the position of a point on the ground in terms of the coordinates of the image, measured from the centre, is given by:

$$\begin{pmatrix} X^* \\ Y^* \\ Z^* \end{pmatrix} = M^t \begin{pmatrix} X \\ Y \\ Z \end{pmatrix} \qquad \ldots\ldots (1)$$

where M^t is the transpose of the direction cosine matrix:

$$M = \begin{pmatrix} M_{11} & M_{12} & M_{13} \\ M_{21} & M_{22} & M_{23} \\ M_{31} & M_{32} & M_{33} \end{pmatrix} \qquad \ldots\ldots (2)$$

For:

$\omega =$ rotation around the X^* axis

$\phi =$ rotation around the rotated Y^* axis $\ldots\ldots (3)$

$\kappa =$ rotation around the Z^* axis

map. Errors will be correspondingly greater with small-scale maps. Accuracy of measurement of position on the film depends on the device used, on the stability of the film base material, the rigidity of the camera, and the geometric distortion of the lens. Measurements are never to be made on ordinary photographic paper, then:

$$M_{11} = \cos\phi\cos\kappa$$
$$M_{12} = \cos\omega\sin\kappa + \sin\omega\sin\phi\cos\kappa$$
$$M_{13} = \sin\omega\sin\kappa - \cos\omega\sin\phi\cos\kappa$$
$$M_{21} = -\cos\phi\sin\kappa$$
$$M_{22} = \cos\omega\cos\kappa - \sin\omega\sin\phi\sin\kappa \quad \ldots\ldots(4)$$
$$M_{23} = \sin\omega\cos\kappa + \cos\omega\sin\phi\sin\kappa$$
$$M_{31} = \sin\phi$$
$$M_{32} = \sin\omega\cos\phi$$
$$M_{33} = \cos\omega\cos\phi$$

With X_c, Y_c, and Z_c as the camera coordinates in the same system as used in (1), then:

Ground coordinates X_g and Y_g are given by:

$$X_g = X_c + X^*(Z_g - Z_c)/Z^*$$
$$Y_g = Y_c + Y^*(Z_g - Z_c)/Z^* \quad \ldots\ldots(5)$$

and the ground height Z_g, calculable when two or more images are available, is given by:

$$Z_g = \frac{(X_c'' - X_c')Z^{*'}Z^{*''} + Z_c'X^{*'}Z^{*''} - Z_c''X^{*''}Z^{*'}}{X^{*'}Z^{*''} - X^{*''}Z^{*'}}$$
$$\ldots\ldots(6)$$

where the primes indicate the values obtained from the respective images.

A least-squares iterative technique, following Schmid in Tewinkel *et al.* (1966), will be used to approximate camera position and angles. The errors relative to the film plane are to be minimized. In IBM SSP form (IBM, 1968), using the notation of Tewinkel *et al.*:

$$||L_j - B + X_j|| = min_j = ||R|| \quad \ldots\ldots(7)$$

For IBM SSP program LLSQ, the equivalent notation is: $L_j = B_j$, $B = A$, and $N = 6$, $L = 1$, and $M = 2*$ Number of control points. AUX (1) returns the error at the film plane squared. It can be used by substitution in (5) to calculate the rms ground error. The elements of the residual matrix R, for a given image point, are:

$$r_x = L_1 + b_{11}d\omega + b_{12}d\phi + b_{13}d\kappa$$
$$- b_{14}dX_c - b_{15}dY_c - b_{16}dZ_c$$
$$r_y = L_2 + b_{21}d\omega + b_{22}d\phi + b_{23}d\kappa \quad \ldots\ldots(8)$$
$$- b_{24}X_c - b_{25}dY_c - b_{26}dZ_c$$

where r_x and r_y are the residuals to be minimized. It is usually presumed that the focal length z is known. If need be, a similar equation for r_z can be derived. The differences between the coordinates of a control point and the camera position are defined as:

$$X_D = X_j - X_c$$
$$Y_D = Y_j - Y_c \quad \ldots\ldots(9)$$
$$Z_D = Z_j - Z_c$$

Then the matrix products M_1X, M_2X, and M_3X are defined as:

$$M_1X = m_{11}X_D + m_{12}Y_D + m_{13}Z_D$$
$$M_2X = m_{21}X_D + m_{22}Y_D + m_{23}Z_D \quad \ldots\ldots(10)$$
$$M_3X = m_{31}X_D + m_{32}Y_D + m_{33}Z_D$$

for each control point.

The variables in the least-squares problem are the changes in ω, ϕ and κ, as well as the changes in camera position, X_c, Y_c, and Z_c as defined by equations (8). The partial derivatives with respect to M of ω, ϕ, and κ obtained by differentiating (4) are:

$$\frac{\partial M}{\partial\omega} = \begin{pmatrix} O & -m_{13} & m_{12} \\ O & -m_{23} & m_{22} \\ O & -m_{33} & m_{32} \end{pmatrix}$$

$$\frac{\partial M}{\partial\phi} = \begin{pmatrix} -\sin\phi\cos\kappa & \sin\omega\cos\phi\cos\kappa \\ \sin\phi\sin\kappa & -\sin\omega\cos\phi\sin\kappa \\ \cos\phi & \sin\omega\sin\phi \end{pmatrix}$$
$$\begin{pmatrix} -\cos\omega\cos\phi\cos\kappa \\ \cos\omega\cos\phi\sin\kappa \\ -\cos\omega\sin\phi \end{pmatrix} \quad \ldots\ldots(11)$$

$$\frac{\partial M}{\partial\kappa} = \begin{pmatrix} m_{21} & m_{22} & m_{23} \\ -m_{11} & -m_{12} & -m_{13} \\ O & O & O \end{pmatrix}$$

and with $g = M_3X$, the coefficients of (8) become:

$$L_1 = \frac{1}{g}(X*M_3X - Z*M_1X)$$

$$L_2 = \frac{1}{g}(Y*M_3X - Z*M_2X)$$

$$b_{11} = \frac{1}{g}\left(X*\frac{\partial(M_3X)}{\partial\omega} - Z*\frac{\partial(M_1X)}{\partial\omega}\right)$$

$$b_{12} = \frac{1}{g}\left(X*\frac{\partial(M_3X)}{\partial\phi} - Z*\frac{\partial(M_1X)}{\partial\phi}\right)$$

$$b_{13} = \frac{1}{g}\left(-Z*\frac{\partial(M_1X)}{\partial\kappa}\right)$$

$$b_{14} = \frac{1}{g}(X*M_{31} - Z*M_{11})$$

$$b_{15} = \frac{1}{g}(X*M_{32} - Z*M_{12})$$

$$b_{16} = \frac{1}{g}(X*M_{33} - Z*M_{13})$$

$$b_{21} = \frac{1}{g}\left(Y*\frac{\partial(M_3X)}{\partial\omega} - Z*\frac{\partial(M_2X)}{\partial\omega}\right) \quad \ldots\ldots(12)$$

$$b_{22} = \frac{1}{g}\left(Y*\frac{\partial(M_2X)}{\partial\phi} - Z*\frac{\partial(M_2X)}{\partial\phi}\right)$$

$$b_{23} = \frac{1}{g}\left(-Z*\frac{\partial(M_2X)}{\partial\kappa}\right)$$

$$b_{24} = \frac{1}{g}(Y*M_{31} - Z*M_{21})$$

$$b_{25} = \frac{1}{g}(Y*M_{32} - Z*M_{22})$$

$$b_{26} = \frac{1}{g}(Y*M_{33} - Z*M_{23})$$

The calculation scheme is shown in the flow diagram (Fig. 6). Here a departure is made from the method described in Tewinkel *et al.* (1966). In the original technique, the solutions of the least-squares problems are subtracted from the last computed value of camera position and angle in the loop. If this is done with extreme obliques and if the initial estimates of camera position are very far from the true ones, instabilities in the solution may result. It is then possible for a false minimum to be reached. Most of the instability develops during the first few iterations. In the scheme shown, the least-squares solution values are multiplied by a fraction, starting at $1/e$ and rising exponentially to 1 in ten iterations. Although this results in a greater number of iterations, the behaviour of the system is much more stable.

For the calculation of ground coordinates for any image point, the matrix product routine MPRD (IBM, 1968) was used, but any equivalent routine will do as well.

A copy of the program is available on request.

REFERENCES

IBM (1968). *System/360 Scientific Subroutine Package* (360A-CM-03X), Version III, *Programmer's Manual* (Order Nr. H20-0205-3), pp. 160–4.

Tewinkel, G. C., Schmid, H. H., Hallert, B., and Rosenfeld, G. H. (1966). Basic Mathematics of Photogrammetry, in Chapter II, *Manual of Photogrammetry*, 3rd Ed. American Society of Photogrammetry, Falls Church, Va., USA.

Some pitfalls in the interpretation of air photographs

D. R. Wilson

Synopsis

Most archaeological sites are only visible from the air in certain conditions of lighting, crop growth, etc. The appearance of crop marks in particular is brief, uncertain, and sporadic. It is important to distinguish archaeological marks from those caused by geological features, agricultural operations, and other modern activities. Some of these can be very misleading. Ten examples are illustrated; the writer gives reasons for disbelieving their superficial resemblance to genuine archaeological sites.

Books and papers on air reconnaissance for archaeology are generally illustrated only with the clearest and most informative of the author's photographs. This is not simply a question of professional pride: a photograph requiring the highest expertise to achieve may well show marks that are too faint for reproduction by any normal economical method. Furthermore, when readers are unfamiliar with the detailed techniques of air photography, only the clearest examples will be immediately intelligible. In view of the current costs of reproduction and printing, the only defensible policy is to 'print the best'.

It should be appreciated, however, that a reader with little aerial experience gains a very misleading impression from the archaeological air photographs he sees published. He tends to believe that:

(1) in the appropriate season, archaeological sites come into view in great abundance;
(2) crop marks, when visible, are clearly defined and readily intelligible;
(3) even allowing for crop rotation and unrewarding seasons, the whole country can be recorded in a very few years.

How often does an air photographer hear the words "By now there cannot be any new sites left for you to discover!"

The truth is very different. The number of fields displaying traces of archaeological sites at any one time is a minute proportion of the whole. Even on the river gravels, notoriously favoured by early man for settlement and by air photographers for reconnaissance, the incidence of visible sites in a typical summer may be limited to two or three fields in a parish. The upper Thames valley is undoubtedly the area in which crop marks appear most often and in the greatest abundance; here, in an exceptionally good season, it has been my fortune to see crop marks at a density of one field in three. This, however, is a very special case. On unresponsive soils nothing may be visible at all except in freak conditions.

Most of the marks that do appear in crops are not caused by archaeological features at all, but by variations in geology and by routine agricultural practices. The main geological factors causing differences of growth within a single field are soil depth, drainage, and pH value of the ground-water. The differences may be caused by erosion and downwash, by the presence of old creeks in reclaimed land or of roddons in the Fens, by frost-wedge polygons in former periglacial areas, and by the succession of hard and soft strata in the underlying bedrock. All of these are phenomena familiar to the aerial observer through their characteristic patterns in soils and crops. Marks produced by modern agricultural activity are even more diverse. The air photographer must learn to recognize the distinctive marks of field drains, fertilizer application, vehicle tracks, intensive grazing, irrigation, and former woodland. In addition, there are the narrow trenches for water pipes and the broad trenches for North Sea gas, the runways, dispersal pans, and perimeter tracks of abandoned airfields, the earthworks and concrete platforms of former army camps and depots, and the aiming marks of military ranges. It is against this background of non-archaeological 'noise' that archaeological features must be isolated and identified.

Nor are crop marks necessarily well defined during much of the time that they are visible. They often appear gradually, coming slowly 'into focus' as the differential between undisturbed subsoil and archaeological features becomes more pronounced. Outlines are at first blurred, and the finer details are lost in a pattern of vague and indistinct shapes. Definition may increase over a period of several weeks, but be lost again within a day as a result of heavy rainfall. Tonal contrast also varies according to the stage of growth, increasing to a maximum when the field is partly ripe, leaving crop marks of pits and ditches showing green against a yellow background, and then, as the crop marks themselves change colour, dropping again to a

The author is with the Committee for Aerial Photography, University of Cambridge

Fig. 1   Cropmarks S.W. of Dagnall, in Edlesborough parish, Bucks. (SP 988149), 19 June 1951.
Photo: University of Cambridge, Crown Copyright reserved

The field in the photograph exhibits several linear marks which evidently reproduce the tracks of agricultural vehicles. One of these tracks runs right up to a circular mark in the top left corner, resembling a ring-ditch, and merges into it, describing a complete circle before curving away again to the right. Note that the breadths of the vehicle track and of the apparent ring-ditch correspond precisely and that the crop is darker in tone where the track has in fact crossed over its own line. This 'ring-ditch' is evidently no more than the place where a tractor has turned in a wide circle; indeed the same track goes on to describe much of a second circle of similar diameter before the mark fades away and is lost to view.

These tractor circles are some of the commonest misleading features encountered in archaeological reconnaissance. They often occur on the edge of a field, and in this position their real character can seldom be determined with complete certainty. In doubtful cases of this kind the following test may be applied: if identical crop marks re-appear in a subsequent season, they are not the ephemeral effects of one year's tillage, but can be accepted as having an archaeological origin (unless, of course, there is reason to suppose a geological expanation).

lower value. When cereals are fully grown, they are easily shaken by the wind, reducing definition on a breezy day, while summer storms may flatten whole fields together.

When crop marks are poorly developed, over-ripe, or battered by wind and rain, they may prove difficult to interpret even in the most general terms. If the marks themselves simply cannot be seen clearly enough, this is an obstacle that the most experienced interpreter cannot overcome. The only remedy is to photograph the site again in better conditions, either later in the season, or in another year when the marks appear again.

It is sometimes forgotten that in aerial reconnaissance the interpretation of archaeological sites begins with the photographer himself, as he decides which marks are likely to be archaeological and which sites are most worthy of photography. The photographs which the ground archaeologist sees have already been selected and composed by his airborne colleague; he can, in effect, only see the sites through another person's eyes. In other words, the initial interpretation has already been completed, and all he can do is to refine it—or reject it.

Few of the points made in the preceding paragraphs can be sensibly illustrated on the printed page. There is little value in printing uninformative photographs of poor crop marks or badly preserved earthworks, merely to establish that such sites exist. There are some sites, however, that are not merely unhelpful but positively misleading. They may deceive both the air photographer and his colleague on the ground, and discussion of representative examples may help to prevent unhappy errors. I have therefore selected a dossier of ten misleading photographs from the Cambridge University Collection and given the

probable interpretation; but it remains for the reader to decide if he is convinced.

REFERENCES

Bowen, H. C. (1972). Air photography: some implications in the South of England. *In* Fowler, E. (ed.), *Field Survey in British Archaeology*, 38–49. London.

Royal Commission on Historical Monuments (England). (1960). *A Matter of Time*. London.

Fig. 2   Idmiston Rings, Wilts. (SU 222366), 22 April 1954.
Photo: University of Cambridge, Crown Copyright reserved

This large circular enclosure, when seen from the air, forms one of the more impressive monuments on Salisbury Plain. The outer ring is 400 m in diameter and is divided into eight equal arcs; the inner ring measures 200 m and comprises four arcs. The line of round barrows just outside the NW perimeter contains recognizable 'Wessex' types, and one might easily be led to suppose that the Rings belonged to the Late Neolithic/Early Bronze Age. Close proximity, however, does not necessarily imply a significant association. Although the round barrows are indeed of 'Wessex' types, they cannot have been deliberately sited on the edge of the Rings, since these are known to have been constructed more than 3½ millennia later. The Rings, in fact, are not ritual enclosures of prehistoric date, but early 20th century military earthworks, designed for training in infantry manoeuvres.

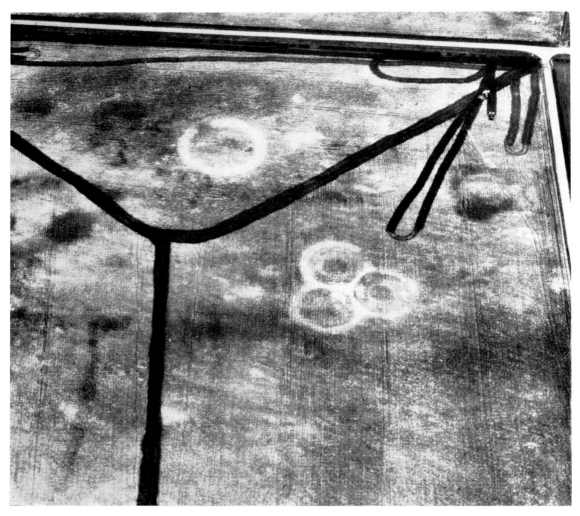

Fig. 3   Soil marks of ring earthworks ENE of Bishop Wilton, Humberside (SE 825564), 12 May 1969.
Photo: University of Cambridge, copyright reserved

Similar groups of ring earthworks have been recorded in terms of crop marks or soil marks not only on the Yorkshire Wolds, but also in East Anglia on the margin of the Fens and in the Trent valley south of Derby. In contrast to this largely eastern distribution, a good example survives as earthworks near Cradley (Hereford and Worcester), 5 km NW of the Malvern Hills. Typically, these groups of earthworks comprise three small rings (not usually conjoined), a single larger ring (not, however, exceeding 30 m in diameter), and a small narrow rectangle, all with entrances. The earthworks at Cradley, however, lie on top of medieval ridge-and-furrow, and although there is a superficial resemblance to disc or ring barrows, the age of such earthworks is not so great that their purpose is unremembered: they are the site of searchlight batteries of the 1939–45 War. The eastern bias of the distribution is therefore related to the direction from which a threat was then principally expected. Such sites are most likely to deceive when seen as crop marks, especially if they are a little indistinct, but the characteristic grouping of rings of two sizes will usually arouse suspicion.

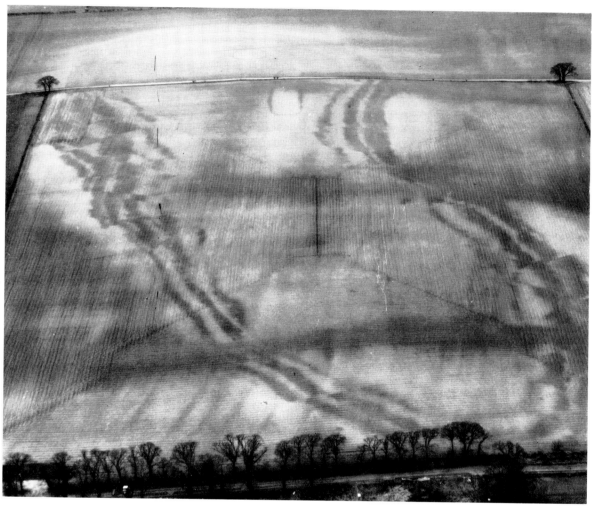

Fig. 4   Soil marks SSE of Bassingbourn, Cambs. (TL 341425), 31 January 1973.
Photo: University of Cambridge, copyright reserved

This site lies less than 2 km from the Icknield Way, on a low chalk knoll *c*. 200 m long. Although it was described as a 'camp' on older editions of Ordnance Survey maps, the resemblance to a hill-fort is misleading and the 'ditch system' is, on close inspection, distinctly bizarre. The lines of 'ditch' are not continuous, but are divided into numerous short lengths, which are abruptly staggered. The whole system is dislocated along a number of clearly defined straight lines, which can only be explained in terms of geological faulting. What the soil marks show, therefore, is not a system of Iron Age fortifications, but the alternation of hard and soft layers at the base of the Middle Chalk, outcropping on the slopes of the knoll. Similar effects, as of ploughed-down defences, may also be produced in limestone by the presence of bands of clay, e.g. near Upper Coscombe, Glos., in the Cotswolds (Bowen, 1972, 39, pl. iv).

Fig. 5   Crop marks SE of Navan, Co. Meath (N 903635), 13 July 1964.
Photo: University of Cambridge, copyright reserved

The site lies in the old park at Dowdstown House, now largely converted to arable. Two circular ditched enclosures contain the crop marks of numerous pits, suggestive of prehistoric settlement. In the foreground of the picture is a strip bounded by a sizeable ditch, also dappled with crop marks of pits. This strip, however, extends along the margin of the former park and can scarcely be related to prehistoric settlement; evidently it marks the belt of woodland by which the park was once mostly enclosed. This is confirmed by reference to Sheet 13 of the Ordnance Survey half-inch map of Ireland (partially revised 1962), on which the actual strip of wood is shown. Similarly, the larger crop-mark enclosure can be identified on the map with a former clump of trees. Thus, the enclosures are not prehistoric and the pits in their interiors were not for storage or for rubbish, being actually caused by dragging out tree-stumps after the trees had been felled in modern times.

Fig. 6   Crop marks W of Tibbermore, Perthshire (NO 040236), 31 July 1967.
Photo: University of Cambridge, copyright reserved

The very distinctive pattern of regularly spaced dark marks is strongly reminiscent of the rows of post-pits of a timber-built Roman military granary. The site lies just over 2 km north of the Roman military road along the Gask Ridge connecting the forts at Strageath and Bertha. But the hypothetical granary would measure approximately 25 × 50 m, with posts more than 6 m apart. Although large military granaries of this type can reach a length of more than 40 m (e.g. at Usk), the spacing between their posts is normally no more than *c.* 1·5 m. Furthermore, such a massive Roman storehouse, even if structurally plausible, would never have stood in isolation, but would have been included in a fort or other defended enclosure. No traces of military defences have ever been recorded at this site. A better explanation of the marks is that they result from an unusually regular arrangement of muck-heaps. During the period before the heaps were spread the ground on which they stood would have received a higher concentration of manure, thereby causing a distinctive pattern of crop growth in the ensuing season.

Fig. 7   Crop marks of a square ditched enclosure WNW of Lakenheath, Suffolk (TL 659855), 4 July 1969.
Photo: University of Cambridge, copyright reserved

The regular shape and rounded corners of the enclosure invite comparison with a Roman temporary camp. The occurrence of such a camp in the low-lying Fen area, 5 km from its margin, would have been a discovery of some historical importance; but account must be taken of other crop marks, visible within the enclosure, forming a system of radial curving lines something like a sectional view of the vanes of a turbine. Enough of this pattern can be discerned to identify a characteristic type of decoy, once common in the Fens and still surviving in a few places,

e.g. north of Newborough, Cambs. (TF 200079). A central piece of open water leads to a number of funnel-shaped radial channels, which are netted over. Wildfowl are enticed to the central pool, then driven up the channels to be caught or killed. In this example the whole complex was surrounded by a boundary ditch. After the decoy had fallen into disuse, it was filled in and levelled off, and the existing road to the nearby farm was constructed over it. But the area is still called Decoy Fen and the farm itself is named Old Decoy Farm.

Fig. 8 Vertical photograph of soil marks in the Fens E of March, Cambs. (TL 460960), 26 April 1968.
Photo: University of Cambridge, copyright reserved

A grid of regularly spaced rectilinear ditches appears to define an ancient system of square fields, each 160 m square. These regular fields contrast with the irregular groups of fields and native hamlets known to be typical of the Fenland in the Roman period, and suspicion is aroused by the way in which the supposed early field system relates so precisely to the modern field pattern. The marks of the 'ditches' always run into the corners of modern fields, bisecting the angles exactly. Furthermore, they are limited to the area in which the modern fields are square; beyond these limits the marks merge directly into the 'envelope-pattern' of modern cultivation in the surrounding fields. (The 'envelope-pattern' is produced by agricultural operations which follow a spiral course, as opposed to going up-and-down the field; examples can be seen in Figs. 1, 3, and 4.) The diagonal marks are thus related to modern, rather than ancient, agricultural divisions; their apparent association in an extensive regular grid results from several lines of square fields being grouped together.

Fig. 9   Crop marks WNW of Store Anst, Ribe amt, *Jutland, 27 June 1967.*
Photo: University of Cambridge, copyright reserved

The great barrow cemeteries of the Danish Bronze Age are usually more dispersed than this, often strung out along a prehistoric trackway, but Iron Age and Migration Period cemeteries are often more concentrated. The apparent ring ditches here are not just closely spaced: where the marks are clearly visible, they actually overlap. The basic element in the pattern, repeated over two fields with varying strength and clarity, is a dark disc inside a concentric dark ring. Some marks have faded to the point where only the disc is visible; others are so strong that the disc and ring have coalesced. Neither the

spacing nor the variations in appearance seem appropriate to the crop marks of ploughed-out round barrows. What they suggest is rather the effects of irrigation with a line of rotary sprinklers in which the two jets are not accurately adjusted, leaving a narrow ring of soil not fully watered.

The use of a larger size of sprinkler can produce the semblance of a ditch of very large diameter, as appropriate to a henge monument. Such large circles may well run across field boundaries in the most convincing manner, but they too are shown to be spurious by occurring in groups which overlap.

Fig. 10 Crop marks NE of Ramsey, Cambs. (TL 318897), 15 June 1973.
Photo: University of Cambridge, copyright reserved

Lines of parching in a cereal crop might seem to indicate the presence of buried foundations belonging to a large rectangular building. The fragmentary plan and broken lines could easily be taken as evidence for the damage being caused by ploughing. But although the light-toned marks to left of centre are the most obvious in the photograph, they are only one part of a regular grid of crop marks which criss-crosses most of the field. The marks consist of broken lines, double in one direction and single in the other. Patterns of this kind were very common in cereal fields in the Fens in the early summer of 1973, and they evidently result from some agricultural process which became general among Fenland farmers at that time. Whatever the exact nature of the process involved (presumably a form of 'subsoiling'), it is still unexpected that a small part of the field should produce such clear *light-toned* marks, when the remainder is showing crop marks that are dark. Such reversals of expected tonal values occur occasionally among archaeological crop marks also (cf. RCHM (England), 1960, pl. 5a); they are not repeated from season to season and must be ascribed to a chance combination of factors rarely operating together.

Aerial reconnaissance in northern France   Roger Agache

Synopsis

Aerial reconnaissance in northern France, which started in 1960, has produced interesting results, in spite of the slender resources available (club aircraft and 24 × 36 mm cameras). In the wet clay regions, where a bocage *landscape dominates, it was primarily medieval evidence that could be studied. On the chalk borders of the plateaux there are thousands of filled-in Iron Age and Roman ditch systems, which have for the most part been deciphered in winter conditions from soil marks, since intensive use of fertilizers make crop-mark observations increasingly difficult.*

Finally, and pre-eminently, countless vanished foundation plans, notably from the Roman period, have been photographed in the deep and fertile soil of the rich plains of limon: fana, *large rural sanctuaries, some* vici, *and, more especially, more than a thousand villas of the Early Empire, all (or most) of which reveal identical rectangular plans (two long rectilinear courtyards, usually orientated towards the rising sun). This dispersed distribution, made up of large estates, is completely at odds with the traditional settlement pattern of these rich cornlands, where the villages markedly cluster together. It would appear that this regrouping of settlement, around a relatively small number of villas, dates to the Late Empire. An atlas of the typology and development of the ancient settlement pattern is in the press.*

In France there is no official organization devoted to aerial archaeology. There are only independent investigators who, sometimes assisted by financial subventions, fly over their areas in search of ploughed-out evidence. They all operate in collaboration with aeroclubs and use small-format cameras of 24 × 36 mm, in order to obtain a maximum cost effectiveness. Most of them work closely with Professeur R. Chevallier (University of Tours and Ecole Pratique des Hautes Etudes), a French university teacher who has for more than 18 years coordinated this research and endeavoured to make the public authorities aware of the problem. He has been responsible for the organization of a series of exhibitions and meetings.

My own surveys began in April 1960 over the Somme. More recently I have extended my flights to Picardy, the Nord region, and latterly to upper Normandy. The Société de Préhistoire du Nord has published several collections of photographs in special issues of their *Bulletin* (Agache, 1962, 1964, and 1970), and an analysis of the principal results was published in the 1970 issue. A summary has appeared in *Antiquity* (Agache, 1972). Finally, a collection of large-scale maps with a gazetteer of levelled sites, plans, and photographs is in the press (Agache and Bréart, 1975).

An educational film has been made in order to demonstrate to students the effectiveness of frequent flights at different seasons, the various types of diagnostic features on buried sites in spring, summer, or under the bare soils of winter.*

In those regions where grassland predominates, the *bocage*† landscape has excellently fossilized medieval structures which re-appear in the modern field divisions. This is the case, for example, in the north-east part of the area surveyed, and especially in the Avesnois. For example, at Ors the outline of a large medieval fortress which has been completely levelled is a striking sight from the air (Fig. 1). The same applies to Normandy, where many mottes and baileys can often be observed, together with interesting ancient field systems. Unfortunately, current reorganization is irretrievably destroying hedges, thickets, hollow ways, and anything which official documents describe as "obstacles to rational exploitation of the soil". This has sometimes allowed wily peasant-farmers to obtain generous subsidies for the ploughing out of barrows or mottes in order to "rationalize" their land!

The best results have always come from Artois and Picardy, with their great mass of flinty chalk forming the sub-soil, as on the other side of the Channel, although the position is the inverse of the English situation, since the chalk here is covered almost everywhere by a thick deposit of *limon*.‡ St Joseph has remarked (1962, 280) that the conditions for aerial detection are very different from those that apply in England. In these rich rolling plains of *limon* divided into enormous fields of considerable age, the conditions for observation are standardized over vast areas, since this land has been comprehensively worked and there are virtually no pastures, woods, or trees, except on the outskirts of villages. These fine plains are cut into by relatively deep valleys which break up the monotony of the landscape. Many of the valley bottoms, such as those of the Somme and its tributaries, are of peaty soils, which cover the alluvial gravels and form marshes that are ill-suited to aerial survey. However, in the Aisne and the Oise, there are patches of alluvial plain where the gravels outcrop; here the soils are very favourable to the revealing of crop sites, as on the other side of the Channel, and Monsieur Boureux has obtained excellent results in the Aisne valley.

The same applies on the plateau edges and certain parts of the bank of the Somme, where the chalk outcrops and good conditions exist for the discovery of filled ditches either as crop marks or as soil marks in winter, when for short periods hundreds of ploughed out circular barrow ditches, many Iron Age

---

*Copies of this colour film (16 mm, sound, 32 minutes' running time), entitled "Archéologie aérienne du Nord de la France" may be hired or bought from the Service du Film de Recherche Scientifique, 96 Boulevard Raspail, 75272 Paris, France—CEDEX 06. An English-language version will be ready in the summer of 1975 from the Scientific Film Service, c/o French Institute, 15 Queensberry Place, London SW7.

†A countryside of small fields divided by hedges and spinneys, typical of north-west France

‡The *limon* of northern France is a fine-grained loam of Quaternary age, originally wind-deposited like loess, but subject to some secondary re-sorting by rain-wash. The nearest British equivalent would be 'brick earth'.

Fig. 1   Ors (Nord). In this bocage *country, the field boundaries show up perfectly the outlines of a large medieval fortress built in 1255 and levelled in 1428. Persistent rain has filled the ancient moats which are, however, barely perceptible on the ground*
Photo: R. Agache

Fig. 2   *Liercourt-Erondelle (Somme). Soil marks in bare chalky soil in winter reveal the plan of a ploughed-out Roman camp, lying immediately behind the Belgic oppidum, the large earthen bank of which can be discerned at the top of the photograph. Preliminary excavations suggest that this was an auxiliary camp from the period of Caesar. It may have been one of the bases for the preparations for the landings in Britain.*
Photo: R. Agache

enclosures, and complex ditch systems surrounding timber-built farmhouses, and also, occasionally, small villas with stone foundations, stand starkly revealed. From among the important discoveries that have been made on these chalk soils, special mention should be made of a Roman camp adjoining the *oppidum* at Liercourt-Erondelle (Fig. 2) and two other legionary camps near the headwaters of the Noye, one at Folleville (Fig. 3) and the other at Vendeuil-Caply. Aerial survey on the rich *limon* plains poses completely different problems. These deep fertile lands had the reputation of being unsuitable for the detection from the air of levelled sites. It is certainly difficult to make out filled ditches in this soil. On the other hand, the recognition of foundations is comparatively easy: in winter with deep ploughing the shares scrape the foundations and bring up fragments of white chalk which stand out against the dark background of *limon* (Figs. 4 and 5).

Moreover, if there has not been a heavy application of fertilizer, it is possible to see at the end of spring and in early summer some distinct differences in colour in the cereal crops; the locations of walls and pavements are clearly visible, because they are less fertile. The same conditions apply in Normandy, where there is currently a trend towards converting pasture to arable. In the early years, the farmers apply little or no fertilizer and the cropmark sites are very distinct, as at Vieux-Rouen, where a very fine villa was discovered in this way. The main building (Fig. 6), with internal courtyards, is of a completely exceptional type in this region.

More than a thousand villas have been discovered by aerial reconnaissance (Fig. 7), and the main building is always long and narrow. It is fronted by a corridor with sometimes one or two corner towers. Occasionally there is another corridor on the other side.

The importance of aerial reconnaissance lies in its having revealed the complete layouts of villas, i.e. not only the dwelling house but also the ancillary buildings. The major unexpected feature has been the density and surprising uniformity of the rectangular plans of the villas (Figs. 8 and 9). Some 90–95% of the medium-sized and large villas are laid out in exactly the same way: in front of the main building (or the 'axial house', since it almost always lies on the long axis of the complex) there is the first courtyard *(pars urbana)*, often flanked by buildings which are sometimes linked by a corridor. The fourth side is closed by a wall beyond which stretches a second courtyard *(pars rustica)*, the length of which is usually three times that of the first. The ancillary buildings, most commonly unconnected, are ranged in two long straight lines. On one side there is a second smaller dwelling (the 'lateral house'), which was probably the residence of

Fig. 3   Folleville (Somme). Roman legionary camp levelled by ploughing and discovered from winter air photographs.
Photo: R. Agache

the *vilicus*. It should be noted that, in the largest complexes, this second dwelling is fairly extensive and is located in the *pars rustica*. On the other hand, in the less extensive villas, it is situated in the *pars urbana*, adjacent to the main dwelling. Sometimes it has a less elaborate layout (basilican plan), but in other cases its plan and dimensions are close to and almost identical with those of the axial house. J. T. Smith has suggested that this may represent a case of two owners jointly exploiting a single farm.

Finally, the small villas had only one courtyard and a single axial dwelling. One curious fact that should be mentioned is that four or five large complexes have been studied which have the layout of villas but no trace of a main dwelling house.

There are, in addition, certain rare examples of farms in which the working buildings are not properly aligned and, in two or three cases only, of farms where the working buildings are ranged opposite the main dwelling, in a dispersed manner, within an enclosure delimited by complex systems of more or less rectilinear ditches. Finally, there are certain randomly arranged small complexes of subsidiary structures (*circa villam*, not *in villa*). These may be examples of hazardous installations, such as bakeries, sited according to the precepts of the Roman agricultural writers (e.g. Columella, I, 6). All the large villas demonstrate the ancient layout, very similar to that

of Anthée, near Namur (Belgium), though on a smaller scale. It is important to note that in the early years our aerial reconnaissances gave the impression that small groups of buildings were more common in northern France. In fact, it is very difficult to observe from an aircraft the overall layouts of large establishments, since they spread over several fields where observational conditions vary according to the crops under cultivation. This means that one can usually see only a very small part of villas clearly.

The same may be said to apply to earlier excavations carried out without the aid of air photographs, where local archaeologists believed that they had excavated a villa, whereas they had only unearthed one dwelling and a few buildings. The vital contribution of air photography has been to reveal the extraordinary homogeneity of these large rural complexes, which are absolutely rectangular and all of the same type.

Some *vici* have been discovered, but the most astonishing finds have been those of enormous isolated sanctuaries associated with rural theatres. These are very characteristic of northern Gaul in the Roman period.

Excavation is, of course, necessary to date all these buried complexes accurately, but at the present time it can be said that the majority of the villas, the sanctuaries, and the occasional *vici* are from the Early Empire.

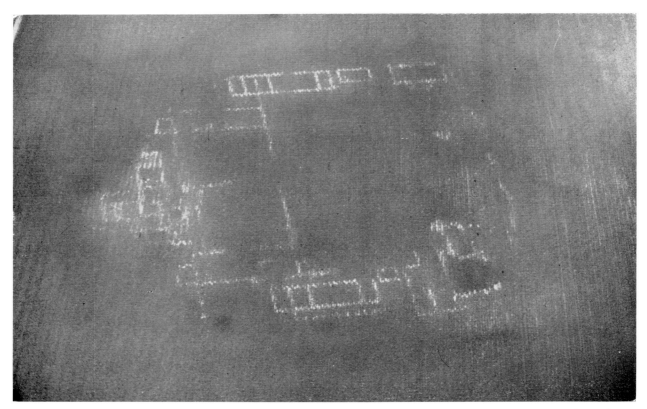

Fig. 4   Grivesnes (Somme). Winter flights over the fertile limon *plains soon after deep ploughing revealed the outlines of many Gallo-Roman villas with two courtyards. This example is less elongated than the rest (total length 120 m)*
Photo: R. Agache

Fig. 5   Warfusée-Abancourt. Winter photograph of a large destroyed villa of characteristic outline (length 320 m)
Photo: R. Agache

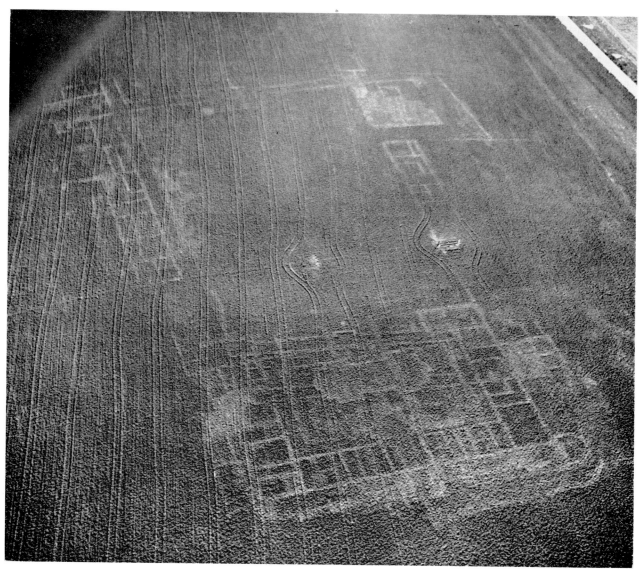

Fig. 6 *Vieux-Rouen-sur-Bresle (Seine-Maritime). Following a period of drought and in the absence of fertilizer, cereal crop marks revealed the plan of a large villa, a veritable rural palace, the main building of which was c. 95 m × 60 m. Winter photographs revealed, on the same site, another villa with a slightly different orientation and a much narrower layout, of the normal "long" type that is found almost everywhere.*
Photo: R. Agache

The reason why they are so well visible is that they were fossilized by premature destruction at the time of the first great wave of invasions (in the second half of the 3rd century AD) and were abandoned.

It thus would appear to emerge that the countryside and the rural landscape were totally restructured at the end of the 3rd century AD. A large number of establishments were finally abandoned at that time, the rural settlement being regrouped around a small number of sanctuaries or more often of villas (Fig. 10), which gave rise to the traditional villages that have survived to the present day.

These Late Roman settlements are thus rarely visible from the air, but wherever a hamlet or a village has disappeared in the Middle Ages or in recent times one always finds the remains of Gallo-Roman villas, *vici,* or sanctuaries. When the modern village is very small, it may happen that the villa that antedated it can be observed from the air (Fig. 10).

This reorientation of the settlement pattern at the end of the 3rd century is doubtless the origin of the complete disparity that can be observed from the air in these rich cornfields between the present pattern, which is nucleated around large villages, and the rural settlement of the Early Empire, almost exclusively made up of very large isolated farms, bearing witness to a pattern of large landholding units (Fig. 11).

However, there was also a restructuring of the landscape, since all the ancient establishments viewed from the air in the plains are unrelated to existing field boundaries or to the course of the older roads. On the other hand, razed medieval buildings seen from the air are all integrated into the present landscape, and are still skirted by roads and field boundaries.

The principal achievement has thus been to reveal this Gallo-Roman rural settlement, about which nothing was previously known. The first distribution map of villas was published recently (Agache, 1973). In

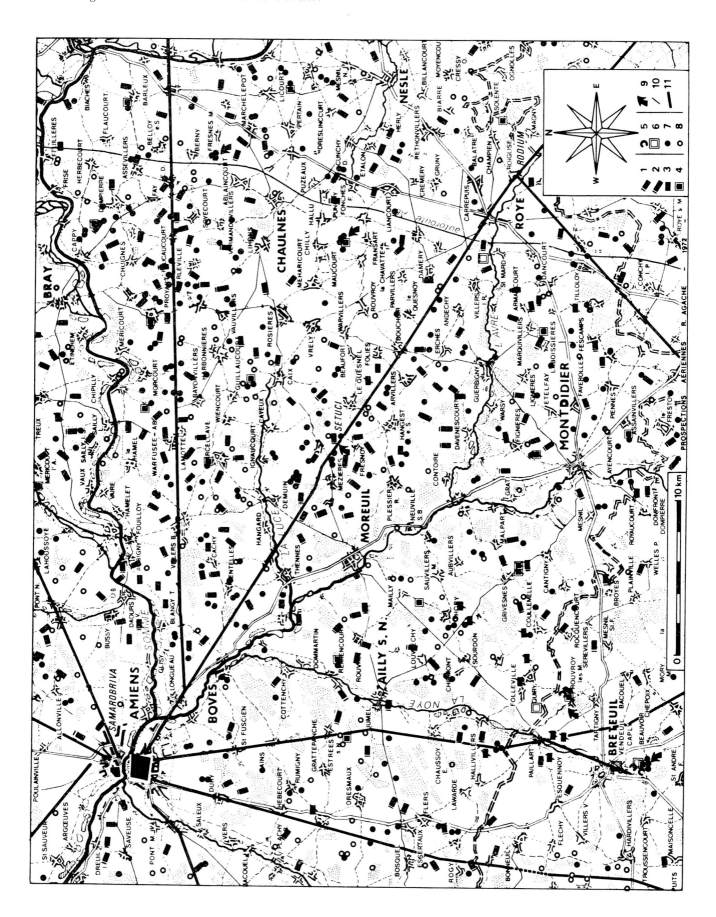

addition, many important isolated establishments, built entirely in wood and clay, have been discovered from the air, mainly on the edges of the chalk plateaux. There is proof that certain of these were contemporary with the villas, but others seem to antedate them, which supports the idea of the existence of large estates dating from the time of Gaulish independence.

Future aerial reconnaissance will be concentrated on the study of these native farms. In addition, efforts will be made to detect the agrarian systems of the Roman period. Some photographs have already revealed unmetalled roads flanked by ditches which lead up to villas and, surrounding these, three types of field have been identified:

1 Rectangular fields that are relatively large and not elongated, i.e. almost the same shape as villas;

2 Fields—or rather gardens (perhaps orchards or vineyards?) that are very long and narrow, situated immediately adjacent to and aligned with the outbuildings of villas;

3 Irregular enclosure systems, often delimited by curvilinear ditches, which are doubtless stock enclosures. Long straight converging lines leading from the entrances of these enclosures represent the narrow ditches, where palisades would have been erected, probably for directing the herds.

Fig. 7 Principal levelled remains discovered by aerial reconnaissance in the wide plains south–east of Amiens (results of air survey by R. Agache, 1973)

    1 Gallo-Roman villa. The orientation is shown. The line indicates the position of the main dwelling.

    2 Large Gallo-Roman villa: the total length of the courtyards exceeds 250 m.

    3 Complex of Gallo-Roman structures of regular form, or Gallo-Roman villa of unknown plan.

    4 Sanctuary.

    5 Gallo-Roman theatre, the orientation of which is shown.

    6 Legionary camp.

    7 Gallo-Roman buildings of unknown purpose.

    8 Dark area marking a vanished settlement of unknown period, but probably ancient.

    9 The arrow indicates the presumed locations of places referred to in the Antonine Itinerary or the Peutinger Table.

    10 The line indicates the hypothetical nature of the structure shown.

    11 Main Roman roads.

The plan of Samarobriva *is that of the mid-3rd century AD.*

All the structures shown on this map were discovered by air survey, with the exception of the Roman roads, the plan of Samarobriva, *and the important ancient complex of Vendeuil-Caply.*

Most of the settlements and sanctuaries included on the map seem to have been destroyed in the second half of the 3rd century AD. Most of the Late Roman settlements are hidden beneath present-day buildings

Finally, in collaboration with Professor J. K. St Joseph, who did us the honour of inviting us to take part in the surveys that he carried out in France in 1973, we intend to extend these flights to neighbouring areas. It is a matter of urgency to increase the number of flights greatly before it is too late, because, at the present time, in whole regions archaeological structures are being irrevocably destroyed. The appalling reorganization schemes, involving systematic levelling by bulldozer of hedges, woods, windbreaks, slight rises in the ground, and even barrows and medieval mottes, result in the disappearance of countless traces of the past. Even more serious is the deeper and deeper ploughing (to say nothing of 'sub-soiling' with chisel ploughs, a devilish invention of agricultural technocrats) which will, in a few years, have destroyed most of the buried evidence in the plains of northern France: not only will it be impossible to excavate them, but even the traces of them will no longer be visible from the air. For aerial reconnaissance in France it is now a case of "now or never".

[Translation by Henry Cleere]

REFERENCES

Agache, R. (1962). Vues aériennes de la Somme et recherche du passé. *Bulletin Spécial de la Société de Préhistoire du Nord*, Musée d'Amiens (93 plates).

Agache, R. (1964). Archéologie aérienne de la Somme. *Ibid.*, Musée d'Amiens (178 plates).

Agache, R. (1970). Détection aérienne de vestiges protohistoriques, gallo-romains et mediévaux dans le Bassin de la Somme. *ibid.*, Musee d'Amiens (390 plates).

Agache, R. (1972). Aerial reconnaissance in Picardy. *Antiquity*, **46**, 113–119.

Agache, R. (1973). Carte de l'habitat antique de la Somme d'aprés les prospections aériennes. *Revue du Nord*, No. 216, Université de Lille.

Agache, R., and Bréart, B. (1975). Atlas d'archéologie aérienne . . . . . *Société des Antiquaires de Picardie*, Musée d'Amiens (in the press).

St Joseph, J. K. (1962). Air reconnaissance in northern France. *Antiquity*, **36**, 74–89.

Excellent accounts of aerial reconnaissance in France are given in:

"Archéologie aérienne" (Proceedings of International Colloquium organized by R. Chevallier), 1963, SVPEN, Paris.

"L'archéologie aérienne: vision fantastique du passé". Special issue of *Archéologia*, 1973, Paris (with contributions from many specialists and an introduction by R. Chevallier).

Fig. 8   Cappy (Somme). Winter re-appearance in the middle of the fertile limon *plains of Picardy of a very typical large villa, with its two courtyards. (Note the completely distinct site of the present-day settlement, grouped as a village in the valley)*
Photo: R. Agache

Fig. 9 Estrée-sur-Noye (Somme). The present-day settlement is nucleated along the Roman road. In the foreground can be seen the outline of a large Gallo-Roman villa with two courtyards disposed geometrically, facing the main dwelling
Photo: R. Agache

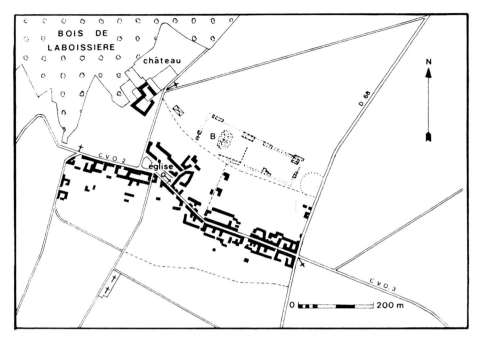

Fig. 10   Laboissiére (Somme). The ancient villa discovered by air survey is shown by dotted line. There is obviously a connexion with the traditional Picardy village. It seems that in the Late Empire this village (perhaps of Germans) developed outside and parallel to the enclosure wall and thus evidently at a time when the latter was still in existence (in ruins at least)

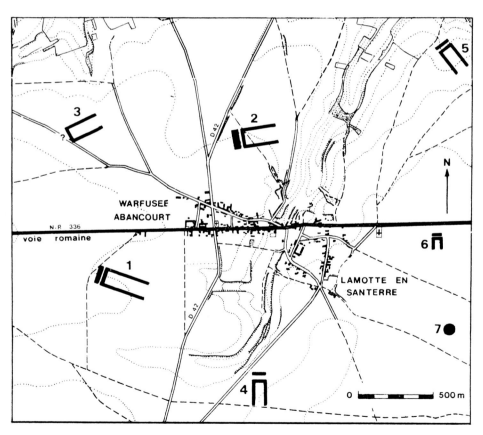

Fig. 11   Sketch map showing the distribution of the villas discovered from the air in the Santerre plains along the Samarobriva-Augusta Viromanduorum *road. The main building is shown by a line, except in No. 3, where there was apparently none. The rectangular courtyards are drawn to scale. There are unidentified Gallo-Roman foundations at No. 7. These villas are all located at a certain distance from the Roman road. It may be that the reorganization of the ancient settlement pattern along this road is attributable to the redevelopment by the* Laeti *of land abandoned after the first great invasion during the second half of the 3rd century AD*

Recent archaeological discoveries in Belgium by low-level aerial photography and geophysical survey

C. Léva and J. J. Hus

Part 1 Aerial reconnaissance and low-level photography for archaeology (by C. Léva)

Synopsis

The present paper, while far from being exhaustive, aims to make known a number of recent archaeological discoveries obtained by means of low-level aerial photography.[1] For certain sites independent control and supplementary details have been provided by geophysical survey, using an electrical resistivity meter and/or magnetometer.

Ten years of systematic research by air photography have shown that, even in Belgium, granted regular and well organized flights, loam (limon) soils yield results of interest for archaeology, as well as for other disciplines.

The variability of climate typical of Belgium allows good results to be obtained at various times of year, especially in winter conditions[2] (bare soil, melting snow, or hoar-frost) or indeed in the course of a very rainy season.

Where sites have been discovered by air photography and subsequently explored by trial trenching or limited excavation, their archaeological character has been clearly established in every case.

The first part of the paper is completed by a series of plates illustrating vanished sites, mostly on heavy loam soils.

Occasional flights and photographs

Our first air photographs, taken over the Roman site of Taviers (Léva, 1958) in 1954, were experimental.[3] This was the time in Belgium when people began to glimpse the possibilities offered by aerial reconnaissance and air photography as the complement of archaeological fieldwork on the ground. An over-naive reaction saw the technique as a marvellous, slightly magical, device for capturing on a single flight in a few photographs the whole plan of a site or vanished structure. This was, admittedly, a case of "haste who must". . . . Excellent results were obtained, for instance at Lommel (Mariën, 1952, 313, fig. 294), Saint-Servais (De Laet, 1958, 224, pl. 63; De Laet and Glasbergen, 1959, 192–3, pl. 47; De Laet, 1974, 430, fig. 209), Fontaine-Valmont (Faider-Feytmans, 1956, pl. vi, vii, ix; Ministère des T. P. R., 1956, 21; Faider-Feytmans, 1960, pl. iii-vi), Oeudeghien, Strée, Nederbrakel (Ministère des T. P. R., 1956, 27-8), Damme, Waha, Clairefontaine (Mertens, 1962), and Assebroek (Ameryckx, 1955; Anon., 1964; Verhoeve and Daels, 1970, 15, fig. 11); and these did in fact catch the imagination of archaeologists and historians. For the most part these views came from vertical cover obtained for non-archaeological purposes (usually cartography, town-planning, or photogrammetry) and this explains their limited number. Government-sponsored flights seldom take place in winter, which

is the season proved to be archaeologically most rewarding. One made do therefore with selecting a print here or there from the photographic cover at the Institut Géographique Militaire or at the Service de Topo- et de Photogrammétrie of the Ministry of Public Works.[4] While this procedure was undoubtedly serviceable and economic, the returns were poor and sporadic. The indispensable complement of high-level photography is the acquisition of low-level views, oblique as well as vertical, at suitable times for the recording of archaeological detail. It has to be recognized that such views virtually did not exist.

As the outcome of some admirable efforts in official quarters several special sorties were arranged, but these were considered to be costly and ineffective, and the organizers became discouraged. This was certainly to throw in the towel too soon. The spectacular results of our neighbours in Britain, France, and Germany, where the soils are different and less unfavourable, led to the belief that in Belgium nothing would be gained by further trials. What *was* gained was a notable delay in this particular field.

It is thus that we conceived the idea, widely regarded as being rash, if nothing worse, of ourselves undertaking this research in the public interest, subject to unavoidable limitations of scope and, of course, very much at our own risk.

From experimental beginnings to systematic organized reconnaissance

Ten years ago we started reconnaissance flights from the airfield of Suarlée-Temploux (6 km from the city of Namur), taking low-oblique air-photographs along the great Roman road from Bavai to Cologne (Mertens and Despy-Meyer, 1968, Annexe 1, 20; Mariën, 1967) in the hope of new archaeological discoveries.[5]

From the beginning these experimental flights displayed the full range and complexity of the difficulties to be overcome. These difficulties arose especially from the type of soil, a heavy loam *(limon)*, from the fragmentation of the landscape into numerous small fields, and from the often unfavourable weather; there were also the problems of securing aircraft and pilots, not to mention our own inexperience.

It was first necessary to learn the job, and it was not until the second half of 1965, after about 100 hours of flying, that the first positive results were obtained. Even then it was not so much the hoped-for Roman structures that came to light as the ephemeral or more permanent traces of sites ranging in date from the

*Superscript numerals in the text refer to the notes on pp. 95–97

Fig. 1   Brussegem, Brabant Province: ring-ditch of unusual size in ripe wheat, seen from the east, 5 August 1972

Photo: C. Léva (No. D. 3088)

This ring ditch, 45 m in diameter and probably Neolithic in date, is located a short way from the north edge of the Roman road linking the old villages of Asse and Elewijt. The terrain forms a ridge on which several centuries of erosion have almost completely destroyed any archaeological remains. The ditch itself is 1·60 m wide and 0·80 m to 1·25 m deep (see Fig. 2).

Neolithic ring-ditches of great size, i.e. those measuring more than 30 m in diameter, can only be detected by low-level aerial photography on vegetation or bare soil. In Belgium the outstanding examples, all previously unknown, are those at Brussegem,[8] Ernage (Fig. 3), and Moxhe[9] (see below, p. 86).

Neolithic to the present day. As a consequence the question arose of what course to follow, our means being limited and our special interest being in Roman settlement along the Chaussée Brunehaut. We were then, as to this day, the only Belgian air photographer/archaeologist carrying out research in this field and there was a great temptation to consider no more than our own project, as anyone engaged in research well might. We found ourselves, however, confronted nearly every day by all kinds of transformation in the landscape, in the urban zones just as much as in the countryside, and day after day this shocking panorama brought home to us the frightening advances of

modern development, destroying for ever vast tracts in which knowledge of the ground was mistakenly thought to be complete.

We felt genuinely concerned and responsible *vis-à-vis* researchers of many disciplines, who are so often in search of low-oblique views of a kind we could rapidly obtain for them, to serve as the indispensable complement of vertical air photographs and cartographic and cadastral surveys. From that moment, despite a certain insufficiency of means, we have laboured summer and winter systematically at this task. We have gone on photographing without break, year after year, features of every kind, building up a

Fig. 2 Brussegem, Trench 3, from the west: the northern part of the ring-ditch shown in Fig. 1, with plough-soil removed

The two poles on the right mark the position of an entrance, 2 m wide, facing north, without any visible postholes. Exploration of the central parts of the ditch disclosed only a small patch of burnt soil. Geoelectrical survey by J. Hus showed no anomaly in the interior of the circle, and a subsequent excavation of one-third of the whole revealed only a few pottery fragments, a chip from a polished stone axe, and some charcoal, all from the ditch. The soil filling the ditch was unfavourable to pollen conservation,[10] while the charcoal was too dispersed and structureless to be of any value.[11] Thus the purpose of the circle remains temporarily enigmatic, awaiting further work when the land is again available.

valuable photographic collection which now contains thousands of pictures in black and white, colour and infra-red 'false-colour'. This substantial photographic archive is of considerable interest to our universities and scientific institutes and, provided that there is adequate protection against loss and deterioration, it can be made available for research. The State would have to be prepared to bear the cost, however, and thereby ensure the continuation in future of a programme begun and carried out over the past ten years by private enterprise.

Reconnaissance and photographic flights have been undertaken regularly from the airfields at Suarlée-Temploux, Grimbergen, and Charleroi-Gosselies.

The aircraft were hired from aero-clubs and flying schools. Our dependence on the availability of machines, however, despite the good-will of all concerned, proved a serious handicap in the summer months and at week-ends. One knew only too well the uncertainty of the weather, the changing condition of the ground, and the chances of cultivation: it was often necessary to be able to take off without delay, virtually at a moment's notice. The aircraft usually used were high-wing monoplanes, such as the Piper Cub 90 HP, Super-Cub 136 HP, Cessna 150, Cessna 150 Aerobat, or Cessna 172. We have now obtained for permanent use a Piper Tripacer PA 22, a high-wing four-seater plane powered by a 150 hp engine and fully equipped

Fig. 3   Ernage, Namur Province: soil-marks of a ring-ditch, from the north-west, 25 April 1973

Photo: C. Léva (No. D. 3784)

This ring-ditch, measuring 32 m in diameter and assumed to be Neolithic, was detected on bare loam soil in Ernage near the watershed between the basins of the Meuse and Escaut rivers. A trial trench disclosed a ditch very similar to those at Brussegem and Moxhe. The electrical resistivity data were processed by computer and converted into 'contours' which faithfully reflect the photographic image and define the exact location of the ditch on the ground. The site is not under threat and it will repay careful excavation.[12]

for VFR and IFR flights, which makes it possible to fly in almost any weather. This machine, registration OO–PEL, based at Grimbergen, is equipped with a special camera door in the underside for vertical photography and is modified for oblique photography from the cabin.

Three professional pilots have gained long experience of this kind of work with us. It is in fact essential always to have a qualified pilot available who is used to working with the photographer as a team.

The camera we have been using is a Hasselblad 500 EL, with six 12-exposure magazines and four 70-exposure magazines. The lens usually used is a Planar $1 : 2 \cdot 8$, $f = 80$ mm; we also have a Sonnar $1 : 4$, $f = 150$ mm. The picture size is 60 mm square. The films most commonly used are (monochrome) Kodak Plus-X, (colour) Agfa CT-18, and (false-colour) Kodak IR-FC. In choosing which film or films to use we have found that the best guide is the experience of the operator in relation to the time of photography, the visibility, the temperature, and the character and condition of the ground. The same applies to the choice of filter(s).

Fig. 4   Oplinter, Brabant Province: soil-marks of a circular enclosure, from the south-south-east, 28 October 1968
Photo: C. Léva (No. D. 793)

This circular feature, about 30 m in diameter, with a probable access corridor on the south-east, was seen in sandy loam soil, newly sown and drying out just after a shower. The photograph shows white patches where the soil has recently dried, the remainder being still wet. The ground slopes towards the south-east, and the immediate surroundings have given up remains dating from Neolithic to Roman times.

Enclosures of this type going back to the Middle Bronze Age but in most instances distinctly smaller in diameter, are well known in Holland and Germany. The site has not yet been excavated, and the only surface finds were a few flints.

Development of the films is carried out by two specialist laboratories able to handle great lengths of film both in black and white and in colour and, if necessary, to do the work as soon as we return from the airfield. The contact prints, inter-negatives, and enlargements are made in our own laboratory.

The photographs are classified in alphabetical order of the names of parishes *(communes)*; also recorded are local place-names, parcel-numbers in the cadastral survey, references to military maps, and a note of the disciplines to which the photographs relate. In this way it becomes easy to find among a mass of documents those which, for example, concern a given geographical location or refer to particular subjects such as Roman roads, sandstone quarries, or abandoned iron-ore mines.

Fig. 5   Hévillers, Brabant Province: vertical photograph of soil-marks, 1 March 1971
Photo: C. Léva (No. D. 4054)

These two square enclosures were detected in the drought of 1971 on the bare soil of a large cultivated plateau sloping southwards, NNE of Mont-Saint-Guibert. The marks disappeared the day after the picture was taken; there are no archaeological remains on the surface, and no geophysical survey has been done to date.

This complex, probably of protohistoric date (below, p. 88), seems so far to be unique in Belgium. It deserves systematic excavation because of its proximity to other sites, especially Court-Saint-Étienne.

Prehistoric monuments and recent aerial discoveries

We have published elsewhere (Léva, 1973) a survey and several plates (of which some are reprinted below) illustrating our researches in relation to the prehistoric and protohistoric periods from Neolithic to Roman.

Since then we have amassed a considerable number of new photographs of circles. Those sites with some relief still evident can be detected at any time; those which have been completely levelled are only visible occasionally. They are not characteristic of any single period and can only be dated by excavation. A really new discovery, however, not previously described, is the recognition in Belgium of large circular ditched enclosures of prehistoric or protohistoric date,[6] such as those at Brussegem (Figs. 1-2), Ernage (Fig. 3) and Moxhe, with diameters respectively of 45, 32, and

52 m. All three circles have been successfully investigated by J. Hus in detailed geoelectrical surveys (for Ernage see below, p. 99). Circular ditches of such size have not, to our knowledge, been previously reported in Belgium. This provides a brilliant illustration of the value of low-level air photography backed by geophysical survey.

Circular features of more modest size include the numerous *tumuli* of the Campine, now mostly levelled. These are most readily detected in February–March, when new grass shows green over the usual surrounding ditch before active growth is resumed in the pasture in general. Aerial reconnaissance at this season, both of meadows and of newly tilled ground on the Campine's sandy soils, is in our opinion our last remaining chance of cataloguing and preserving

Fig. 6 Sauvenière, Namur Province: a line of unmelted snow indicates the position of a buried, unmetalled, Roman road, looking north-west, 4 February 1969

Photo: C. Léva (No. D. 941)

The modern Gembloux–Jodoigne highway crosses the photograph from left to right and is itself crossed very obliquely by the Roman road from Bavai to Cologne (foreground), which is now only in use by local farmers. Near the intersection it meets another Roman road, of earthen construction, now buried, marked by the white line slanting across the centre of the photograph. Melting snow has remained longer over the compacted earth of this hidden road, which is one or two degrees lower in temperature than the adjoining ground. The difficult discovery of an earthen road buried in earth was made possible by photography at precisely the right moment. Further

photographs show the length of the road to be at least 750 m; its northward continuation was picked out by water standing on the surface during heavy rain, the loam covering the road being less permeable than the neighbouring soil. This phenomenon only occurs on loam *(limon)* which has been left untouched for a certain time and has compacted naturally.

See Hus below (p. 102, Fig. 19) for the results of electrical resistivity survey carried out here in July 1974. These results were confirmed by a trial trench[13] which exposed the unmetalled road buried at about 1·40 m beneath the surface.

the Urnfields of this region.[7] We have all the necessary equipment for a project of this kind (Mertens, 1961), but the decision to set it in motion and to meet the cost depends upon Government departments. Such a project would only be truly effective if it was systematic, if it was planned in the long term, say over a period of four or five years, and if it involved close co-operation between the flying team, photographic laboratory, draughtsmen, and field surveyors. Successful results depend on a fully co-ordinated 'combined operation', effective on a number of different levels.

One only has to look at the way such things are done in Britain. In Belgium it is high time that specialists in air photography came together to plan common action for the conservation of their national archaeological heritage.

Aerial reconnaissance of the *tumuli* of the Ardennes has scarcely yet begun, but recent flights make it clear that there is need for a joint project here also.

In known areas of prehistoric mining, such as the parishes of Avennes, Moxhe, Braives, Orp-le-Grand,

Fig. 7   Tongeren (Tongres), Limbourg Province: part of the earthen ramp carrying the aqueduct of Atuatuca Tungrorum, *seen from the west, 13 March 1970*

Photo: C. Léva (No. D. 1843)

Atuatuca Tungrorum, modern Tongeren (Tongres), already in the first century AD had an aqueduct made of a long earthen ramp, now known as 'Beukenberg' (Baillien, 1962, 127–8; Mertens, 1964, 14–15, fig. 5). This was probably about 8 km long, drawing water from a spring at Otrange near the Geer river and following the slope of the ground all the way to the city. In the foreground the ramp shows clearly as a band of drier earth (lighter in tone); it has been flattened and spread by a combination of natural erosion and ploughing. Excavation by the Provinciaal Gallo-Romeins Museum at Tongeren in November 1970 showed that the original width of the base of the ramp was 30 m, as opposed to 50 m at the present day (Vanvinckenroye, 1971). The site is now occupied by a building erected since the time of photography in 1970.

Jandrain-Jandrenouille, Meeffe, Spiennes, and Obourg, it is worth photographing circular areas of subsidence in periods of heavy rainfall, since these often mark the entrances of ancient flint mines.

Circles occurring more or less in isolation have been encountered in meadows and grassland in various localities on the loam *(limon)* soils. Their form is not always perfectly regular, but that does not exclude an archaeological origin. Cases of fungus rings are easily eliminated, since these almost invariably occur together in some numbers. They grow from year to year, and their diameter goes from less than 1 m to about 15 m. When two or three rings merge into one another, they disappear within the area of overlap and combine into aberrant forms. Single circles maintaining a constant diameter in photographs taken over two or three consecutive years are thus almost certain to have an archaeological origin.

Among sites of subcircular or oval form a memorable example appeared at Oleye, near Waremme, where a ditch was revealed from the air on the bank of the Geer during a flight made over melting snow. The shape is probably oval, but the known outline is as yet incomplete; the sector shown on the photograph has been confirmed in a geoelectrical survey by J. Hus. This ditch surrounds a known Omalian (i.e. Danubian) settlement, where excavations by J. Haeck are still in progress. This discovery demonstrates the advantage of reconnaissance over the heavy loams of the Hesbaye at a time when they are snow-covered. The snow generally melts more slowly over such ditches because of a variety of factors, of which the principal are the different compactness, permeability, and degree of freezing of the filling.

The chief discoveries of square and subrectangular features have been at Hévillers (Fig. 5) (Léva, 1973, 41) and at Grand-Manil near Gembloux in a field of ripe flax. Enclosures of this type often occur within larger circuits of more or less rectangular plan. So far there has been no geophysical survey at any of these sites. Subject to confirmation by excavation, we provisionally suppose them to be of protohistoric date on the basis of their resemblance to known examples elsewhere. It can at least be observed that the

Fig. 8   Gottignies, Hainaut Province: soil-marks of a large Roman building, from the south-west, 19 October 1967 Photo: C. Léva (No. D. 484)

In Belgium it is uncommon for Roman buildings to appear in terms of a pattern of linear marks caused by their buried foundations. The hundreds of villas whose locations are known have mostly been revealed by large areas of damp soil, whose appearance is brief and sporadic. Furthermore the land pattern is very fragmented, and current reorganization adds still further complications for research. Thus the present site, first seen in 1967, is even today not fully known, no traces being visible in the adjoining plots of land. It is evidently a large building-complex, and a Roman road coming from Bavai aims straight for the site before vanishing a short distance to the south. No excavation has yet taken place.

Grand-Manil complex has a different orientation from the Chaussée Brunehaut and that the outer circuit, which is not completely visible, may well cross the Roman road at an angle, thereby implying a pre-Roman date. The circuit surrounding the two enclosures at Hévillers is only visible at times when the enclosures themselves are not; it still remains to establish that all the features there are contemporary. These ancient features can be readily distinguished from those produced by modern agricultural schemes such as are typical of the environs of Gembloux.

We will be giving elsewhere an account of the traces of the Roman, Merovingian, medieval, and modern periods, as well as of sites of importance for military history (cf. Figs. 6–14). (For the Roman period see also Léva, 1973, 42–5.) However, we felt it would be useful to add here some comments on the application of air photography to industrial archaeology.

Industrial archaeology

Great Britain, which was the first country to experience the immense and dramatic adventure of the Industrial Revolution beginning in the 1740's, was also the birthplace of industrial archaeology. Excellent works on the subject have been produced by Hudson (1963), Buchanan (1972), and Bracegirdle (1973).

In Belgium the flowering of this new science is recent. The pioneer in the field is undeniably Georges van den Abeelen, at present lecturer at the Institut supérieur d'Histoire de l'Art et d'Archéologie at Brussels (van den Abeelen, 1973) and, with Marinette Bruwier, joint promoter of the National Conference of Industrial Archaeology held on 27–28 May 1973 at Mons and Hornu.

Thus it came about that in August 1967 he suggested that we should photograph the workshops of Grand-Hornu at Hornu (Fig. 15), and that we undertook to make a more systematic record, taking every opportunity for photography, of the monuments and remains of industrial archaeology still visible on Belgian soil.

As a result there now exists an abundant documentation of aerial views covering a great variety of sites, of which the following are only a few:

   Spiennes: Neolithic flint mines at "Camp-à-Cayaux".

Fig. 9   Liberchies, Hainaut Province: crop-marks of the south-west corner of a Romano-Celtic temple, from the south-west,
8 July 1970

Photo: C. Léva (No. D. 1659)

In the wheatfield below the road the traces of two parallel walls turn in a right-angle. These belong to a Romano-Celtic temple, with a square *cella* surrounded by a colonnaded gallery. On the excavation site across the road several fragments of the columns were found buried in a ditch. The whole temple area is surrounded by a great precinct-wall, which is not visible in the photograph because it lies in other crops. The temple lies on the northern edge of the Gallo-Roman *vicus* of Luttre-Liberchies and was first discovered in the excavations of M

Pierre Claes (Claes, 1964, 1965, 1970; Claes and Léva, 1972). The plan is completed by the air photograph, which reveals in addition a circular mark about 6 m in diameter, that proves to be of geological rather than archaeological origin.[14] The unripe wheat is distinctly taller where it grows over the wall-foundations, because of their chalk content, and also over the circular feature, because this forms an island of loam surrounded by sandy soil.

Jandrain-Jandrenouille: Neolithic mine-pits.
Tongres: aqueduct supplying the Roman city of *Atuatuca Tungrorum* (Fig. 7).
Antoing: monumental Roman burial-chamber built of Tournai limestone, in the hamlet of Billemont.
Marilles: Roman tile-kilns (Léva, 1966, and Hus below, p. 98).
Rognée: iron slag used in the construction of the Bavai-Dinant Roman road.
Saint-Denis et Isnes: simple furnaces; charcoal-burners' hearths of the Austrian period, following deforestation.
Suarlée: iron ore mine-pits; traces of demolished industrial buildings; quarries of sandstone and black marble.
Andenne, Seilles, and Couthuin: quarry-pits for pipe-clay; zones of subsidence indicating the site of abandoned mine galleries; medieval potters' kilns at Andenne.

Sclayn: lime-kilns.
Hornu: coal mine, workshops, and industrial housing at Grand-Hornu (Fig. 15). This is an outstanding monument of the Industrial Revolution in Belgium and one of the most remarkable in Western Europe (Bruwier *et al.,* 1968, 1969; Hudson, 1971, 17; Roelants du Vivier, 1972; van den Abeelen, 1973, 29).
Vedrin: lead mines.

A great number of places, mostly along the Sambre and Meuse channels, possess abandoned coal mines with ruined installations and slag-heaps, some of which have gone for the construction of motorways and are now completely vanished. The Borinage, the region of Charleroi, and the Liège basin, when seen from the air, exhibit an unbelievable density of past industrial enterprises of every possible kind, of which unfortunately an important number are now in ruins. Some are associated with extensive industrial housing

Fig. 10   Tourinnes-Saint-Lambert, Brabant Province: general view of Roman vicus, *looking north-east, with soil-marks of a Roman barrow, 21 October 1967*

Photo: C. Léva (No. D. 534/2)

The Roman burial-mound has been completely levelled and was previously unknown. The white outline is caused by fine clay being deposited over the centuries and remaining in the soil round the perimeter of the original barrow. This mark is only visible from the air on bare soil during the short period of drying out. All other indications of the existence of the mound were probably destroyed unwittingly several years ago, when the present owner hauled away to a dump the grave goods brought to light by deep ploughing of the field.[15] The barrow lay near a Roman road running southwards from the *vicus* to connect with the great Roman road from Bavai to Cologne (Amand, 1969, 4, fig. 1; Lassance, 1974, 34, fig. 1).

Five other levelled *tumuli* have been discovered in the neighbourhood, again by air photography. Their siting in the countryside appears to have been determined by the pre-existing pattern of roads and land-divisions.[16]

schemes, as at Bois-du-Luc in Hainaut. These establishments bear witness to a glorious industrial past from which the whole of Belgium has benefited. Some of the sites, selected as typical examples, undoubtedly deserve to be restored and preserved from demolition.

Air photography also takes note of humbler monuments which are on the way to disappearing, such as windmills, watermills along our rivers, and rare examples of other wind-driven machinery, used for pumping water from wet ground or generating electrical power.

The changing communications network also requires attention. There are now, of course, hundreds of roads and lanes disused since the land reallocation now taking place and also many railway lines which have been taken out of use. Did not Belgium, around 1900, have the highest railroad density in the world with her 4568 km of railways, besides 2643 km of connecting local tramways? The plane thus sometimes sees, for instance at Rêves near Nivelles, the plough retaking possession of the site of a railway line, or again, as in Thieusies, sturdy bridges of metal or brick, isolated in the countryside, giving passage only to the peaceful cows of a neighbouring farm.

On bare soils large reddish patches appear in rainy periods on the outskirts of built-up areas. These often mark the site of artisans' brick kilns, of which the

Fig. 11   Jodoigne, Brabant Province: vertical photograph of soil marks of three circles, 21 October 1967. North is at the top
Photo: C. Léva (No. D. 509)

The three circular marks on the photograph probably indicate the sites of three levelled *tumuli* beside the Roman road connecting Namur to Tirlemont via Taviers. The soil is a heavy loam and the ground slopes towards the bottom right-hand corner (south-east) of the picture. There is an accumulation of soil, brought down by hill-wash, at the base of the southern *tumulus*. This mound appears fully white because it is not yet wholly flattened, whereas the other two barrows display only outlines of white, showing that they have been completely levelled (cf. Fig. 10). These marks appear only briefly and sporadically, requiring a combination of bare soil and slight moisture on a rapidly drying surface. It was only by a remarkable coincidence that the present photograph could be obtained, seeing that three different fields had all to be in bare soil and equally moist at the same moment.

waste products were left undisturbed. Non-circular blackish patches, found mostly in Hesbaye, are often due to the presence of pits for the extraction of phosphate mined during the last war. Pink, rusty, yellowish, or whitish patches usually denote geological outcrops where sand, ironstone, chalk, etc., are present.

Ancient peat-cuttings and quarries for sand, marl, marble, sandstone, limestone, shale, pipeclay, etc., are found scattered throughout the country in accordance with the occurrence of the geological beds. Whether open, flooded or filled, these are also, like old brickyards, sites of industrial archaeology. They also must be photographed before it is too late, so that

Fig. 12 Thieusies, Hainaut Province: crop-marks of two curving concentric ditches in ripe wheat, from the north-west, 13 July 1973

Photo: C. Léva (No. D. 3810)

The photograph is taken at an important Middle Neolithic site north of Mons excavated by Professeur Dr P. Vermeersch, Service of Prehistory, Catholic University of Louvain (K. U. L.). The site lies on a sandy loam plateau at the confluence of two small incised streams and is cut off by a large curved ditch which crosses the promontory from one steep margin to the other. This ditch was first detected on vertical air photographs. Concentric with its inner edge and about 20 m distant a second, narrower, ditch has been discovered by low-level oblique photography. The existence of these two ditches has been confirmed by electrical resistivity surveys and by cuttings made in 1973. To avoid losing the position of the ditches after the crop was harvested, two of the excavators, directed by radio from the air, placed rods in the ground to mark the spot. The two figures are visible as white spots just below the broad dark-toned mark of the larger ditch.

Further research eventually revealed that the ditches were of Merovingian-Carolingian date.

Fig. 13   Walhain-Saint-Paul, Brabant Province: the castle ruins, from the north-east, 13 February 1971

Photo: C. Léva (No. D. 3378)

The castle of Walhain, situated to the south of the modern village, is today an abandoned ruin. It did, however, know a glorious past and was the seat of a powerful domain whose origin goes back to the 12th century (Génicot, 1973, 131, p. xi).

This aerial view, taken in winter looking into sun, displays to perfection the breadth of the surrounding moat and of the *basse-cour,* with its entrance clearly visible (upper left).

future generations may be reminded by the pictures of these places that here courageous men have worked and strained mightily in the hope of preparing a better future.

Acknowledgments

On the completion of this work we pay tribute to the active and invaluable assistance of all those who have helped to bring it to a successful conclusion.

From 1964 until now the reconnaissance and low-level photography have been carried out in partnership with private and professional pilots. We thank them all very warmly, and more especially the airfield commandants Roger Lefebvre, François Goosse, the instructors Frans Péllissier, Pierre De Maeght, Bernadette Bihin, Commandant Paul Christiaens of the Belgian Air Force, and the pilots Guy Gheysens and Hubert Denoncin.

Our appreciation goes equally to the Directing Staff and members of the Administration de l'Aéronautique, of the Institut Géographique Militaire, and of the Service de Topo- et de Photogrammétrie of the Ministry of Public Works, who have so often smoothed our path and really contributed to the success of our work.

A great number of willing and enthusiastic diggers have worked conscientiously with us on electrical and magnetic surveys, excavations, and *sondages* which have confirmed the results of air photography on a

Fig. 14   Wépion, Namur Province: crop marks of pentagonal enclosure, from the north-west, 9 July 1968
Photo: C. Léva (No. D. 619)

A previously unknown pentagonal enclosure found in a ripening wheatfield at Wépion called 'Ris-de-Flandre' is all that remains of a fortification erected on this high point, perhaps at the end of the 17th century. It is a historical fact that Louis XIV camped not far from here before capturing the stronghold of Namur. Perhaps this forgotten military bulwark was one of the forward posts encircling the fortified city. Another photograph taken on bare soil about 60 m away revealed a straight line ending in a right angle and aligned on one of the angles of the pentagon (Anon., 1972; Lassance, 1974, 34, fig. 2). Isolated fortifications of this kind do not generally appear on scale models of the city because of their distance from the main fortress.

series of sites. These researches have been theirs, and to them is due a good share of the credit. We thank them here most heartily.

Our special gratitude goes to M J. Hus who for some years has been devoting a very large part of his free time at week-ends and holidays to geophysical surveys on the different sites. Part 2 of our paper (Hus below, p. 98) is eloquent testimony of the importance of his collaboration and of the scientific support kindly offered by the Institut Royal Météorologique of Brussels and by the Centre Géophysique of Dourbes. We are also indebted to the owners and tenants of the lands where we were kindly permitted to excavate: M and Mme P. Delacroix, M and Mme E. Lariviére, M and Mme L. Evilard, Baron and Baronne van Oldeneel tot Oldenzeel, and M and Mme L. Laduron.

Finally, last but not least, there remains the very pleasant duty of thanking the organizers of the Air Photography Symposium held in London in 1974 for the opportunity of presenting to the Symposium some of the results obtained in Belgium and of setting them out in this place. Our gratitude goes especially to Professor J. K. St Joseph, Mr D. R. Wilson, Dr G. Webster, and Mr J. Hampton. Especial thanks are due to Mr and Mrs David Wilson for their work in translating the text and in improving it in the process.

NOTES

1   In Belgium there is still no legislation on the protection of archaeological sites and on excavation. Publication of air photographs is for this reason sometimes a matter of some delicacy. Consequently it will be appreciated that some of the photographs published here are given locations that are not precise.

Fig. 15   Hornu, Hainaut Province: 19th century industrial complex, now disused, from the south-south-east, 17 August 1967

Photo: C. Léva (No. 1211)

The deserted coal-mine of Grand-Hornu, a kind of *colosseum* from the early Industrial Age, is seen here before its restoration by the architect Henri Guchez. This monumental ensemble, unique of its kind, was a veritable 'conglomerate' before the invention of that term. Besides the coal-mine, it consisted of metal workshops erected between 1820 and 1835 by the French architect Bruno Renard, foundries, a sugar refinery, and a residential quarter for the workers, the whole being built on the orders of Henri de Gorge-Legrand, one of the first great coal exploiters of the Borinage (see above, p. 90 with references). Grand-Hornu also even owned the first surface railroad of Belgium. The coal was transported by rail in wagons drawn by horses. This innovation provoked the anger of the existing wagon-drivers who, in 1831, fearing the competition of the new railroad, incited the population to riot. The machinery was wrecked and the business plundered. It was, however, rapidly rebuilt and continued in operation until the 1950s.

This remarkable industrial complex, filmed by the BBC in 1973 for a popular science programme, must now find its final destiny. In a region where industrialization was so early and so dense as in the Borinage an ensemble of such importance can only be truly appreciated in its setting through the aerial view.

2   The prime importance of winter flights has been brilliantly demonstrated by our French colleague Roger Agache. His truly spectacular results in the Somme Basin have heightened the reputation and the quality of French research. Among his many publications an excellent overall picture is given by his *Map of the ancient settlement of the Somme as revealed by air reconnaissance* (Agache, 1973b).

3   We are anxious to pay tribute here to the memory of J. Mutsaerts, pilot of Namur, who kindly carried out several flights on behalf of the Société archéologique de Namur, especially over the *vicus* of Taviers. This work resulted in the discovery of a rectangular feature in the western part of the parcel Sect. A, 154[b]. The marks did not correspond to any tangible remains in the soil, which in this locality tends to be difficult, and they have never re-appeared. By contrast, the site of the late-Roman fortlet and the Roman road, sited in parcel Sect. A, 156[c], have re-appeared regularly.

4 We have the most agreeable duty of offering very special thanks to the Directing Staff of these two Services for so often having allowed us to consult their vertical cover. Vertical photographs, like large-scale plans both ancient and modern, and maps including that of Ferraris, provide a basis for the location of sites. More and more often these are found to have been obliterated by recent land reallocation.

5 The venture on which the author embarked at this time could not have been continuously pursued but for the efforts, often freely given, of a great number of individuals, to whom the warmest of collective thanks are here given.

6 The only example previously known was that at Assebroek near Bruges, of unknown date (see above, p. 81). There are fine specimens abroad: see Agache (1973a), 19, Cocquerel; Schmiedt (1973), 96–7, fig. 1, Lucera; Günther (1973), 182, fig. 1; Benson and Miles (1974), 84–7, map 27, Figs. 13–14, pl. 5.

7 It is right to stress here the importance of the co-ordinated efforts made in recent years by the National Excavation Service (Service National des Fouilles) under the dynamic impetus of its Director, M Heli Roossens, and the School of Archaeology of the University of Ghent, directed by Professor S. J. De Laet.

8 We thank Professor R. Paepe, of the Free University (VUB), Brussels, for valuable advice and information which he was kind enough to give us during his visit in the field.

9 We are anxious to express our indebtedness to Professor M. E. Marien, of the Free University (VUB), Brussels, and to Mme Ulrix, of the University of Liège, for the interest they displayed in our work on this site, which lies south-east of the spot known as 'A la Tomballe'.

10 We thank very heartily Professor W. Mullenders, Director of the Laboratory of Palynology and Phytosociology of the University of Louvain, and also Professor A. V. Munaut, for their frequent collaboration during our researches and excavations on many sites.

11 We thank nevertheless M E. Gilot for the various radiocarbon determinations which he has been kind enough to undertake for us during different excavations.

12 Examination of the profile and filling of the ditch bears witness to a relatively complex stratigraphy in the view of Professor P. Vermeersch, who visited the site.

13 We are anxious to thank Professors R. Paepe and A. V. Munaut and M E. Gilot for their valuable collaboration ever since this time. We owe to M J. Hus the electrical and magnetic surveys which enabled us to site the trial trench in precisely the most favourable spot within the field.

14 We thank M J. Hus and Professor P. Vermeersch for examining this circular feature. Electrical resistivity survey was carried out by the former, while borings and soil-samples taken by the latter led to the determination of the feature as being of geological origin. Part of the circle was excavated to a depth of 2 m. It formed a vertical-sided shaft filled with pure loam *(limon)* entirely surrounded by a soil of ferruginous sand. It was evidently a solution-hole.

15 We received this information from M Georges Heldenbergh, who has been carrying out systematic excavations in this *vicus* for several years. We give him hearty thanks for a long association both as collaborator and as correspondent. The local farmer was unaware of the destruction he was causing, and no excavation could take place just because at this time the site was still unknown. It is, however, reasonable to conclude that the remains belonged to a Roman *tumulus*.

16 Certain *tumuli* were deliberately sited beside a road or at a cross-roads. A number of circular marks, which undoubtedly represent levelled *tumuli*, have been detected along Roman roads, such as the highways between Bavai and Cologne and between Tienen and Tongeren, thanks to low-level air photography in winter and spring on bare soil (Amand, 1971).

REFERENCES

Abeelen, G. van den (1973). *L'Archéologie industrielle* (2e ed.) Bruxelles.

Agache, R. (1973a). L'archéologie aérienne dans le nord de la France: perspectives nouvelles. *Document Archéologia*, **1**, 40–5, 9 figs.

Agache, R. (1973b). Carte de l'habitat antique de la Somme d'après les prospections aériennes. *Revue du Nord*, **55**, 15–16, pl. iii.

Amand, M. (1969). *Nos tumulus splendeurs impériales (= Archaeologicum Belgii Speculum*, 2). Bruxelles.

Amand, M. (1971). Etudes sur nos tumulus. *Les Etudes Classiques*, **39**, 484–92.

Ameryckx, J. (1955). Merkwaardige oudheidkundige vondst te Assebroek. *Biekorf*, **56**, 205–9, fig. 1–3.

Anon. (1964). *Ur-Schweiz*, **28**, p. 1 of cover and 78, fig. 52.

Anon. (1972). *Sabena Revue*, **37**, 89.

Baillien, H. (1962). De drinkwatervoorziening te Tongeren. *Het Oude Land van Loon*, **17**, 127–44.

Benson, D. and Miles, D. (1974). *The Upper Thames Valley: an archaeological survey of the river gravels* (Oxfordshire Archaeological Unit Survey, 2). Oxford.

Bracegirdle, B. (1973). *The Archaeology of the Industrial Revolution*. London.

Bruwier, M., Meurant, A., and Piérard, C. (1968). Un monument d'archéologie industrielle: les ateliers et la cité du Grand-Hornu. *Industrie*, janvier, 39–56.

Bruwier, M., Meurant, A., and Piérard, C. (1969). Le Grand-Hornu. *Industrial Archaeology*, **6**, 353–68.

Buchanan, R. A. (1972). *Industrial Archaeology in Britain*. London.

Claes, P. (1964). Liberchies Bons-Villers: temple gallo-romain. *Archéologie*, 73.

Claes, P. (1965). Liberchies Bons-Villers: temple gallo-romain. *ibid.*, 60–62, fig. 5.

Claes, P. (1970). Liberchies Bons-Villers: temple gallo-romain. *ibid.*, 10.

Claes, P. and Léva, C. (1972). Le vicus des Bons Villers à Liberchies. In: *Le Trésor de Liberchies* (by M. Thirion), 1–24, figs. 1–10, pl. B–E and i–vii. Bruxelles.

De Laet, S. J. (1958). *The Low Countries*. London.

De Laet, S. J. (1974). *Prehistorische Kulturen in het zuiden der Lage Landen*. Wetteren.

De Laet, S. J. and Glasbergen, W. (1959). *De Voorgeschiedenis der Lage Landen*. Groningen.

Faider-Feytmans, G. (1956). Les fouilles du site romain de Fontaine-Valmont (Hainaut). *Mém. Public. Soc. Sciences Arts Lettres Hainaut*, **71**, pl. vi, vii, ix.

Faider-Feytans, G. (1960). Le site sacré de Fontaine-Valmont. *Mém. Public. Soc. Sciences Arts Lettres Hainaut*, **74**, = *Fouilles du Musée de Mariemont*, **1**, pl. iii–vi.

Génicot, L. (1973). *Histoire de la Wallonie*. Toulouse.

Günther, K. (1973). Die Abschlussuntersuchung am neolithischen Grabenring von Bochum-Harpen. *Archäol. Korrespondenzblatt*, **3**, 181–6, fig. 1–2, pl. 38–9.

Hudson, K. (1963). *Industrial Archaeology*. London.

Hudson, K. (1971). *A Guide to the Industrial Archaeology of Europe*. Bath.

Lassance, W. (1974). Plaidoyer pour la sauvegarde de notre environnement archéologique. *Propriété terrienne*, no. 313, janvier, 34–7, figs. 1–5.

Léva, C. (1958). Le site gallo-romain de Taviers. *Annales Soc. archéol. Namur*, **49**, 5–40, figs. 1–6.

Léva, C. (1966). Un four de tuilier à Marilles. *Bull. Cercle archéol. Hesbaye-Condroz*, **6**, 113–14.

Léva, C. (1973). Archéologie aérienne en Belgique. *Document Archéologia*, **1**, 40–5, 9 figs.

Mariën, M. E. (1952). *Oud-België van de eerste landbouwers tot de komst van Caesar*. Antwerpen.

Mariën, M. E. (1967). *Par la Chaussée Brunehaut de Bavai à Cologne* (Musées royaux d'Art et d'Histoire). 2e éd. Bruxelles.

M[ertens], J. (1961). Archéologie et photographie aérienne. *Archéologie*, 152–3.

Mertens, J. (1962). Archéologie et photographie aérienne en Belgique. *Bull. Soc. française Photogrammétrie*, **5**, 4–8. [This short paper not only gives a faithful account of the history of archaeological research from the air in Belgium, but makes judicious comments, most of which are still relevant today. — C.L.]

Mertens, J. (1964). Enkele beschouwingen over Limburg in de Romeinse tijd. *Archaeologia Belgica*, **75**, 1–42.

Mertens, J. and Despy-Meyer, A. (1968). *La Belgique à l'époque romaine* (Service National des Fouilles, *Cartes archéologiques de la Belgique*, 1–2). Bruxelles.

Ministère des Travaux Publics et de la Réconstruction (1956). *Activité des Services de Topographie et de Photogrammétrie 1952–1956* (brochure prepared for the 8th International Congress of Photogrammetry, Stockholm 1956). Bruxelles.

Roelants du Vivier, F. (1972). *Les Ateliers et la Cite du Grand-Hornu de 1820 a 1850: un exemple d'urbanisme industriel à l'aube du machinisme* (mémoire du licence, ronéotypé). Louvain.

R[oosens], H. (1960). Kempische urnenvelden. *Archéologie* 417, pl. ii.

R[oosens], H. (1962). Luchtverkenning in de Kempen. *ibid.*, 19–20, pl. iiia.

Schmiedt, G. (1973). Panorama des applications de la photographie aérienne en Italie dans le domaine de la topographie historique. *Document Archéologia*, **1**, 96–107.

Vanvinckenroye, W. (1971). Tongeren: waterleiding in romeinse weg. *Archéologie*, 13–14.

Verhoeve, A. and Daels, L. (1970). *Circulaire vormen in Binnen-Vlaanderen ten westen van de Schelde* (= Belgisch Centrum voor landelijke Geschiedenis, pub. 18). Gent-Leuven.

Part 2   Magnetic and electrical survey—powerful aids for the location and confirmation of archaeological features seen on air photographs (by J. J. Hus)

Synopsis

Some preliminary results are given of magnetic and electrical survey of archaeological features discovered during aerial reconnaissance over Belgium.

A magnetic survey of the Roman tilery at Marilles shows that irregular marks and spots seen on air photographs may reveal geometrical features of archaeological interest.

Results of electrical resistivity traverses over a linear and a circular feature are presented, and the utility of geophysical prospecting methods for location, determination of extent, and confirmation of features is demonstrated.

Magnetic survey at the Roman tilery at Marilles

In 1966 C. Léva started the excavation of two Roman kilns discovered during fieldwork by J. Mercenier at Marilles (50° 41′ 50″ N, 4° 57′ 40″ E). Kiln no. 1 was rectangular with sides about 6·25 m × 5·85 m and had been used to produce roofing tiles and probably floor tiles and hypocaust elements (Léva, 1966).

As kilns usually are grouped and rarely appear in isolation, we decided to carry out a magnetic

exploration of the site in order to find other baked structures of similar character. The area lent itself to magnetic survey very well, since man-made disturbances were absent in the immediate surroundings.

A rapid preliminary survey was executed with a portable fluxgate magnetometer (SCINTREX Model MFD-2) measuring the vertical field component. For accurate measurement this magnetometer needs to be levelled on a tripod, but a precision of approximately 10γ can easily be obtained when the instrument is being carried [1γ = 10^{-5} Oe]. After some minutes of recording an important anomaly was detected at a distance of about 20 m from the excavated kilns in an area so far unexplored. A measuring grid (22 m × 22 m) with a mesh size of 1 m was set out around the anomaly and the total magnetic field was measured at every grid intersection with the ELSEC proton magnetometer (Aitken, 1961).

Figure 16 represents the non-smoothed total magnetic field measured along Traverse P 5. The geographical azimuth from *A* to *B* is 17° 00′. The measured profile is seen to be typical for a traverse passing approximately north–south over an inclined magnetic dipole

*The author is with the Institut Royal Météorologique, Bruxelles

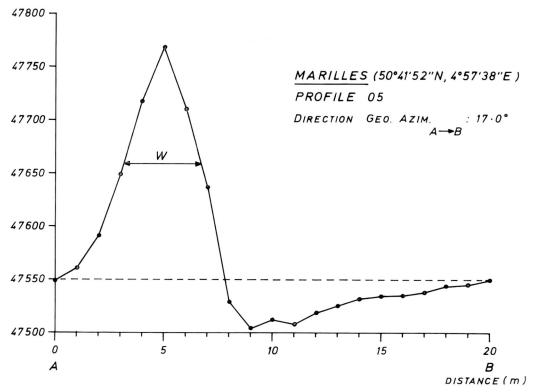

Fig. 16 *Magnetic profile over a probable Roman kiln at Marilles*

at our latitudes (Aitken, 1961). The inclination of the earth's magnetic field at the surveyed area is 66° downwards. The width *W* (Fig. 16), between the two points at which the anomaly has half its maximum value, is in this case approximately equal to the width, rather than the depth, of the anomaly. The computer-processed data of this survey and the results of the application of filter techniques will be published later. Re-examination of air photographs of this area taken by C. Léva revealed on some of them a reddish-coloured spot at the site of the anomaly. This red spot is caused by the higher iron-oxide content of the topsoil immediately above the anomaly and is clearly visible on the ground when the topsoil is wet.

The measured anomaly strength (roughly 250γ) and the estimated anomaly width (about 3·5 m) seem to indicate the presence of another buried kiln.

This example shows that reddish spots on air photographs may be the result of local concentrations of iron oxides in the topsoil and may indicate buried baked structures of archaeological interest.

Electrical resistivity survey over a circular feature

During an air reconnaissance flight over the *limon*-covered zone of Belgium a faint circular mark (Fig. 3) was found by C. Léva at Ernage (50° 36′ 00″ N, 4° 41′ 10″ E).

Some of the first questions to suggest themselves when features are recognized on air photographs concern the exact location, the dimensions (especially depth) of the features, and lastly (but not for us least) the archaeological interest. We are convinced that

geophysical prospecting methods can be very helpful in answering such questions, and we therefore planned an electrical resistivity survey of the area.

The survey made use of the Bison earth resistivity meter (Model 2350 A), using the Wenner configuration. We will not repeat here the principles of electrical surveying, which are explained in numerous good textbooks (Keller and Frischknecht, 1970; Lasfargues, 1957; Hesse, 1966). Our first step was to make four parallel trial traverses to localize the feature. Each traverse had a length of 60 m and measurements were taken at every metre. One of the traverses was repeated with several different electrode separations to find the best response.

Figure 17 shows part of this last traverse passing over the east side of the circular feature. The earth resistivity decreases with depth over the feature, but elsewhere an inversion can be seen. This can be explained by the higher moisture content of the topsoil compared with the soil horizons immediately beneath. It should be noted that the survey took place in November and that the topsoil was damp. The curve for an electrode separation of 1 m shows abrupt fluctuations where the inner electrodes pass over the feature. This can be attributed to distortion of the current path by the proximity of the feature to the individual rods (Clark, 1963). Once the circular feature was precisely located, a measuring grid of 38 × 38 points with a mesh size of 1 m was set out around the feature and an electrode separation of 1 m was selected. This resistivity survey was conducted at a moment when no sign of the feature could be seen from the air.

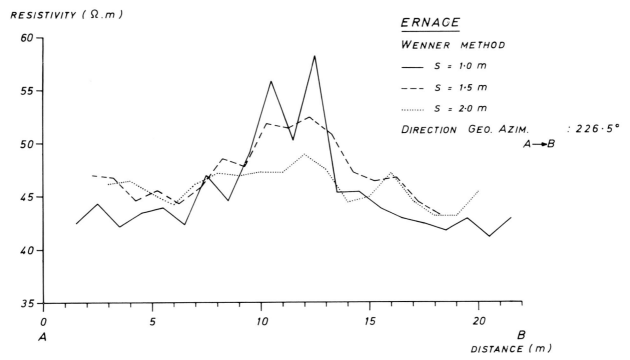

Fig. 17   *Electrical resistivity profiles at three different electrode separations on a line across the east side of a ring-ditch at Ernage*

Figure 18 shows a computer plot of the lines of equal resistivity, after calculating the power spectrum and after filtering the data in the wave number domain (cf. Scollar and Krückeberg, 1966; Scollar, 1970; Black and Scollar, 1969). We found an overall mean apparent resistivity of 51 Ω-m, a maximum value of 80·1 Ω-m, and a minimum of 37·5 Ω-m. The circular feature is clearly visible on the resistivity plot and it is evident that no other anomalies are present.

The aerial and resistivity surveys were followed by a trial excavation across the northern part of the circular feature. This allowed it to be identified as a ring-ditch. The ditch was filled with a light-coloured deposit more compact than the natural soil. In order to conserve the site for further scientific investigations, we expressly limited our excavation to a single trench measuring 6·0 m × 1·0 m × 1·8 m.

Electrical resistivity traverses over a linear feature

In July 1974 an electrical resistivity survey was carried out at Sauvenière (50° 36′ 05″ N, 4° 44′ 00″ E) near Gembloux over a linear feature (Fig. 6) discovered by C. Léva during an aerial survey flight (Léva, 1973,42). Our main purpose was to locate this feature as accurately as possible and to obtain more information about the horizontal extent and depth. We also wanted to follow its course in the fields to the north where it was no longer visible from the air.

Some preliminary traverses with different electrode separations were done as usual, to find the separation most likely to give the best results, and to ensure that the density of measurements was adequate to give the information required. The Wenner method with an electrode separation of 1 m was finally chosen. We measured the resistivity at every metre along each of six traverses; the distance between traverses was 40 m and the length of each was 47 m. The six lines were laid out perpendicular to a small road connecting the

farm of Coninsart (Fig. 6) with the intersection of the Chaussée Brunehaut and the highway from Gembloux to Jodoigne (N 21).

The exact location of the traverses is given by full lines on Fig. 19. The resistivity maxima can be seen to fall approximately on a straight line. On the fourth traverse from the south the feature is not clearly indicated, and this agrees well with its appearance on the air photograph at the same place (Fig. 6). We found a mean apparent resistivity of 29 Ω-m, which is typical for loamy soils, and estimated the width of the feature as about 6–6·5 m at a depth of 1 m.

A trial trench across the linear feature on the line of the second traverse from the south revealed the existence of an unmetalled road buried about 1·4 m below the surface. The road material was light-coloured and more compact than the natural soil, closely resembling the filling of the circular ditch at Ernage, which lies only 3·5 km away. In both cases the resistivity 'high' can be explained by the lower porosity and lesser ionic content of the deposit.

CONCLUSION

These few examples show that geophysical prospecting methods (especially magnetic and electrical traverses) can be used for the accurate location of features detected during aerial surveys.

The prospecting instruments now on the market have attained such precision that they can give good results at almost any time of year, even when short-lived marks are no longer visible from the air.

Not only can features be located, but an estimate can be made of their horizontal extent and depth below the surface.

These methods are the means of rapidly providing independent control for the irregular and patchy marks often seen on air photographs, which may in

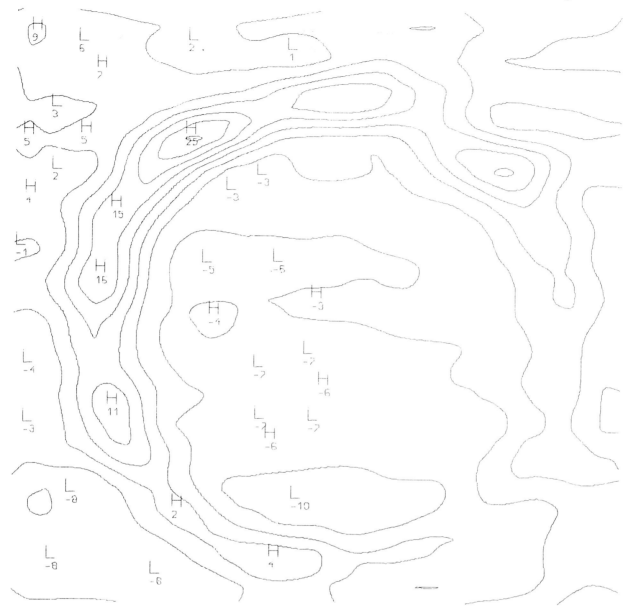

Fig. 18 Computer plot of lines of equal resistivity at Ernage. (The computer program is designed principally for meteorological data; the letters H and L, indicating areas of higher or lower pressure, should be understood in this context as referring to higher or lower resistivity)

the end reveal geometrical man-made features of archaeological interest.

We think that an aerial survey combined with an electrical and/or magnetic survey should precede every archaeological excavation, because they give guidance to the director of the excavation in planning his work, and because they are non-destructive.

Geophysical prospecting, in its ground and aerial aspects, results in a document such as Fig. 18, which not only presents a valuable general ground-plan, but also constitutes a powerful argument when defending the interests of the site.

ACKNOWLEDGMENTS

I wish to express my thanks to M C. Léva, who drew my attention to this subject and gave me access to his file of aerial photographs.

I am grateful to Professor Dr A. De Vuyst of the Geophysical Centre at Dourbes of the Royal Meteorological Institute of Belgium (Institut Royal Météorologique), who was kind enough to lend the prospecting instruments, for his support; to Professor Dr J. Van Isacker of the Royal Meteorological Institute at Brussels for the computer time placed at our disposal; and to Dr F. De Meyer for the computer plot.

I wish to thank the sons of Baron van Oldeneel tot Oldenzeel, Mlle A. M. Sacré, MM A. Demeffe, C. De Puydt, H. Heldenbergh, A. Mercier, and O. Witlox for their assistance during the surveys and excavations. We are also indebted to the landowners M and Mme Thyrion-Marique, MM L. Evilard and L. Laduron for their kind permission to investigate their lands. This project, which has been carried out during weekends and holidays, would have been impossible without their collaboration and encouragement.

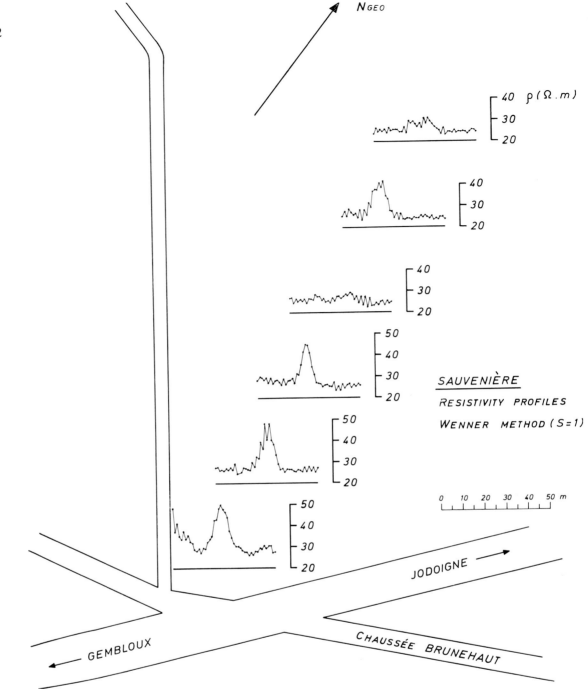

Fig. 19   Resistivity profiles over a buried unmetalled Roman road at Sauvenière

BIBLIOGRAPHY

Aitken, M. J. (1961). *Physics and Archaeology*. New York and London.

Aitken, M. J. (1963). Magnetic location. In: *Science in Archaeology* (Ed. by D. R. Brothwell and E. S. Higgs), 555–68. London. [See also 2nd ed. (1969), 681–94.]

Black, D. I. and Scollar, I. (1969). Spatial filtering in the wavevector domain. *Geophysics, 34,* 916.

Chevallier, R. (1966). Quelques méthodes modernes de prospection archéologique. In: *Etudes d'archéologie aérienne* (by R. Agache, R. Chevallier, and G. Schmiedt, = Ecole pratique des Hautes Etudes, *Mémoires de Photo-interprétation*, 2), 89–124.

Clark, A. (1963). Resistivity surveying. In: *Science in Archaeology* (Ed. by D. R. Bothwell and E. S. Higgs), 569–81. London. [See also 2nd ed. (1969), 695–707.]

Hesse, A. (1966). *Prospection géophysique à faible profondeur: applications à l'archéologie.* Dunod.

Keller, V. and Frischknecht, F. C. (1970). *Electrical Methods in Geophysical Prospecting.*

Lasfargues, P. (1957). *Prospection électrique par courants continus.*

Léva, C. (1966). Un four de tuilier romain à Marilles. *Bull. Cercle archéol. Hesbaye-Condroz,* **6,** 113–14.

Léva, C. (1973). Archéologie aérienne en Belgique. *Document Archéologia,* **1,** 40–5.

Scollar, I. (1965). A contribution to magnetic prospecting in archaeology. *Archaeo-Physika,* **15,** 21–92.

Scollar, I. (1970). Magnetic methods of archaeological prospecting — advances in instrumentation and evaluation techniques. *Phil. Trans. Roy. Soc.* **A 269,** 109–19.

Scollar, I. and Krückeberg, F. (1966). Computer treatment from archaeological sites. *Archaeometry,* **9,** 61–71.

Air photography and the development of the landscape in central parts of southern England

H. C. Bowen

Synopsis

The prime object of this essay is to illustrate how aerial photography makes possible a study of the development of widespread landscape patterns in those areas where open countryside and a favourable geology and land treatment reveal a relatively ample picture of former arrangements. Here it is the Chalk of south central England where patterns of prehistoric land allotment, in particular, are displayed over thousands of square kilometres, with implications for economic practice and change, and a suggestion of notable organization. Consideration is given to the fact that some archaeological soil marks may be virtually undetectable except on air photographs.

The purpose of this essay is to parade some particular advantages of aerial photography in studying the development of landscape patterns in areas where extensive archaeological remains are visible from the air. My illustrations are mostly taken from the open Chalk lands of south central England, a region which contains a wealth of complex patterns so far matched only in the Fens, the East Riding of Yorkshire, and on certain of the river gravels. My concern will be to show how air photographs are an essential aid in evaluating the past development of the landscapes.

The particular advantages I shall focus on are:

   (i) *the ability to display pattern* at all scales from the simple circularity of a 20 m ring-ditch to complexes which, arbitrarily preserved to view within my chosen area of more than 5000 km², can, not unusually, extend almost unbroken for perhaps 50 km². The existence of complex patterns over such wide areas would otherwise be quite unappreciated.

   (ii) *the ability to plan*, from air photographs, a mass of detail which either could not be achieved otherwise or only with such difficulty that it ceased to be a practical proposition.

   (iii) *the revealing of detail* otherwise not likely to be discovered at all and perhaps not recoverable by any other means whatsoever.

Some of the consequences deriving from these virtues are that categories of sites and recurring relationships come to be recognized, that the importance of a site may derive from its position in a pattern, that the range of possible patterns and their incidence can be tentatively analysed and points selected for specific investigation by all other means, and that suggestions can be put forward for what, on the basis of pattern analysis, *should* exist but cannot yet be verified.

To offset these merits many caveats may be voiced. One of these is that archaeological features in certain situations are highly resistant to air photography—a reminder, should it be needed, that fieldwork on the ground is still absolutely necessary.

Our first indication that the development of the landscape is not haphazard but subject to organization, however arranged, comes from the distribution of burial mounds and 'ritual' monuments in England. These occur in clear concentrations and within these concentrations it is frequently apparent that individual monuments were precisely sited for particular reasons.* Aerial photography has done much to advance our knowledge of these matters.

Before considering even more complex patterns of human origin, a brief excursus may be made to remind ourselves, in looking at rare survivals of elements of the primeval landscape, how air photographs can provide pictures of detail virtually impossible to plan (Figs. 1–3). The air photographs, taken long since from naval helicopters, show a beach in south Pembrokeshire (now incorporated in Dyfed) where a river still scours the sand towards its 'mouth' in the lea of an old headland, shown as an eroded anticline. The scouring exposes alluvium, seen in the photographs as dark patches, under the boulders that lie over part of the beach. An oak tree, 13 m long, seen centrally on Fig. 2, is the clearest of the remains of the now submerged former 'Atlantic' phase forest of oak, alder, and willow.†

Aerial photography is correspondingly best able to provide plans of another survivor of the primeval landscape, the so-called sarsen stones, this time within the Chalklands of our main study where they are sometimes found in dramatic scatters among the survivors of our earliest recognizable fields (cf. RCHM (England), 1970, Ancient Field group 5). It is, however, the fields themselves which are the most widespread evidence for the former shape of the landscape. I shall have much more to say of them, but for the moment it should be remembered that they were formerly very extensive indeed. Total destruction can be admitted in areas of intense historic development, but over the Downs air photography, especially, enables us to see where they formerly existed from even very slight remains. It is now therefore possible to look for and assess those areas where cultivation seems never to have been practised. These can be regarded, perhaps, as areas of very early permanent pasture, but the reason for such segregation, or non-arable use, can be clearly complex. The area north of Stonehenge is worth considering from this point of view.

The author is with the Royal Commission on Historical Monuments (England).
*RCHM (England) (1960), Fig. 2, and (1970), especially pp. 423–9.
†I am indebted to Professor F. W. Jane for an analysis of wood samples and to Professor G. W. Dimbleby for an analysis of pollen:
  cf. Bowen in Fowler (1972)

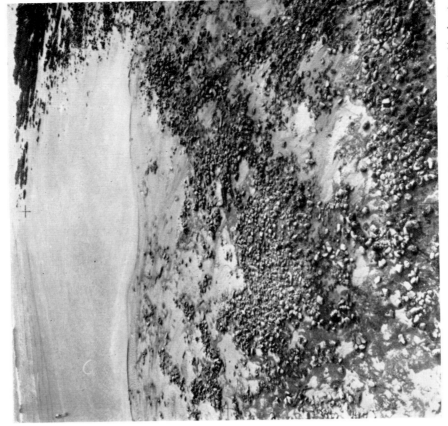

Fig. 2   Steep oblique air photograph of the area of submerged forest (Fig. 1), showing patches of alluvium and an oak tree in the centre
Photo: Royal Navy; Crown Copyright reserved

Fig. 1   Low oblique air photograph of beach at Wiseman's Bridge (SS 147059), Dyfed, Wales, from the east, showing area of submerged forest exposed among boulders around old river in the middle distance (1958)
Photo: Royal Navy; Crown Copyright reserved

The photograph of Stonehenge itself (Fig. 4) is the earliest archaeological air photograph known in this country, taken in 1904 from an Army observation balloon. It displays the enormous merits of good old air photography, not least in displaying former sources of destruction such as the much worn route right across the monument and partly down the ceremonial Avenue extending north–east from it, a nice reflection of fairly recent attitudes even to the most famous monuments in our landscape!

The Avenue, as carefully surveyed (and for 0·5 km as straight and precise) as a Roman road (curiously matched here by the apparently 18th century AD embanked highway, never finished, crossing it at right-angles) is the indicator which shows that there can never have been any but the lightest disturbance of the sward here. The Avenue has no sign of plough-soil piled against it or of plough-erosion from it (Fig. 5). So, in an area of intense prehistoric development, there are no 'Celtic' fields. The ground was therefore segregated for reasons powerful enough to preserve it inviolate to this day, a piece of primeval pasture that should, in my opinion, never be broken up.

Fig. 3 Ground photograph of oak tree in Fig. 2, looking east. Roots in foreground; figure near tree-top
Photo: H. C. Bowen

In my personal model of landscape evolution, ritual and funerary monuments (with which I would include causewayed camps) *generally* are the earliest surviving

Fig. 4 Steep oblique air photograph of Stonehenge (SU 123423), from Royal Engineers' balloon
Photo by courtesy of National Monuments Record

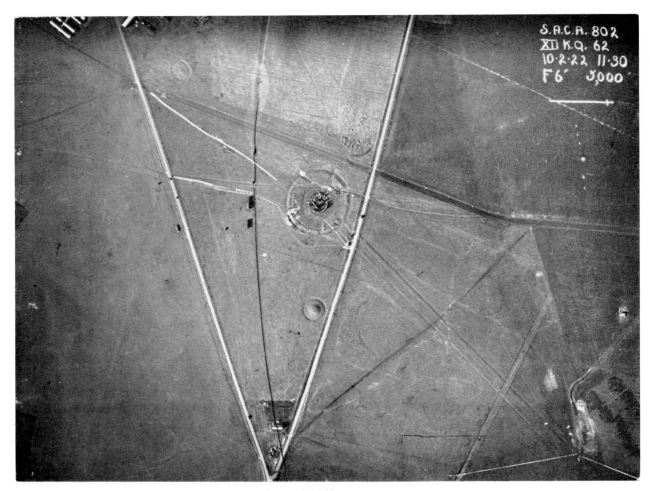

Fig. 5   Vertical air photograph of Stonehenge and area (1922)
Photo: Royal Air Force; Crown Copyright reserved

features. I should like to develop this point and suggest that in south central England surveyed blocks of arable fields are the next to appear.

Twenty-five kilometres north–east of Salisbury, RCHM has made a plan of all the visible archaeological features within 70 km² (Fig. 6). These largely survive as earthworks. The air photographs used, all excellent, include old verticals taken by the US Army Air Force, commercial verticals by Hunting Aero Surveys, a new vertical series by the Cambridge Committee for Aerial Photography, and overlapping obliques taken by the National Monuments Record (RCHM).

On the plan the black lines represent ditches, mostly with corresponding banks. Red lines show 'Celtic' fields. It is apparent that the fields occur in roughly rectangular blocks arranged on different axes (cf. Bowen, 1972, 45). These seem independent of the aspect or slope of the ground and were surely laid out by rough survey (as opposed to the precision which was available, as we have seen, at Stonehenge and its Avenue). Sidbury is a hill-fort of 7 ha. Extending out from it in four directions are long ditches which divide the surrounding area into large enclosures, the smallest of which is 20 ha, and one of which takes in the Bronze Age necropolis of Snail Down, as presumably, pasture.

To the long ditches I shall give their usual name of 'ranch boundaries'. They are found in different concentrations within the area of perhaps 4000 km² between the rivers Stour in Dorset and Meon in Hampshire. In this instance they are clearly in some phase related to the hill-fort, but evidence elsewhere (possibly applicable here) suggests that many originated in what I might call the Middle Bronze Age. Here they lie *across* orderly blocks of 'Celtic' fields in seven different parts and bound the fields in three others. It is the repetition of this relationship in many examples which makes me regard 'Celtic' fields as marking the earliest large-scale organized development of this south British landscape.

Among the fields are two long barrows which are integrated with the pattern. Since long barrows are massive and have a clear axis, the fact that the field blocks are on the same axis shows that in such instances they are justifiably regarded as the reason for the fields being on that particular axis.

The inferred change from arable to pasture, indicated by 'ranch boundaries' splitting 'Celtic' fields where there is no evidence for subsequent lynchet formation, is sometimes accompanied by evidence showing that the new linear boundaries were developed in more than one phase. On Knoll Down, Damerham (Hants.),

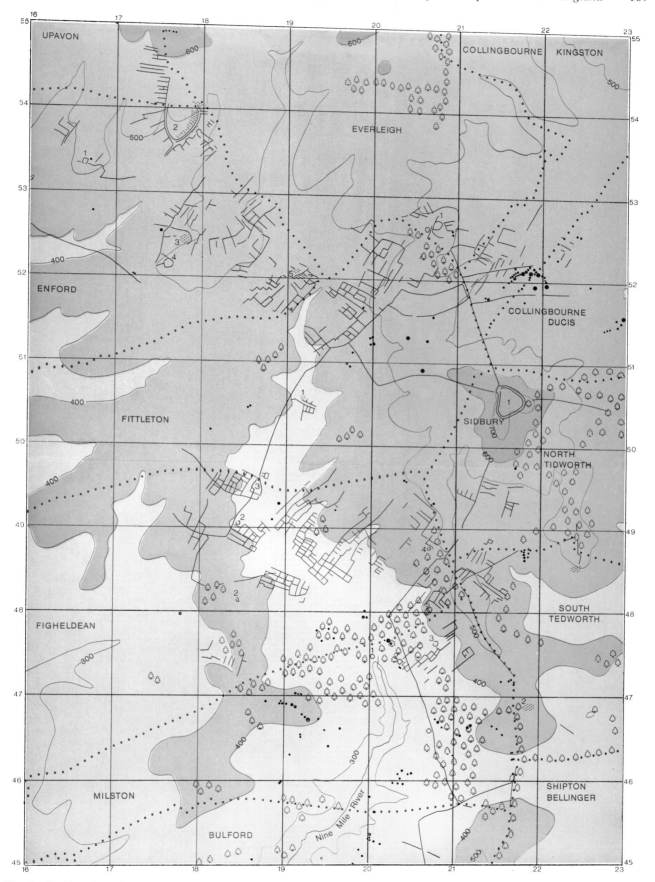

Fig. 6   Prehistoric and Roman remains in the area of Sidbury hillfort (SU 217506), Wiltshire. Experimental plan made for RCHM (England) as forerunner of series to accompany Wessex Inventories (by permission of the Commissioners). Snail Down is at 217521

Fig. 7   Oblique air photograph of 'Grim's Ditch' on Knoll Down (SU 087187), Damerham, Hampshire (14 April 1970)
Photo: National Monuments Record; Crown Copyright reserved

1·5 m high, is a testimony to long cultivation suddenly ended, once more, presumably in the interests of pasture. A very thin dark line extends west 16 km south–west of Salisbury, a very large 'ranch boundary', its bank, and ditch 13 m across, curving in a bow splitting 'Celtic' fields with lynchets up to from the knuckle of the large 'ranch boundary' at the east end of the bow. It seems reasonable to regard this thin line, which marks a small ditch, as an early phase of the linear boundary system. It is visible only on air photographs in this immediate area and, of course, only survives where it has not been destroyed by the big ditch (Fig. 7).

It has already been suggested that 'ranch boundaries' apparently springing from hill-forts may ante-date the hill-forts but still perhaps be associated with them in a late phase of control, as demonstrated long ago by Professor Hawkes at Quarley Hill (1940). Elsewhere I have shown that the ditch on Knoll Down

appears to be making for the multivallate hill-fort of Whitsbury, 3 km to the east, on which three other 'ranch boundaries' converge (Bowen in Fowler, 1975). The suspected continuation is now known to exist for much of the gap. It is of a size which matches the narrow ditch suggested as a first phase on Knoll Down. There are good archaeological reasons for regarding the earliest 'Celtic' fields in this south–west area of Hampshire as at least Middle Bronze Age (Bowen, 1961, 35 and fig. 3) and the 'ranch boundaries', therefore, despite the ultimate association with Whitsbury, as probably *originating* well within the Bronze Age.

So far we have accepted that dark lines showing as soil marks (and excluding plough marks) represent ditches which could be discovered by excavation to have been dug well below the level of the bed rock. Let us now look at a linear feature close to those discussed above. About 1 km south–west of Knoll Down it approaches

Fig. 8 Crop marks of linear feature approaching the settlement on Blackheath Down above Soldiers Ring (SU 077177), Hampshire (16 May 1971)
Photo: National Monuments Record; Crown Copyright reserved

an Iron Age and Romano-British settlement, curving uphill with 'Celtic' fields abutting it, but its position in the local pattern suggests that it might be an element of the 'ranch boundary' system. It appears on air photographs both as a soil mark and as a clear crop mark. The crop marks in Fig. 8 show the settlement displaying features that are repeated on many other air photographs of 'native' settlements. Surface finds are mostly of the Roman period. Excavation by the South Wessex Archaeological Association in 1972 showed that, in the event, the 'ditch' was only some 15 cm deep below the chalk surface and tentatively can only be called a worn hollow-way, probably serving the settlement.

Being warned by this example, I am now coming to the problem I promised of how on earth we should interpret certain other soil marks.

Figure 9 shows a pattern of what appears to be pairs of parallel ditches (the inner line of the right-hand pair being double) in an area of intense Iron Age and Romano-British settlement west of Micheldever Wood, about 40 km east of Salisbury and north of Winchester. The chalk here is capped by patches of sandy clay

which obscure the soil marks in places, but in favourable conditions they are visible on the ground, where not so capped, and could in fact be surveyed with precision if the air photograph was used to direct the surveyor to the right marks! A broader dark mark curves away from the bottom left of one pair of lines at X (Fig. 10). Routine augering showed that this thick line was clearly a ditch. Select augering elsewhere of the pairs of lines could show no distinction in depth of soil from the natural all round, which varied from 35 cm to about 60 cm. Under the soil lines the depth was generally about 35 cm.

Figure 10 is a select diagrammatic transcript of the features. Mr A. J. Clark tested these geophysically in the course of his survey along the proposed line of the new extension of the M3 motorway. He found no significant magnetic reaction directly above the lines but noted a slight reaction uphill of them. These features will be excavated later this year by the M3 Archaeological Excavation Committee.*

Excavation on another site has conclusively demonstrated the total absence of any depression in the

*Excavation has now shown that these marks are generally above slight ditches. The second line in from the right, noted as 'double', is found to be marked by very slight 'ditches' up to 15 cm deep, one of which was not present at all in places. I am indebted to Mr P. J. Fasham for this information.

Fig. 9   Oblique air photograph of soil marks of roughly parallel pairs of lines, west of Micheldever Wood (SU 524373), Hampshire (29 January 1971)
Photo: National Monuments Record; Crown Copyright reserved

bedrock to match soil marks of what conventionally, from the indications on air photographs, would be regarded as ditches.

The site concerned is near Andover, 30 km north–east of Salisbury. A photograph (Fig. 11) of it shows, top right, the ditched enclosures around an Iron Age and early Romano-British settlement which, as an aside on the development of the landscape, partly lies across the so-called Harroway, a probable Saxon road following the ridge-top along the hedges on the right of the picture. It has just been excavated by Mrs Sara Champion (to whom I am indebted for much of this information) and Southampton University Archaeological Department on behalf of the Department of the Environment. It is a matter of concern to any prospective builders that every small black circle is a pit frequently 2 m or more deep. Extending south from the settlement is a meandering long ditch which

is earlier at least than the middle Iron Age phase of the settlement and can be called a 'ranch boundary'. On the near side of the 'ranch boundary' are the marks I want to draw attention to. They are up to 200 m long, the individual lines in places about 75 cm wide. They splay out towards the south but roughly run along the contour of a gentle north–east slope. The uphill edges of the thin lines are generally sharp and clearly defined, while there is a general smearing on the downhill side.

A very rough transcript, based on a number of air photographs, shows that at least one of the lines bends sharply at right-angles, so again could not be plough-formed (Fig. 12). I shall call such a collection of lines a 'parcel'.

Mrs Champion used a mechanical grader to strip a swathe 100 m long across the lines of this parcel, now

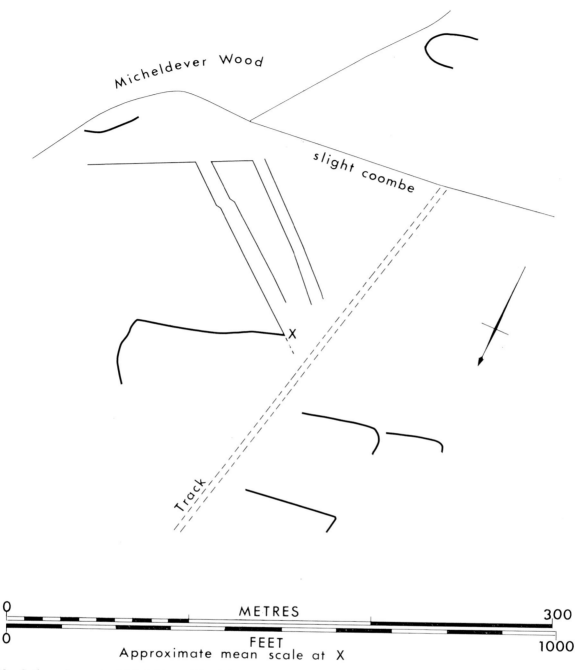

Micheldever Wood

slight coombe

Track

| 0 | METRES | 300 |

| 0 | FEET | 1000 |

Approximate mean scale at X

Fig. 10 Soil marks west of Micheldever Wood (SU 524373), Hampshire: diagrammatic transcription from Fig. 9

invisible under rough pasture but clearly locatable The 'ranch boundary' could be seen in the swathe but of the parcel there was no sign whatsoever in the chalk bedrock. The thin top soil was about 23 cm deep. Despite a series of investigations by means of geophysical survey and laboratory analysis,* there is virtually nothing that corresponds to the soil marks. Nor has it been possible to 're-create' the soil marks in the small area involved by selective scraping. So here indeed is a twofold problem:

First: if certain marks appear only on air photographs and, presumably, in the topsoil, how can they be verified and their original nature determined? I have been told of other examples of this phenomenon suspected elsewhere, on gravels as well as on chalk.† Dr Ian Stead tells me he has been puzzled on a chalk

*By Mr A. J. Clark and Dr Helen Keeley respectively.
†Mr David Miles of the Oxfordshire Archaeological Unit has written to me that the most obvious example of this was at Appleford (Benson & Miles, 1974, map 34, circle at 523936) where a fairly clear crop mark of an inner penannular ring to a circle could not be detected by careful excavation in the deep topsoil, over 0·75 m thick, or in the bedrock gravel.

Fig. 11   Oblique air photograph of Iron Age and Romano-British settlement (SU 33954638), linear ditch and unexplained near-parallel straight lines adjacent to the Harroway west of Andover, Hampshire (6 March 1969)
Photo: National Monuments Record; Crown Copyright reserved

site in France by the purely topsoil existence of certain regular features seen on air photographs of a site he excavated at Alincourt in the Ardennes. When the soil is removed in such sites, all the evidence goes as well. The *second* and more particular aspect of the problem, exemplified on the Andover site, is that we have evidence for some activity within the landscape marked by parcels of lines which are unexplained. The only archaeological dating suggested at Andover is provided by the association with the 'ranch boundary', but all this means, strictly speaking, is that the lines are later than it. (There is evidence, provided by Mr Max Dacre from a nearby site, of a similar linear ditch being still recognizable on the surface and probably accepted as a boundary, but suffering mutilation, in the 6th century AD). The parcel of

lines could relate in some way to part of the pattern of medieval fields that once covered this ground.* Air photographs, however, provide us with many other sites of close-set parallel dark lines, only one or two closely akin to Andover, but some forty of them representing equally mysterious parcels. They are generally close to prehistoric or Romano-British settlements, and at least three I know are crossed by parish boundaries, a clear pointer to a pre-medieval date. It is premature to pursue this subject in any detail, but it is relevant to draw attention to something like the Andover parcel in a remarkable photograph of Mr Hampton's of a chalk ridge north of South Wonston, not very far from Micheldever (Fig. 13). In the middle of this photograph are splaying close-set lines undoubtedly integrated with a prehistoric and

*Comparison with an estate map ([Crawford], 1922, pl. facing 304) makes this feasible, but two major difficulties remain. Why parts of the lines are at right-angles and so not plough-produced? And why only this one anomalously splaying 'furlong' should survive, one moreover for which there is a probably pre-medieval analogy described below?

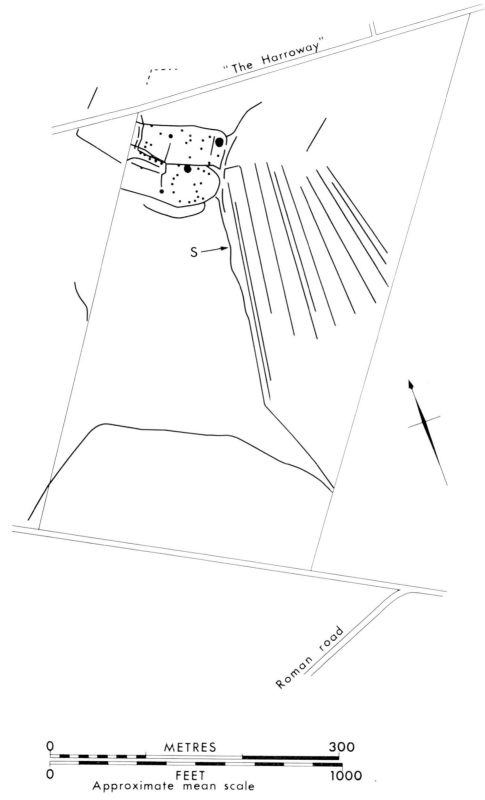

"The Harroway"

S →

Roman road

0   METRES   300
0   FEET   1000
Approximate mean scale

Fig. 12   Soil marks west of Andover, Hampshire, at SU 33954638: diagrammatic transcription from Fig. 11

*Fig. 13   Steep oblique air photograph of complex of features, Neolithic to Iron Age, at South Wonston (SU 470367),
Hampshire (4 March 1971). The arrow points to a pit alignment*
Photo: National Monuments Record; Crown Copyright reserved

Romano-British pattern and probably ending against that rarest of all things on the Chalk, so far, an undoubted pit-alignment (most common in the river gravels). The probable date is latest Iron Age or early Romano-British. There is also in this photograph a whole range of antiquities representing development of the landscape from the Neolithic and ending today in intense arable cultivation which has totally flattened most of the features.

At the highest point is a probable long barrow *not* quite integrated with 'Celtic' fields, but at the angle of one of the fields, in a typical position, is a round barrow. The enclosure from which 'Celtic' fields spring is surely prehistoric. There are close-set parallel lines, of uncertain description but not medieval, other than our splaying parcel, top right of the photograph overlying some 'Celtic' fields. The narrow wide-set pair of lines top right is more likely to be Roman than anything else but, again, repeats a pattern found in other places nearby—and nowhere excavated.

The chronological focus of my essay is ancient and modern. I have touched on some aspects of the development of the landscape in ancient times. I must largely miss out the intermediate phases, that is, much of the Roman and virtually all of the medieval, and I shall now move briefly to the modern, or at least post-medieval.

About 160 km NW of Salisbury is Minchinhampton, on the limestone of the Gloucestershire Cotswolds. The Common north of the town is almost flat, now devoted to a golf course, some grazing, and gentle public recreations such as flying kites—another of which I shall now fly! The whole area of fifty or so hectares is covered in earthworks, most of them small and of slight relief. I noted the fact on the ground but Professor St Joseph found it from the air in ideal conditions and has provided an archive of hundreds of superb air photographs. I illustrate one which is by no means his best (Fig. 14). The earliest recognizable widespread works are boundary banks and scarps,

Fig. 14   Oblique air photograph of earthworks on Minchinhampton Common (SO 855010), Gloucestershire (5 February 1964)
Photo: University of Cambridge; copyright reserved

probably Iron Age. The biggest are the Bulwarks, very prominent. I want to draw attention to the large number of long and a few round mounds, which we call 'pillow-mounds' (probably for breeding rabbits sometime between the 15th and 18th centuries AD) and to the 800 or so small open pits with attendant mounds. The plotting of these pits is beyond any reasonable ground survey yet is easy on air photographs (e.g. Fig. 15), a close study of which shows that their distribution is virtually the same as that of the 'pillow-mounds' and that both are contained by slight enclosure banks that are definitely later than the probable Iron-Age features, which continue to the top half of my plan (Fig. 16). This distribution then, only discernible with the use of air photographs, goes a long way to fixing those curious pits in the same bracket as the 'pillow-mounds' and thus all feasibly post-medieval. Most previous interpretations have relied on geological or natural phenomena. I should very much like to end with a suggestion that a characteristic of the 'pillow-mounds' here, seen

clearly on air photographs, helps to solve a mystery of the chalk downland near Salisbury, first surveyed on the instruction of Sir Richard Colt Hoare in the early 19th century but now generally known only from a superb photograph taken by O. G. S. Crawford (Fig. 17).

Narrow grooves divide a typical Minchinhampton pillow-mound into segments (Fig. 15). Crawford's photograph shows what he called 'biscuits', many characterized by similar grooves. Surely they are all 'pillow-mounds' but of an unprecedented elaboration which is itself pleasant to ponder in the development of this piece of landscape? They all lie, of course, on top of 'Celtic' fields.

A recent NMR photograph shows what the area looks like today, modern ploughing erasing the mounds and preserving only a view of the underlying 'Celtic' fields (Fig. 18). It provides an interesting twist to the theme that we cannot have too many air photographs—and that they need to be used critically.

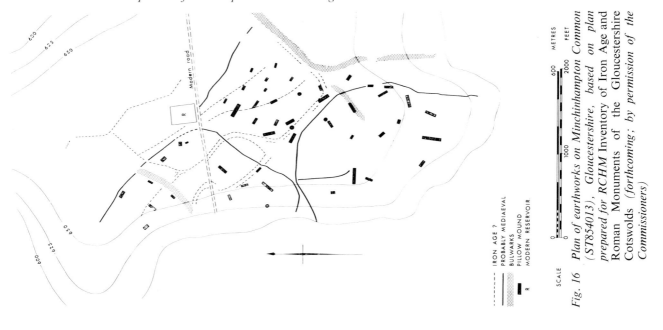

IRON AGE ?
PROBABLY MEDIAEVAL
BULWARKS
PILLOW MOUND
R   MODERN RESERVOIR

SCALE

Fig. 16   Plan of earthworks on Minchinhampton Common (ST854013), Gloucestershire, based on plan prepared for RCHM Inventory of Iron Age and Roman Monuments of the Gloucestershire Cotswolds (forthcoming; by permission of the Commissioners)

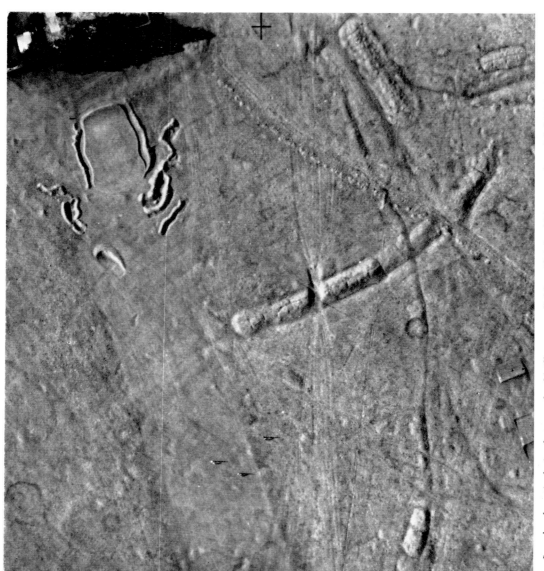

Fig. 15   Low-level vertical air photograph of 'pillow mound' (? artificial rabbit warren) at SO 85570073 in Fig. 14 (8 April 1964)
Photo: University of Cambridge; copyright reserved

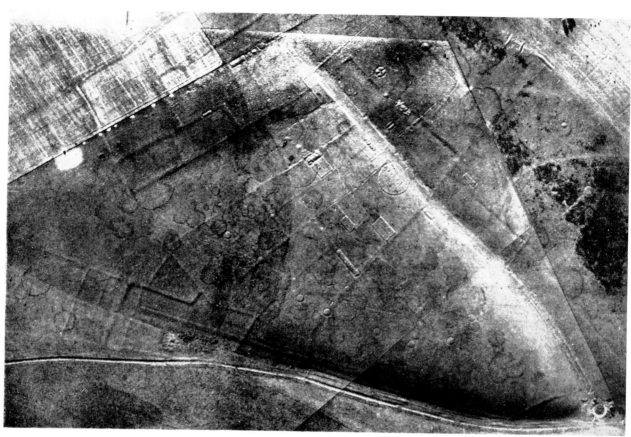

Fig. 17 Vertical air photograph of earthworks on Steeple Langford Cow Down (SU 037094), Wiltshire, before ploughing (15 July 1924). Modern road near reservoir extreme bottom left
Photo: O. G. S. Crawford, by courtesy of National Monuments Record

Fig. 18 Mosaic of recent oblique air photographs of Steeple Langford Cow Down (Fig. 17), after ploughing (20 April 1968)
Photo: National Monuments Record; Crown Copyright reserved

REFERENCES

Benson, D., and Miles, D. (1974). *The Upper Thames Valley*, Oxford.

Bowen, H. C. (1961). *Ancient Fields*, London, British Association for the Advancement of Science.

[Crawford, O. G. S.] (1922). *Papers Proc. Hampshire Field Club*, **9** (1920–24), 291, with plate facing p. 304.

Fowler, E. (ed.) (1972). *Field Survey in British Archaeology*, London, CBA.

Fowler, P. J. (ed.) (1975). *Recent Work in Rural Archaeology*, Bradford-on-Avon.

Hawkes, C. F. C. (1940). The excavation at Quarley Hill 1938, *Procs. Hampshire Field Club*, **14**, 136–190.

RCHM (England) (1960). *A Matter of Time: an archaeological survey of the river gravels of England*, London, HMSO.

RCHM (England) (1970). *Dorset:* Volume II, *South East*, London, HMSO.

The organization of aerial photography in Britain

John Hampton

Synopsis

The identification of buried features by aerial photography is limited by a number of factors. This results in fragmentation of evidence and the subsequent need to bring together all photographs for critical analysis. The functions of the National Monuments Record include the collection of significant photography, and aid to those who take and use air photographs for archaeological purposes. Future needs will require more aerial photographers trained in archaeological techniques, photo-interpreters, and cartographers to translate the vast mass of photographs now available.

The contribution made by aerial photography to archaeology since the 1920s has revolutionized the concept of numbers. Large areas of the countryside can now be shown to have been more intensively occupied than was once thought. In particular types of soil photography has recorded an almost continuous occupation since about 3000 BC, in which each succeeding phase has created a landscape by destroying, re-using, or building according to current needs. This process of evolution, which still continues, has left a palimpsest of remains from all periods which forms the potential for aerial reconnaissance, and at the present time only air photography can record its immensity and almost infinite complexity. Yet, for a variety of reasons, it is impossible for the air camera to record the full potential. An understanding of the reasons, and particularly of the often critical series of events that leads to the identification of buried features, is important for the organization of aerial photography and for the use of the evidence it provides.

Buried features with no surface displacement can only be recognized from the air as marks in the soil or as variations in the growth of the crop that overlies them. The difference in soil colours that betrays a silted ditch may show only for a short time after ploughing, for amongst other factors much depends on the moisture content of the soil. In winter and early spring, when most ploughing takes place, the opportunities for reconnaissance flights are significantly reduced: hence it will be that most buried features are likely to be recorded through a variation in crop growth. For this to occur, there has to be a critical situation in which the factors of climate and soil ensure that a buried feature is significant to the growth of the crop. Insensitive crops, the wrong sort of weather for the soil, each in varying degrees, will conspire to mask the hidden feature, and their fortuitous combination will guarantee that growth variations—*crop marks*—caused by buried features will differ in time and space. The differing rates of crop development and the impossibility of forecasting the appearance of a crop mark make it impossible to record any area at one point in time. In fact, reconnaissance flights are made over many years, each producing a facet of the potential, and from these will spring important consequences. The first will be that most photographs are likely to be taken at a time when the crop marks are not revealing the full potential. Secondly, the evidence will be fragmented into large numbers of photographs taken over many years; and thirdly, to form an appreciation of the evidence photographs must be brought together and analysed.

This means that the photo-interpreter is faced with using tens, even hundreds, of photographs for one site: and when it is remembered that something like 1·7 million vertical photographs exist for England and any one may contain archaeological information, the problem of organization becomes immense. Moreover, the collections of air photographs are not static; each year many tens of thousands of photographs are taken for a variety of reasons, and added to these are something like 10,000 specialist photographs of archaeological subjects received by the National Monuments Record. From this shifting sand of source material the archaeologist may cull his evidence.

The author is in charge of the Air Photographs Unit of the National Monuments Record.

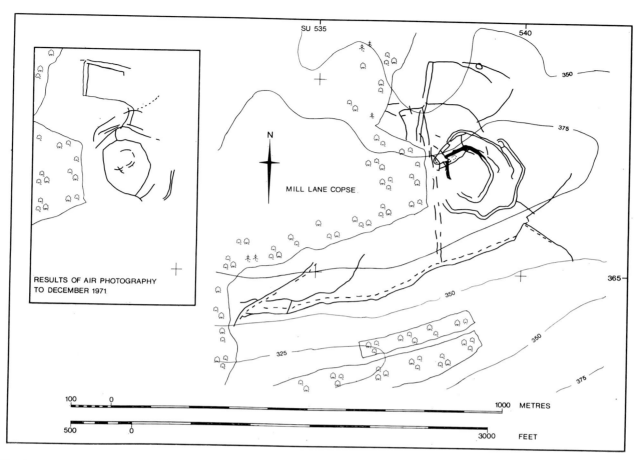

Fig. 1   *Micheldever, Hants. (SU 535365): a plan of ditches etc. derived from over 100 specialist aerial photographs taken between 1967 and 1972, and a selection of vertical 1 : 10,000 RAF photographs. The inset shows the first assessment based on photographs then available. Further amendment to the plan may be expected as more photographs become available, but the degree of amendment is not likely to be as great as that between the two plans shown above. The significance of the features depicted has yet to be determined in archaeological terms*
Crown Copyright

The evidence derived from aerial photography must be seen as a link in the chain of archaeological research alongside documentary sources, fieldwork, and excavation. The only way to present evidence of this nature for critical analysis is through the medium of a map, the common denominator for all these complementary activities. It must be clear that evidence solely derived from aerial photography can only be regarded as an interim statement likely to be amended by the next series of photographs. For a few sites, the degree of amendment may be small: for many it may be large, and this will depend largely on the crop/climate/soil factors that existed at the times of photography. Figure 1 illustrates this process. Clearly the initial assessment (inset) established the existence and accurate position of an archaeological site, but it was not possible to assess its character and extent with any degree of accuracy until concentrated photography had taken place: and it may be that knowledge of a significant percentage of sites so far photographed is still at a state comparable with the first at Micheldever.

The validity of any statement made in cartographic terms must be considered: if the source material is of such variable quality, is it worthwhile creating a subjective statement which, without the arbiter of excavation, must be regarded as interim and tentative? The answer must largely lie in the vast quantity of material now identified through the medium of air photographs. How else can this evidence of past landscapes be seen in the context of topography, except through the medium of a map? And, in spite of its subjective origin, the combined assessment of many photographs is likely to be more reliable than the examination of a single photograph; furthermore, as the areas of past occupation can now be shown to be so large, it is unlikely in the foreseeable future that any but the smallest fraction will be excavated. From the number of sites now known it seems probable that for most the only knowledge of their existence and form will be that derived from air photography, supplemented with such evidence as geophysical surveys and fieldwork will produce.

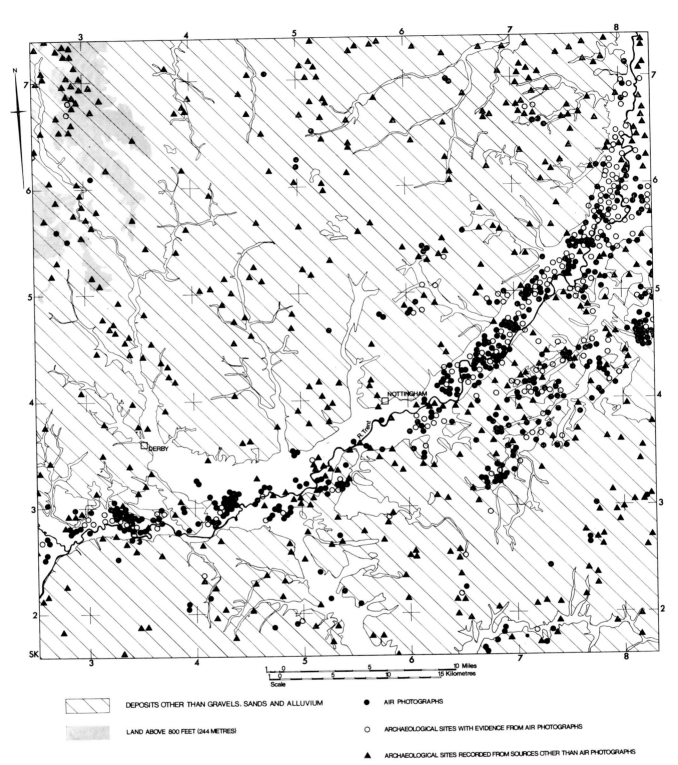

Fig. 2   Distribution of aerial photographs and archaeological sites in the area of the River Trent between Newark and Derby. The vast concentration of photographs and archaeological sites on the gravels should be compared with the paucity of photographs on other soils, although a sprinkling of archaeological sites is attested from other sources. An uncharacteristic distribution of photographs around SU 7040 is analysed in Fig. 3
Crown Copyright

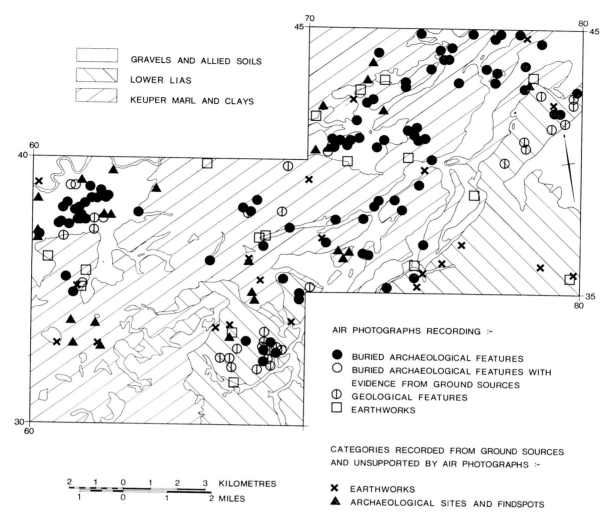

GRAVELS AND ALLIED SOILS

LOWER LIAS

KEUPER MARL AND CLAYS

AIR PHOTOGRAPHS RECORDING :-

● BURIED ARCHAEOLOGICAL FEATURES
○ BURIED ARCHAEOLOGICAL FEATURES WITH
   EVIDENCE FROM GROUND SOURCES
⊕ GEOLOGICAL FEATURES
☐ EARTHWORKS

CATEGORIES RECORDED FROM GROUND SOURCES
AND UNSUPPORTED BY AIR PHOTOGRAPHS :-

✗ EARTHWORKS
▲ ARCHAEOLOGICAL SITES AND FINDSPOTS

2 1 0 1 2 3 KILOMETRES
1 0 1 2 MILES

Fig. 3   *Distribution of air photographs recording archaeological and other information in relation to soils and archaeological data recorded from ground sources. Geological information based on 1 : 50,000 sheet 126 and 1 : 63,360 sheet 142* Crown Copyright

The limitations imposed by geology are most important for the consideration of archaeological evidence derived from aerial reconnaissance. The site at Micheldever was in an area where even in indifferent climatic conditions some crop marks will appear. But in heavier soils only exceptional climatic conditions combined with a sensitive crop will produce any significant evidence, and to consider these limitations an area of the central Midlands is examined in some detail.

The area of the River Trent between Burton and Newark and beyond has been subjected to intense air reconnaissance over a period of fifteen years by James Pickering of Hinckley (Leicestershire), and it is largely the results of his reconnaissance that form the basis for the following analysis. It is in fact an outstanding example of what can be achieved by a private flyer concentrating on a limited area.

Figure 2 shows an area 58 km square (containing *c.* 1300 square miles) traversed by the River Trent from Burton-on-Trent at the south–western extremity to a point about 20 km (13 miles) downstream from Newark in the north–east. To the north–west the

southern edge of the Pennine chain rises to above 300 m. The gravels and alluvium of the river average about 4 km wide and tend to be bounded by Keuper Marl. The distribution of photographs shown in Fig. 2 shows the vast majority sited on the band of gravel and alluvium. Yet the Ordnance Survey has identified a significant distribution of features, sites, and find spots, using sources other than air photographs, on other soils. The lack of photography in these non-gravel areas may be attributable to three causes: the reluctance of heavy soils to produce crop marks, the non-existence of archaeological sites likely to produce crop marks, and the absence of air reconnaissance. It is impossible to say at this stage which of these factors is primarily responsible for the lack of air photographs: suffice it to say there is a *prima facie* case for saying that soils off the gravels have not attracted aerial photography, and this is probably due to the lack of crop marks. But for those who wish to use information derived from aerial reconnaissance in distributional studies the implications must be obvious.

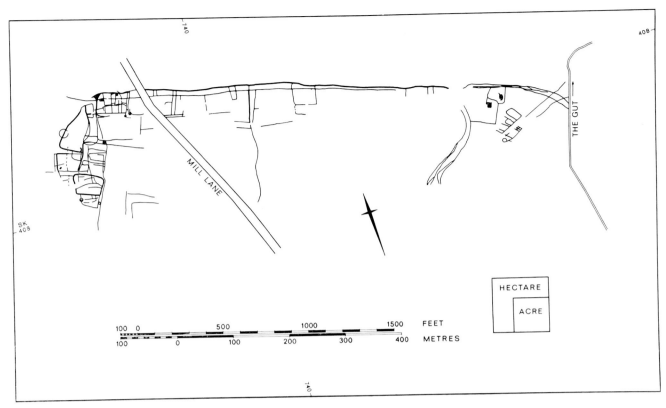

Fig. 4   Aslockton, Nottinghamshire (SK 740408): this plan of crop marks, compiled at the scale of 1 : 2500, is derived mainly from air-photographs taken by J. Pickering, with additional near-vertical photography by the NMR. It represents an assessment of some 22 photographs now available to the Unit, and must be regarded as an interim statement likely to be amended as further photography becomes available
Crown Copyright

An apparent deviation from the general pattern (Fig. 3) occurs south–east of the Trent in an area south and east of Nottingham. Here the ground on the south–eastern bank of the Trent rises to about 30 m (100 ft) above the river south of Nottingham, gradually subsiding to the north–east until it merges into the flood plain of the river south of Newark. The D-shaped area so formed, limited by the river to the north–west and the Lower Lias of the Vale of Belvoir to the south–east, is at its widest point some 10 km (6 miles) wide. It contains Keuper Marl with patches of alluvium and boulder clay. The Lower Lias of the Vale of Belvoir around the southern and eastern periphery of the area includes bands of limestone, and the soil tends to be clayey.

Superficially, the distribution of photographs suggests the possibility of archaeological sites in the vicinity of the Foss Way, and importantly it demonstrates that air surveillance has taken place. Detailed examination revealed evidence of probable archaeological significance in 82% of the photographs taken of 'gravel and allied soils' which occupied 25% of the area. Of the photographs of 'other soils'—75% of the area— only 56% contained similarly caused marks. But even this figure is somewhat misleading: the category 'other soils' (Lower Lias, Keuper Marl, clays) is based on the 1 in and 50,000 geological maps, and it is difficult to determine the precise nature of the soil at a specific locality. At a major site at Aslockton (SK740408) (Fig. 4) the Soil Survey of England and Wales report

the land to be graded as Class II (above average quality) loamy drift over Keuper Marl. This area was described as boulder clay on 1 : 50,000 Geological Sheet 126 and as "drift . . . . . very variable in character . . . . ." by the Memoir. At three other sites apparently on Keuper Marl the Soil Survey recorded the existence of a loamy drift c. 0·5–0·8 m thick, similarly graded as Class II land (Thomasson, 1971).

No attempt has been made to correlate all the sites recorded in this area with the soils, but it seems, as might be expected, that apparently unresponsive areas will contain pockets of good soil attractive to early settlement and capable of producing crop marks. This situation is some measure of one of the problems of aerial reconnaissance. How much flying time should be devoted to apparently unresponsive areas, for unless some flying takes place their response cannot be measured: is it more important to extend to unlikely areas rather than to continually record those already known? For the former many hours' flying may achieve little in terms of quantity, yet be highly significant in other respects. Clearly soils less permeable than the gravels and alluvium are less likely to produce crop marks. According to Pickering much of the area discussed has been under close observation for the past fifteen years, yet some sites off the gravels have only appeared on one or two occasions, particularly in the dry years of 1969 and 1970. All this emphasizes the need for constant observation, with the economic implications thereof. It shows that evidence of man's past settlement is more difficult to obtain in particular soils, and that the absence of sites recorded by conventional camera and human eye does not necessarily indicate an absence of past occupation.

For the archaeologist it will be manifest that the distribution presented by the use of aerial photography is only a measure of soils that produce crop marks. Furthermore, until each component can be assigned to a period, any map produced is no more than a cartographic inventory. Yet, even in a crude undigested form such a map provides a focus on topographical and spatial relationships and is a vital platform upon which the needs of the archaeologist can be based. From a planning point of view a cartographic statement showing the distribution of antiquities is a vital prerequisite for decisions likely to affect their survival, and on this account alone deserves considerable attention. It may be more practical to create maps of crop marks as a medium of communication rather than produce large numbers of photographs, each of which may tell only a part of the story.

Aerial reconnaissance for archaeology is currently undertaken on a national basis by two organizations, with regional surveys carried out by universities and individuals. In Britain Professor J. K. S. St Joseph has been flying since 1949 on behalf of the Committee for Aerial Photography of the University of Cambridge. *The Uses of Air Photography* (1966), edited by St Joseph, describes a wide range of activities for which aerial photography can provide information, and, incidentally, gives some indication of the range of subjects covered by the Cambridge Collection, which now numbers about a quarter of a million photographs, including 'cover' of some 15,000 archaeological sites.

The Air Photographs Unit of the National Monuments Record of the Royal Commission on Historical Monuments (England) was established in 1965 to build up a record of archaeological features and sites through the medium of air photographs. To 1974, the collection contains about a quarter of a million prints, of which about half are specialist photographs derived from flights undertaken by the National Monuments Record and by private flyers who deposit their material with the Record.

Flights by the NMR are based on the twin requirements of the Royal Commission's research programme and the photography of areas of high archaeological interest, where there exists a risk to survival. Great emphasis is placed on the recording of landscapes, and the use of an automatic 70 mm camera makes it practical to record even the smallest ditch.

The very important small band of local flyers who undertake regional surveys have virtually revolutionized the concept of numbers in the areas they have covered. Much of this material is made available to the NMR, who assist on a *quid pro quo* basis. The importance of local flying cannot be over-emphasized, for a person who concentrates on a small area has the advantages of local specialist knowledge of ground and weather conditions and, if the airfield is nearby, achieves substantial savings in transit time. The advent of archaeological units who undertake reconnaissance in their own areas is a much welcomed step in the development of constant observation, as are universities who undertake flying for regional research.

In the non-specialist field there are well established air-survey companies who are able to take vertical photographs and produce maps and plans to the very highest standards. A list of these companies is given in Appendix I: their photograph libraries represent sources of great importance. The average cost of 9 in × 9 in prints is in the 40–60 p bracket, a price which depends largely on the numbers required (a single print can be in the order of £3·00), plus such royalties as the owner of the copyright may require.

The largest single repository of air photographs in the country is the library of the Department of the Environment at Prince Consort House, London. It contains over two million photographs of Britain, including RAF photography from 1944 to the 1960s, and the Ordnance Survey material to 1966. Furthermore, through the medium of a central register, it can give an enquirer some indication of the commercial cover that may be available and advise him of the source to be consulted.

In view of the numbers of air photographs held by these sources the enquirer should indicate very precisely his needs, both in terms of topography and photography. For example, scale and time of photography are all-important in relation to the subject and geology. The relatively small scale of 1 : 20,000 might be useful for field systems, but its use is seriously limited for smaller features. For interpretation 1 : 10,000 is the optimum, with 1 : 7000 or 1 : 5000 ideal for complex areas. The best time of photography must be judged against the background of soil and climate. Crop marks on the heavier soils are to be expected only in particularly favourable conditions, whilst soil marks are related to ploughing and subsequent moisture content. Earthworks with very slight surface displacement require sunlight at a very low angle for their recognition; these and other factors must be considered when selecting photographs. Clearly it is important for the researcher to identify his aims and relate them to the chances of success and the overall cost in terms of time and money. Large-scale search and purchase of existing photography might well be uneconomic if, say, photography has been taken at the wrong times: and the commissioning of new photography may be useless if the time-scale does not allow at least several seasons for the right climatic conditions to occur, or for the farmer to plant a sensitive crop.

For the future the areas of greatest need may be defined as:
1. The ability to identify and bring together all significant photography for critical analysis.
2. The compilation of maps showing crop-mark and other evidence for planning and rescue activities.
3. Specialist training in the field of photo-interpretation.
4. Continuous air observation for areas of archaeological interest and high risk.

(1) The problems associated with the collection of aerial photographs are largely those of resources and numbers. Given a geology which produces evidence of archaeological significance that can be recorded by photography, the specialist photographs held in various collections are likely to give the quickest overall assessment of the ability of the medium. This should not be taken to mean every area with

archaeological potential has received systematic concentrated photography: in fact very few areas have received this attention. Specialist photographs being usually oblique in character may present particular problems of plotting, and vertical photographs must be considered as an aid in this respect, as well as a potential source of information. The numbers of photographs available are enormous: economics demand selection. It is therefore necessary to establish criteria according to the aim of the research and the nature of the geology. Scale of photography is perhaps the first consideration, followed by time. The implications of both factors have already been discussed; suffice it to say it must be for the researcher to decide the most significant conditions for the area, and a history of the recent climatic conditions would be an invaluable aid for the selection of air photographs. A function of the Air Photographs Unit of the National Monuments Record is to bring together all photographs important to archaeology and a start has been made in indexing and collection.

(2) The construction of maps showing crop marks and other evidence must have high priority on three counts: as a guide to further photography, as a basis for planning decisions, and as an assessment of archaeological content. Much of this has been discussed above (see p. 119), but it seems that far too little attention has been paid to this aspect in the allocation of resources. It must be emphasized yet again that such a map so derived is but an interim statement likely to be amended by the next series of photographs. All too often a well drawn map can give the illusion of presenting fact, whereas in this particular context it is no more than a statement of the possible or probable. As an aid to a more definitive statement selective excavation at critical points is required to establish the functions and relationships of features recorded.

(3) The interpretation of air photographs is surely a specialist function, for it is desirable for the interpreter not only to be a competent archaeologist but also to have some knowledge of photographic chemistry, physics, soils, plant pathology, geology, and photogrammetry. There is much to be said for an inter-related two-stage technique, with initial specialist translation followed by fieldwork etc. Particularly important in such a situation is a feed-back of information from the fieldworker to air photographer/interpreter giving information on soils, drainage etc. and especially the results of excavation in accordance with the proposal made above. On the photographic side there is a great need for methods of image enhancement. The computerized techniques used by NASA for the moon photographs show the potential, and the development of sensors more sensitive than the conventional camera and film emulsion is vitally important.

(4) 'Constant' observation from the air is largely a matter of economics. The advantages of 'local' flyers have already been referred to, and in this context they can make a valuable contribution. Only local flyers can be aware of the subtle and yet significant conditions in their area. Any flying so undertaken should be clearly linked to particular projects, areas, and ground research teams, for without defined purpose, it can easily develop into a joy-ride for the 'best' sites.

The results of concentrated photography depend on the potential that has survived and the ability of the

soil to reveal the hidden past. To give some concept of numbers an area of Hampshire where the soil is particularly amenable may be cited as an example. The Archaeology Division of the Ordnance Survey revised its records of the County to about 1970, and in 1974 the chalk areas of the county became a research area for the Commission. Concentrated photography by the National Monuments Record has taken place since 1967.

TABLE I   Hampshire 1 : 25,000 map SU 54: Archaeological sites and find-spots

From documentary evidence	110
From air photographs other than NMR	25
'New' sites from NMR photography	65

The total number of photographs for this area of 10 km × 10 km is something in the order of 1200 vertical and 1700 specialist oblique photographs. Such is the quantity of the results to be expected from an amenable soil, and it provides a measure of the storage, retrieval, interpretation, and mapping requirements. Whilst it is true that in this situation the information is being currently assessed for publication, it is also true to say that many other areas similarly endowed with extensive survivals of past landscapes are not being so treated. It seems clear that there exists an urgent need for far greater resources than have hitherto been made available for the communication of information contained in air photographs to the archaeologists and planners. It cannot be over-stressed that this information is part of the basic evidence upon which the archaeologist depends: from it is derived an understanding of the problems of land use, with all the implications of social, economic, and political development. Unless this source material is made readily accessible British archaeology is so much the poorer: an 'embarrassment of riches' awaits discovery.

ACKNOWLEDGMENTS

The writer is grateful to the Royal Commission on Historical Monuments (England) for permission to publish this paper. The views expressed are his own. Thanks are due to Mr A. J. Thomasson of the Soil Survey of England for information on the soils around Aslockton.

BIBLIOGRAPHY

Geological Survey (1908). *Memoir, Sheet 126*. London.
Geological Survey (1909). *Memoir, Sheet 142*. London.
Geological Survey (1969). Map at 1 : 63,360, Sheet 142.
Geological Survey (1972). Map at 1 : 50,000, Sheet 126.
St Joseph, J. K. S. (1966) (ed.). *The Uses of Air Photography*. London.
Thomasson, A. J. (1971). *Soils of the Melton Mowbray District* (Mem. Soil Survey Great Britain). Harpenden.

APPENDIX   A select list of sources of aerial photographs in the United Kingdom

Specialist photography for archaeology

Professor J K S St Joseph, OBE MA PhD FSA
Director in Aerial Photography
11 West Road
CAMBRIDGE CB3 9DP
Telephone Cambridge 57717

The Air Photographs Unit
National Monuments Record
Royal Commission on Historical Monuments
(England)
Fortress House
23 Savile Row
LONDON W1X 1AD
Telephone 01–734 6010 Ext. 58 (Mr J. N. Hampton)

General photography

B K S Air Surveys Ltd
Cleeve Road
LEATHERHEAD
Surrey KT22 7NL
Telephone Leatherhead 74841 (Mr A Baker)

Fairey Surveys Ltd
Reform Road
MAIDENHEAD
Berks SL6 8BU
Telephone Maidenhead 21371 (Mr A W Gardner)

Huntings Surveys Ltd
(Aerofilms Ltd)
Elstree Way
BOREHAM WOOD
Herts WD6 1YZ
Telephone 01–953 6161

Meridian Airmaps Ltd
Marlborough Road
LANCING
Sussex BN15 8TT
Telephone Lancing 2992 (Mr R H Smith)

The Air Photographs Unit
Department of the Environment
Prince Consort House
Albert Embankment
LONDON SE1 7TF
(For England and Wales)

The Scottish Development Department
Air Photographs Unit
New St Andrews House
St James Centre
EDINBURGH EH13 TB
(For Scotland)

Problems of town and country planners   David Baker

Synopsis

Archaeological advice professionally integrated with the planning process is on the increase. Local government reorganization, and the creation of Local Plans and Structure Plans by the new Authorities, will provide opportunities to improve the situation further. Archaeological data, especially that provided from aerial photography of otherwise unknown sites, must become a part of wider development control and development plan information systems. Some preliminary screening and some grading must occur. The use of aerial photographs by Bedfordshire County Council Planning Department is outlined, with special reference to the work of its Conservation Section. Problems of mutual understanding over goals and roles between planner and archaeologist are discussed.

As Conservation Officer in a County Planning Department I am concerned with County level specialist services in archaeology, historic buildings, and Conservation Area designation and implementation. These services are intended to assist the planning process at all its stages through the survey and evaluation of the historic environment; through rescue recording of historic sites and buildings they also attempt to deal with the consequences of some planning decisions.

The integration of archaeological advice with the planning process through the employment of specialists is fortunately becoming much more usual than it was three years ago, when my colleague Geoffrey Cowley was perhaps only the second County Planning Officer to make such an appointment. I must confess to having formal qualifications in neither planning nor archaeology, other than experience; this partly reflects the present situation when archaeologists are still moving towards a professional structure and planners are seeking to regulate professional relationships with many essential specialist disciplines. I am prompted by my brief three years' experience to identify the problems in my title as twofold: some involve a lack of mutual understanding between planners and archaeologists over goals and roles, and some are more simply administrative.

Rumour has it that the world of British archaeology is in a state of self-examination and attempted reorganization: such also is the condition of local government. This conference starts on the day after the appointed day for rearranging the local government structure we have enjoyed for most of this century.*

The author is Principal Conservation Officer, Bedfordshire County Council Planning Department.
*This paper was originally delivered on 2 April 1974.

In recent years archaeologists, whether professionally employed in universities, museums, or elsewhere, or acting in the part-time private sector, have been making increasing efforts to come to grips with existing planning machinery to safeguard the objects of their study and interest in potentially destructive situations. As a result of yesterday's changes, the planning process is largely unaltered, but the machine for administering it has been dismantled and put together in a different way: both its customers and operators have to learn the new procedures. The situation is further complicated by a grave shortage of moving parts: development control sections in the new District Councils are almost universally understaffed and all planning department establishments are under strength. It may be helpful to start with a brief sketch of this new division of planning responsibilities, to clarify how the new procedures may affect the preservation or destruction of archaeological sites.

The planning process before and after 1 April 1974 is intended to determine planning applications, within a framework of statutory plans or regulations and agreed policies. It thus divides into two main activities, development control and plan making, with many ancillary functions. Reorganized local government has two operational levels for both activities: in general the District deals with routine development control and local plan making; the County covers strategic policies and those development control matters which directly involve strategic as well as local considerations. Districts are no longer either rural *or* urban, they are now rural *and* urban. New Metropolitan Counties and Districts cover the great conurbations, but London's arrangements are unchanged. Of course there are exceptions and complications. Mineral extraction and transportation planning are handled by Counties: these are earth-disturbing agencies which greatly concern archaeologists. Some local plans of strategic significance may be made by the County Authority, such as town centre proposals. In some areas the need for staffing economy will require that a County employ specialist officers providing direct services to their group of Districts. In all matters there will be the need for the closest working consultation between new County and District Authorities, whether the new system requires it or not, for mutual benefit and to the end of making the new arrangements work.

The hierarchy of plans governing development control policies is based upon data organized in complex information systems. Within these, archaeological data have a rightful place, though it is one that has not been universally admitted or taken up. At the lower end of the scale, *local plans* lay down the appropriate uses for land in small areas; *structure plans*, usually covering a county or a large conurbation, lay down the broad strategic framework for a group of local plans; the structure plans are themselves conditioned by *regional strategies* and *government policies*. Most local and structure plans have yet to be made. A local plan may cover a group of rural villages or an historic town (or both). It may show the Scheduled Ancient Monuments (whose designation and administration is a Department of the Environment matter), Conservation Areas, and major groups of Listed buildings; their legal identity should create a strong presumption on favour of preservation from destructive alternative land uses. But the legally protected or legally identified elements in the historic environment are only a part of the whole heritage, and only a small proportion of

major archaeological sites. Sites detected or understood from the air are particularly underprotected. However, this hierarchy of plans does give the opportunity for adequate protection, provided that the sites are identified at local level, provided that the structure plan recognizes the principle that conservation is desirable, and provided that there is a favourable national climate in public opinion, backed by the machinery of statute and government circular.

We do not know what advantages and disadvantages the new planning system will show. Conservation interests, including archaeologists, have been alarmed at the prospect of development control decisions being taken at District level, when they had been pressing over many years for adequate staffing provision at County level: the new Districts are much smaller and more numerous than the Counties, and less able to afford such advice even if enough advisers existed nationally to cover the country. On the other side of the coin it should be noted that many of the new District Planning Officers have come from old County Authorities, and at that level replace Engineers and Surveyors who were sometimes less sympathetic to conservation. The new Planning Officers are more likely to have experienced the need for such specialist advice. Also, many of the larger Districts have been able to set up teams covering conservation matters for themselves, and indeed the Secretary of State for the Environment required the new Districts to satisfy him with regard to their conservation arrangements. In archaeology, the trend continues towards the appointment of County Archaeological Officers, but several Districts may employ officers of an equivalent status. Thus, while the system may have been re-ordered, the principles governing it remain unaltered, and it is worthwhile today to discuss the existing relationships of aerial reconnaissance, planning, and archaeology in the new local governmental world.

Planners have always valued aerial reconnaissance and the photographs it produces, for giving overall impressions of land-use and as a supplement to Ordnance Survey Maps. In the former case, public pressure on recreational facilities at a given time can be gauged over a wide area from the air, as can the extent of some kinds of industrial pollution and the impact of various agricultural or extractive processes. Public pressure on a monument can be graphically shown by the encroachment of buildings or by the patter of feet creating a pattern of eroded pathways.

Development Control planning, which must clearly identify a single house plot on a map, relies on the old County 25 in or new 1/2500 scale maps. In spite of the valiant efforts of Ordnance Survey map revisers, there are still significant areas of the country only covered by published maps in the County 25 in series. These lack National Grid lines, nor are they aligned with the National Grid, and they often depict a pre-war landscape. Even the 1/2500 series which replaces them is rapidly outdated by village or town development, hedgerow rearrangement, and all the manifestations of a technically powerful and accelerating lifestyle on these small islands. There are various temporary remedies for this situation: in Bedfordshire, for planning purposes the County Council obtained a complete vertical aerial cover of the County in 1968, a survey which may need to be repeated shortly to take account of subsequent development. In one form the photographs are printed on transparent base for dyeline reproduction within the Planning Department;

the scale is 1/2500, and each sheet is the equivalent of a new-style 1/2500 map. A set of the old County series 25 in map has been cut up and reconstituted in the 1/2500 format of paired kilometre squares, and revised from the enlarged aerial photographs, thus giving the facility of a complete metric format revision. The only unhappy aspect is that the flight was made at a time of year when archaeological features did not show up very clearly; even so, the aerial photographs printed at this enlargement make it easy to check whether some rural sites recorded decades earlier have survived the tractor plough.

Bedfordshire County Council Planning Department acquired a further set of aerial photographs when their Archaeological Officer was appointed in 1972. The two main sources were the Cambridge Committee for Aerial Photography (Professor J. K. St. Joseph) and the National Monuments Aerial Photographic Unit (Mr J. Hampton). Both provided full access to their collections, and copies covering the sites photographed by them were purchased. I would like to pay tribute to their co-operation, and to remark that the Cambridge Collection is having to cope with an avalanche of requests from rescue archaeologists seeking to establish systematic records for their areas; to an outsider there seems to be a danger that other primary purposes of the Collection will be squeezed between staff shortages and these demands.

What part does aerial photography play in filling the total record picture of Bedfordshire archaeological sites?

Figure 1 shows the major sites noted on the Bedfordshire Sites, Monuments and Buildings Record, an information system based upon that pioneered by Mr Don Benson at the Oxfordshire City and County Museum. After two years of collecting information the Bedfordshire Record has over 4,000 items, and reflects the existing state of knowledge on sites, including all that known from aerial reconnaissance. A high proportion of the major sites within that total were actually discovered from the air.

Figure 2 shows how the sites recorded (and mostly discovered by) aerial photography can be divided into crop or soil mark sites and earthworks. The former category predominates.

Figure 3 shows how this aerial information affects the rescue excavation programme in Bedfordshire. A significant number of sites due for destruction are only being recorded because they were discovered from the air.

How is archaeological information from aerial and other sources incorporated into planning information systems for everyday development control use? Some Planning Departments have comprehensive information systems, a few of them allowing for the computerized retrieval of policy and site constraints in respect of planning applications. In Bedfordshire at present a simpler manual system of overlay Constraints Maps is used.

Major archaeological sites are drawn upon these Constraints Maps, a series of 6 in scale which shows all factors that must be considered about an area of land which is the subject of a planning application. These factors include Green Belt land, river flood plains, Grade 1 agricultural land, trees subject to Preservation Orders, Scheduled Ancient Monuments, to name only a few. Thus threats to such major

archaeological sites can be identified as soon as a planning application is received, and in some cases may be known earlier through informal consultations. Archaeological information on these Constraints Maps can be altered in accord with the results of further investigations in the field or from the air. In Bedfordshire this information service is fully co-ordinated with the new Districts.

The involvement of archaeological sites at the heart of the matter is the crucial step forward, but problems do remain. Only known sites can be registered as a Constraint, and other contributors to this volume have shown how much the aerial observer is at the mercy of climate, geology, and crop types. In Bedfordshire we owe much of our knowledge of County prehistory to barley, but Biggleswade brussels sprouts have contributed little. It is also extremely arbitrary to describe some sites as major, and not give that title to others, particularly when the evidence for a minor category may be little more than a scatter of pottery on the surface. There is always the possibility that such minor indications conceal something of much wider significance. Some would advocate the registration of every site of any apparent level of importance. In Lowland England this could have the effect of covering the entire map and diluting the credibility of the archaeological constraint, as well as making consultations based upon it administratively unmanageable.

Planning Committees and their Planning Officers are constantly trying to reconcile conflicting interests for the greater good and in the process cannot fail to upset one or more of them. This Symposium is concerned with a subject that is important, but is nonetheless a minority interest. The familiar but often friendly demons of rescue archaeology—the motorway engineer, gravel magnate, and wicked developer—tend with the worried archaeologist, to be regarded as morally neutral adversaries in the planning process. In the Conservation context, archaeology is only one interest; earthworks may be threatened by proposals to put underground unsightly overhead wires in ancient villages. At the next level Conservation itself, i.e. the attempt to retain the best of the existing and to get the best replacements for what must go, may be found competing with clean-sweep re-development. Even if the archaeological interest can be satisfactorily integrated within the planning machinery, Committees and Officers still have to make the kind of fully informed judgment in which the needs of the extractive industries may be given precedence over those of research into prehistory.

Some archaeological sites are of such importance that they virtually constitute an absolute constraint against destructive development, but these are few in number. Many others could be called important, not just for their academic, but also for their local interest. Others may not be judged to be so important by themselves that a new housing estate should be refused permission, but if they lie under Grade 1 agricultural land in an Area of Outstanding Natural Beauty, the combination of circumstances could ensure their survival, and the location elsewhere of the needed homes.

It is clear what archaeologists want from planners: ideally it is the preservation of important sites, and at least the full consideration of the claim to survive in each case. What do (or should) planners require of archaeologists? The fact that many new County

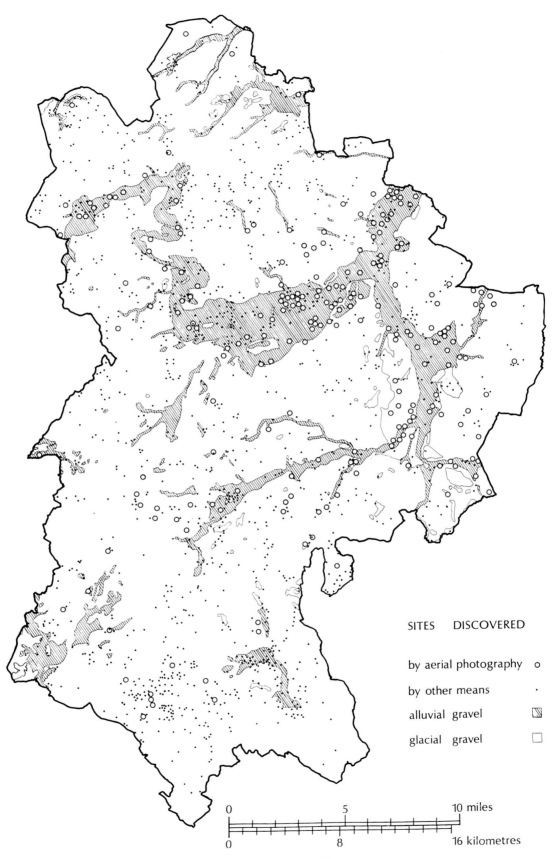

SITES   DISCOVERED

by aerial photography   o

by other means   .

alluvial gravel   ▨

glacial gravel   ☐

Fig. 1   Bedfordshire Sites, Monuments and Buildings Record: sites discovered

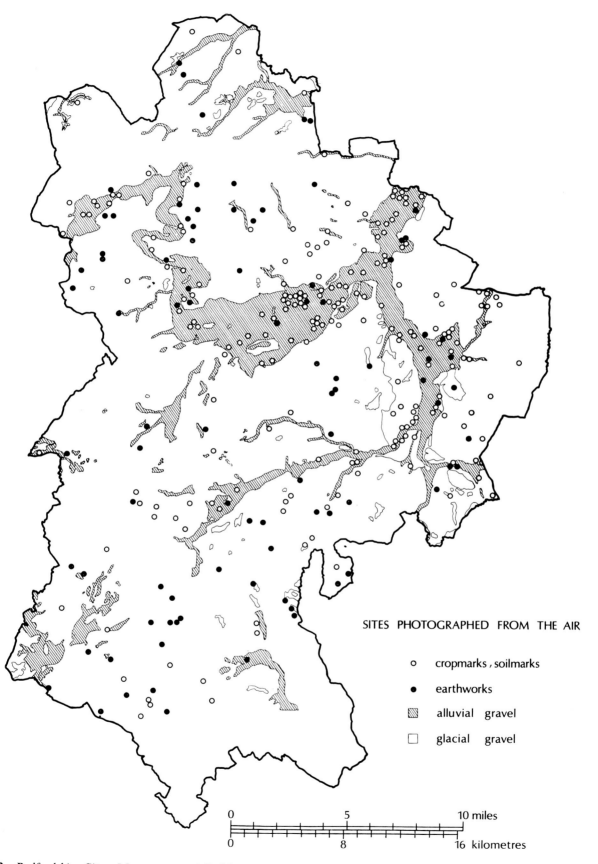

SITES PHOTOGRAPHED FROM THE AIR

○   cropmarks , soilmarks

●   earthworks

▨   alluvial   gravel

☐   glacial   gravel

Fig. 2   Bedfordshire Sites, Monuments and Buildings Record: sites photographed from the air

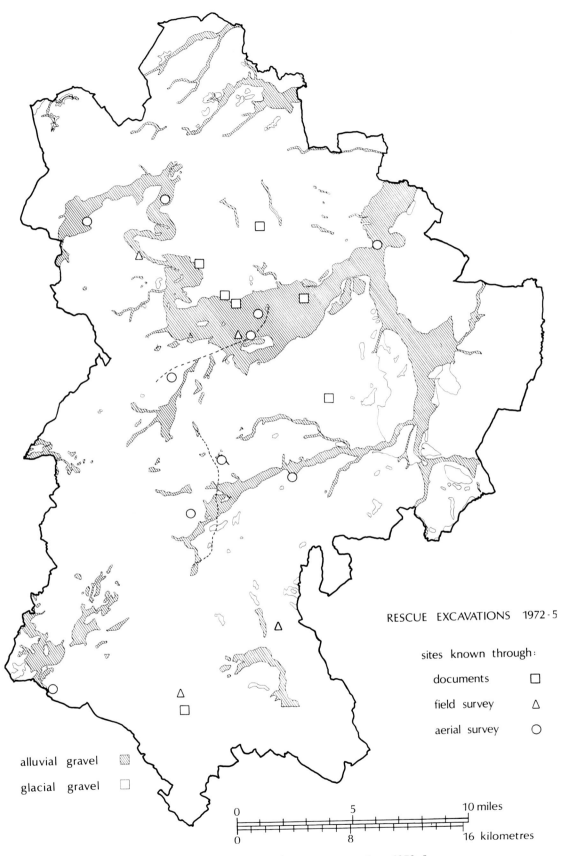

RESCUE EXCAVATIONS 1972·5

sites known through:

documents   □

field survey   △

aerial survey   ○

alluvial gravel   ▨

glacial gravel   □

0   5   10 miles

0   8   16 kilometres

Fig. 3   Bedfordshire Sites, Monuments and Buildings Record: rescue excavations 1972–5

Authorities have not appointed specialist archaeological advice may indicate a failure to require this in sufficiently strong terms from national level, even though a Circular was issued in 1972 suggesting such appointments. Equally it is possible that public archaeological opinion, essential for archaeological reform in a democracy, has not been sufficiently clear about how its interests should relate to planning; too many people still feel that local authority archaeological officers by definition will not win all their arguments (which they should not and cannot) and mistake the inevitable adjudication of planning decision for subversion by tyrannical planning officers pulling rank.

Planners require the archaeological data presented in a form which can be assimilated and assessed rapidly and efficiently. Planners are always in a hurry to complete complicated consultations and reach decisions, and are always being blamed for delays. Aerial photographs showing sites will, by themselves, be useless without the sites fully identified and interpreted. Professional development control planners do not want to make academic archaeological decisions. Little attention will be paid to sites unless they are plotted on a map with accuracy. A set of solely archaeological maps presented to a planning department from outside is unlikely to be consulted for every application, even with the best will in the world: the time does not exist. Thus, assuming that the planning department has some central data system, the archaeological information must be placed on it. Judgments will have to be made about which sites appear important enough for such consideration, and further appraisals are inevitable once a given site is threatened; thus the need for professional and readily available advice becomes clear. If circumstances demand that the archaeological advice must come from outside local government, certain standards must be met and matched by a level of co-operation from planning staff. Sites must be accurately plotted; their continued survival must be verified; the block of data should be given in one block and revisions minimized; they must be graded in some way, however much that process does violence to academic criteria. At least there should be division into:

(a) sites which are so important that they must be preserved at all costs;
(b) sites which are so important that their loss could not be contemplated without full record;
(c) sites where a full watching brief should be carried out during destruction.

All these sites would be important enough to be entered on Constraints Maps: categories (a) and (b) at least should be Scheduled as Ancient Monuments. It also follows that there must be well oiled machinery to follow up planning decisions with the necessary field action. In return, planners can attempt to apply conditions of planning consents affecting archaeological sites, or make informative comments at the time of granting permission.

There is much current debate about the best way to organize archaeological advice for planners and the rescue field programmes that are associated with it. Local government departments, independent units, and county societies figure in varied combinations of suggestions, depending upon existing local circumstances. The Bedfordshire solution, as evolved after local government reorganization, might be of interest as an example where the lead was given by the public sector. The County Planning Department includes a Conservation Section whose responsibilities have already been mentioned. In co-operation with District Councils, who run the main museums, and local societies, a field survey and rescue recording programme is being developed: thus survey, planning advice and necessary action are combined within the same administrative system. It provides a service to other departments, other Authorities, and the general public. The County Council has produced an Aspect Report, covering the 'Historical Environment', as a contribution to the Report of Survey preceding the County Structure Plan. This outlines the current situation with regard to archaeological sites, historic buildings, ancient settlements and landscapes, the controls over them, the threats to them, and advocates a systematic and detailed survey programme over the County, on the ground and from the air. When this survey has been completed the material may form the basis for a Subject Plan.

In conclusion I return to the problem of mutual understanding. Never forget that planning has a high political content: planning Authorities have to attempt a proper distribution of resources and benefits within the community, and there are always many views on how this should be done. Planning Authorities are bound by practical considerations, a responsibility to statute and electorate; archaeologists' responsibility is usually more within the limits of an academic discipline, whose primary concern is the advance of knowledge. The media have made all aware that archaeology is interesting, but not whether it is politically or socially valuable. Planning increasingly reflects a concern with environmental issues, but has tended to exclude archaeology from this.

The historic nature of the environment must be defined, and appropriate planning aims that recognize its existence and needs must be set out.

(a) To identify those items in the physical environment which are of historical and archaeological importance;
(b) To record such items;
(c) To ensure that such items are fully considered in any land-use conflict which may threaten their survival;
(d) To devise appropriate conservation policies for such items;
(e) To facilitate the communication of the nature and the content of the historical environment as a resource for research, education, and recreation.

In summary, we should be seeking to identify, conserve, enjoy, and transmit to the future the significant elements in the historic environment as an heritage in the fullest sense of the word.

The application of aerial photography in the Oxford region

Don Benson

Synopsis

Some recent results, obtained by examining aerial photographs for Oxfordshire, are outlined and discussed. It is stressed that these results arise solely from detailed plotting of crop marks, a process which is made more difficult by some gross delays in dissemination of information. Stages in the collation and documentation are described and the need for regional collections of photographs and their integration into regional or county archaeological archives is noted. The relevance of archaeological aerial photographs to aspects of planning and conservation, excavation, and field survey is briefly discussed.

This paper discusses the use of aerial photographs within one particular area, Oxfordshire, and inevitably much of what is said here will apply to uses and users of aerial photographs within other regions. It is hoped, however, that there will be some benefit in distilling what are often national aspects and problems into a regional point of view, based on experience of work carried out in the Field Department of the Oxfordshire County Museum since about 1967.

Oxfordshire covers some 3,500 square kilometres, containing a variety of subsoil types, including limestone and chalk uplands and clay vales, but dominated by a large section of the Upper Thames Valley with its extensive gravel terraces. The prolific crop marks on these terraces have had an almost magnetic attraction for aerial reconnaissance for many years, largely at the expense of other parts of the County. But at least, one might suppose, the results of this reconnaissance along the gravels are well known? The recent survey of the gravels (Benson & Miles, 1974a)* utterly belies that supposition. It is only through this Survey, by bringing together the results of fifty years of aerial reconnaissance in the Oxfordshire section of the Upper Thames Valley, that we can begin to appreciate the extent, value, and significance of the discoveries.

The Survey is not, and was not intended to be, an academic analysis of the historical evidence revealed by aerial photography. Such an analysis would have delayed the presentation of the basic maps and gazetteer for several years. Rather, it provides a means of assisting individual photographers to disseminate the results of their work, and presents the evidence upon which subsequent research may be developed. Certainly, it is apparent that much recent specialized research has been carried out in ignorance of important data which have been in existence for a number of years.

SOME RECENT RESULTS

It is, nevertheless, appropriate to draw attention briefly to some of the superficial results of aerial reconnaissance in the County. Firstly, and obviously, there is

the enormous increase in site densities, and a major shift in density distributions from the uplands to the river valley. The importance of the gravel terraces is well known, but the extent and variety of settlement is something only recently appreciated. New discoveries, not only on the gravels but also on the alluvium, must lead us to treat the whole of this valley area as one vast archaeological site (Benson & Miles, 1974a, 18). At the same time, these distributions draw attention to the now relative barrenness of the adjoining uplands, and it is clear that for some periods of settlement, though not necessarily for all, the known density distributions must be a distortion of the real regional situation.

Secondly, the content of particular periods has been dramatically expanded. For instance, the number of Saxon settlement sites has been increased from 18 to at least 40. As a result, however, aerial reconnaissance has produced a most unlikely pattern, with 38 settlements and 32 cemeteries on the gravels, and 4 settlements and some 30 cemeteries (and a further 20 possibles) over the whole of the rest of the County. The need for settlement reconnaissance throughout the non-gravel areas is readily apparent. It is inconceivable that such sites should not be associated with the early cemeteries in the north and south–east of the region, or that the associated settlements all lie beneath present villages.

Thirdly, detailed plotting of crop marks has added new dimensions to earlier records: old sites and finds are being placed in new contexts. Again, the Saxon period provides the best demonstrations. A cemetery at Brighthampton recorded by Akerman in 1857 may now be seen as part of a complex containing *Grubenhäuser* and a part at least of the remainder of the cemetery may be identified (Benson & Miles, 1974a, 46, Map 21, 3803). One of the few remaining unworked areas at Stanton Harcourt, now firmly sandwiched between two gravel pits, shows possible *Grubenhäuser* which may be connected with Saxon pottery recovered from the destroyed area immediately to the west, and might be linked with a salvage-recorded inhumation cemetery to the east, or perhaps the 23 secondary Saxon burials in the Stanton Harcourt Barrow 600 m to the south–east. Perhaps the most important illustration of this exercise is at Sutton Courtenay where, in addition to the recognition of further *Grubenhäuser* to the south of the pit marking the site of Leeds's discoveries between 1921 and 1937, we now have a series of presumed Saxon timber buildings which place Leeds's famous Saxon village in an entirely new perspective (Benson & Miles, 1974b). Fourthly, there are aspects of landscape development and land utilization to be considered. Here we must beware of treating the gravels in isolation from the rest of the region, especially in the prehistoric period, when economic and cultural systems transcended

The author is the Keeper of the Field Department, Oxfordshire Museum.
*For convenience this publication is referred to as the *Survey* throughout the rest of this paper.

valley and upland boundaries. Even within the valley, the crop-mark complexes tend to suggest an intensity of human activity which is more apparent than real. In relation to the total land available, the distribution of crop marks of any one period would present a very sparse picture indeed, one which must be even more sparse since all features attributed to that period will not be contemporary. With this in mind, the existing evidence points to very localized, rather than widespread, exploitation of the gravels in successive periods.

In this context it is instructive to consider the gaps in the crop-mark distribution. These gaps are substantial: present crop-mark evidence covers perhaps 25 % of the available surface area. No doubt many of these gaps will be filled, particularly those major areas of several square kilometres where no features whatsoever are known at present. Smaller gaps, including blank areas within crop-mark complexes, are perhaps more interesting. Do these represent, for example, persistent woodland, or waste (in the medieval sense), or long-established pasture, or perhaps arable land whose boundaries and internal divisions may have been too nebulous to be revealed as crop marks? It may be rash to assume that some of these smaller blank areas do not contain concentrated settlements, since aerial reconnaissance has been far too unsystematic and documentation and analysis of climate and vegetational factors in crop-mark development have been too imprecise for us to believe that it is the gaps that are genuine and not our survey techniques which are at fault. Better organized and more disciplined recording, combining aerial and ground survey, would provide a better basis for predicting the content of these apparently 'featureless' areas. Nevertheless, there are hints that some such areas may have been persistently 'featureless'. Studies of the parishes of Stanton Harcourt and Eynsham have shown an almost total absence of early prehistoric sites beyond the area of the medieval open fields (Sturdy, 1973) and this now appears to be true of crop-marked sites of all periods in this one area. Whether this is coincidence or whether it implies that there were in earlier periods less developed areas of land which survived as such into and through the medieval period is a problem that must be explored by examining other areas in the valley in this way. At any rate, a useful and necessary approach is indicated here—one in which we should begin with the present landscape and gradually work back, examining the crop-mark evidence in a variety of historical contexts.

Detailed reconstruction of the changes in land utilization over the whole valley area would be an enormous, if not impossible, task. Localized concentrations of crop marks, however, have much information to offer. Several of these concentrations lie on terraces incised by rivers and streams defining areas whose land-use potential is not constrained by significant variations in ground level or subsoil type. Crop marks in these areas thus present an opportunity for close examination of the factors behind the precise siting of features. The importance of man-made residual elements as a land-use constraint is one such factor which has been discussed elsewhere (Benson & Miles, 1974a, 99-102). Another factor to consider is the extent to which the early clearances determined the pattern of later land use. Already cleared areas must have attracted later settlers and generated further expansion, which perhaps in turn,

had the effect of releasing long-established open ground for intensive settlement, ritual, or burial purposes. This is the impression created by such provocative juxtapositions of crop-marked features of successive periods as the Abingdon causewayed camp and the Radley linear barrow cemetery (Benson & Miles, 1974a, Fig. 15).

Examination of the present aerial and excavation evidence suggests that many of the multi-period crop-mark complexes may owe their origin to the earliest clearances. Continuity of open ground may thus be the key factor. This need not involve continuity of actual settlement or continuity in cultural tradition, but it does require persistent land utilization of a type, or of a variety of types, which would maintain its open nature and provide an attractive base for further expansion.

This model cannot provide an exclusive explanation of the pattern of landscape development of the valley in pre-medieval times; in some areas the process may have begun at a later prehistoric period, though the evidence for complexes without at least an early Bronze Age element in their composition is, at present, slight.

Outside this general picture there are the isolated examples of crop-marked settlement enclosures. Should further aerial reconnaissance and fieldwork fail to enlarge the crop-mark pattern in these areas, we may perhaps come to view such sites, many of which are superficially of Iron Age or Romano-British date, as the unsuccessful assarts of these periods.

COLLATION AND DOCUMENTATION

I have mentioned these aspects if only to emphasize that the real significance of aerial discoveries of crop-marks dates, not from the time they are located or photographed, but from the time they are plotted in detail on a map, juxtaposed with previous plottings and with elemental information obtained from surface finds or excavation. Because of the rate of destruction, this kind of documentation is most urgently required. Rapid collation of the results of aerial photography is essential if the information is to be made available for use *where* it is most needed and *at the time* it is most needed. Unfortunately, this is rarely the case. Many of the data in the Survey, for example, are grossly retrospective and include the plotting, for the first time ever, of some large areas of crop marks, many of which have been long since destroyed (e.g. Benson and Miles, 1974a, 85, fig. 13).

The first task is to identify sources of aerial photographs potentially relevant to the region's archaeology. This is by no means easy, and the extent and variety of material covering the county is somewhat alarming. Sources of oblique photographs include the Allen and Riley collections in the Ashmolean Museum, the Cambridge University Collection, the collections at the National Monuments Record (including photographs by Arnold Baker, Jim Pickering, and John Hampton), and there are also a number of small collections by private fliers, some of whose prints we have been able to obtain. Non-specialist vertical photography includes the Fairey Surveys' collection of the whole of Oxfordshire (2200 prints) carried out in 1962 for the County Planning Department, their 1969 survey of the A34 (covering some 20 km), a survey of the area of the first section of the Oxfordshire M40 by Meridian Airmaps in 1965, and a more recent survey (1973–74) of this Motorway's extension, the whole motorway area covering nearly 60 km of countryside. Several other collections of photographs for road schemes and by-passes are known. The amount of aerial survey commissioned by local authorities is perhaps not fully appreciated by archaeologists. (It is also interesting that estimates for road schemes generally include thousands of pounds for preliminary aerial survey, the cost of which is recoverable by the Local Authority—100% for acceptable Trunk Road schemes, 75% for Principal Roads.) Add to these collections the RAF reconnaissance cover, surveys of large sections of the region by such Statutory Authorities as the Central Electricity Generating Board, and the coverage of select areas of the County for recent Ordnance Survey 1 : 2500 map revision. Since all of these various sources have upon inspection always produced something new, one may begin to see the scale of the problem. Some of the collections are finite and there is thus more chance that the information they contain will eventually be extracted. Others, if not infinite, are at least steadily growing, and at a rate with which it is very difficult to cope.

The next stage is to determine what is actually relevant amongst such collections. The ease with which this is done depends upon, first, the accessibility of the collection and, secondly, the kind of indexing employed. From a regional point of view (and this will obviously be the case in many other areas) our requirements are first and foremost not information on a specific site or a specific type of site, but to discover the existence of sites of which we would otherwise have no knowledge. In this respect, we have found that the system of storage and indexing employed at the NMR is best suited to our purposes.

Next, we have generally transferred information from the photographs on 1 : 10560 maps at the collection source employing someone specifically for this purpose over a three- or four-month period at a time. Although we have not used transparent overlay sheets for this purpose, this would be a better course to adopt.

The selection and purchase of photographs at the time of plotting at the collection source is something we consider necessary in order to make some source material available for regular study and inspection within the region, since the majority of the negatives are not locally held. One needs to refer to the actual photographs time and time again, and there are obviously occasions where there is simply not time to travel to the original source to check detail. Regional collections of such copies may have other advantages in the future in acting as a screen for the major collections at London and Cambridge, relieving some of the consultation pressure, though not necessarily orders for prints! Cost is a difficulty here, not so much for obtaining specialist prints, since, somewhat ironically, we have found that only a limited number of copies of these can be supplied per year, but rather in obtaining for permanent keeping copies of commercial verticals, some of which are currently costing over £3 per print.

The maintenance of regional archives of copies of aerial photographs is one very important way of making the information available for specialist and public use. In Oxfordshire this must be seen as only one part of the Sites and Monuments Record at the City and County Museum (Benson, 1972), a record which now also performs the function of the archive for the Oxfordshire Archaeological Committee. The

photographs themselves would be of reduced value if the prints and the information extracted from them were not integrated into the Record as a whole. The photographs themselves form one unit within this record and they are ordered according to the system employed at the NMR, though at John Hampton's suggestion we will adopt a letter system within each kilometre square to avoid confusion with his own photograph numbers. The record numbers that we allocate to each site in the County are marked on the back of relevant photographs. Cross-indexing according to subject, parish, and a whole range of other attributes is achieved, as for the whole of the Record, by using optical co-incidence cards, a system which will be partly replaced by the eventual computerization of much of our Record data.

The plotting on the 1 : 10560 maps is sketch-plotting by eye, using mainly obliques. Record numbers are subsequently allocated to discrete crop marks according to type of site and period, as far as is possible. Crop-marked areas difficult to disentangle are sometimes given a block of numbers for a whole complex. For complicated areas, where finds and early excavations need to be related to particular marks within a group, plotting is done on 1 : 2,500 maps, though here again accurate plotting is not attempted at this scale, the primary function of these maps being to show more clearly the precise part to which the record numbers relate.

Problems of updating Record Maps from growing individual collections of aerial photographs is something for which we have not yet made any specific arrangements, and the organization of this needs to be worked out. Regular updating is essential. It is also clear that the present system of communication between photographers, collection sources, and local users is hardly adequate. Because of the volume of photographs involved we are unable to cope with the regular transfer of data to the various elements of our Sites and Monuments Record. It is becoming increasingly evident to me that for the various functions I have listed—the identification and regular monitoring of sources, the ordering and purchasing of photographs, the transfer of data to maps, the whole range of cross-referencing tasks required to integrate the information into the Sites and Monuments Record —we need our own regional John Hampton.

PLANNING AND CONSERVATION

Once assembled and integrated into the Sites and Monuments Record, the data from aerial photographs are used in a variety of ways and for a variety of purposes. One task—and it should clearly be the foremost if we are to reduce the number of rescue situations—is to pass the information to the Planning Authorities at a Structure and Local Plan level. So far this has involved a member of the Field Department Staff going to the Planning Department and outlining areas of crop marks on the actual development control maps. This has been achieved for only a small area of the County, but arrangements have been made with the new District Planning Authorities to accept information in this map form. The outlining of areas rather than showing any detail, follows the developing practice of transcribing archaeological information on such maps with the intention that applications will be referred to those competent to deal with the archaeological factors.

Information also needs to be fed into Structure Plans, the level at which broad planning priorities and strategies are determined. At this level, however much we may dislike the idea, archaeology is treated as a resource whose exploitation or conservation must be based on policies and priorities which we archaeologists must be prepared to define, otherwise we shall find them defined for us. Factors such as the present condition of sites have to be taken into account, and here the evidence from aerial photographs is invaluable. Not only does a photograph provide a basic record of a site at a specific point in time (in some cases it is the only existing record and in others it may well remain so), but comparison of photographs taken over a number of years enables us to assess the changing condition of a site. In the absence of detailed ground surveys of earthworks, air photographs are often the only source of such information. The often dramatic evidence that they provide enables a stronger case to be made for the preservation of the remaining undamaged sites, or provide strong arguments for the prevention of further damage. I am sure that the forthcoming survey by the Oxfordshire Archaeological Unit of the effect of ploughing on archaeological sites in Oxfordshire will rely heavily on the aerial evidence. In other cases we have found aerial photographs particularly useful for reconstructing information about the rate of destruction of crop marks, as for example in some of the case studies published in the Survey. Here too aerial photographs helped to provide information about the circumstances of archaeological recording and illuminated aspects of early excavations that were not altogether clear in the published excavation reports.

EXCAVATION

In an area like the Upper Thames Valley, the evidence from aerial photographs clearly has a fundamental role in determining excavation policies. In the past, much of the response to this aerial evidence has been one based on salvage excavation of whichever crop mark was threatened at the time, and the results of this are discussed in the case studies presented in the Survey. Now that the bulk of the available evidence has been plotted on maps, and notwithstanding the incomplete picture that crop marks present, we have at least a basis on which to develop an excavation strategy which will be on firmer grounds than responding to the destruction of a particularly interesting or enigmatic crop-mark type, or even of an individual group of crop marks. We have not yet been able to absorb the full academic implication of the recent survey work and it would be better if all excavation ceased until this is achieved. But hypotheses can now be constructed, and general and specific aims can be formulated to elucidate the successive settlement patterns within the Upper Thames Valley. It is also apparent that, with the quality and extent of the crop-marked evidence we now possess, the excavation of relatively small areas can help to disentangle relationships between sites over very much larger areas, as Peter Fowler and Collin Bowen have shown on the Downland. In the Upper Thames Valley the point has already been made at Northfield Farm, Long Wittenham, where the excavation of a critical intersection between two sets of trackways, one linked to a series of known Romano-British enclosures, the other to a whole complex of 'celtic' fields, demonstrated a sequence (the former post-dating the latter) from

which may be inferred a drastic change in land use over a very much larger area than that actually excavated.

FIELD SURVEY

Prior to excavation, extensive ground survey is needed. Comparison of the detailed maps of crop marks with surface finds shows, for example, one area of the upper Thames Valley between Oxford and Lechlade of some 6000 ha, containing nearly 1500 ha of actual crop marks, which has less than twenty recorded surface finds. The incentive for field-walking, and the necessity to organize this, is obvious. At present, this is something we hope will be developed through a programme of Parish Surveys involving local societies and volunteers. The work will not be confined only to surface finds—and one should not in any case rely solely on such finds to date crop marks. Surface scatters, or even concentrations, may reflect only one of several phases represented by a crop-mark pattern, and in some instances they may belong to a phase which is not represented by any of the features visible on the aerial photograph. Reasonable correlations, however, may be made in some cases (as in the examples mentioned at the beginning of this paper). Of equal importance at a Parish Survey level is the use of the plotted crop marks for the reconstruction of the origins and growth of the Parish. One possibility which is now apparent is that some medieval boundaries may be pushed back to a much earlier period. There is also enormous potential for plotting, within an area where upstanding features are almost entirely absent, of ridge and furrow, or rather the furrows and headlands, these being the principal elements of an open field system which show as crop marks. This is a form of evidence which we were unable to include in the Survey, since it would have obscured detail of earlier features, but the extent of the available crop-mark evidence is such that a separate study of this problem is clearly required. In those areas of the Upper Thames Valley less affected by development, we can now see exciting possibilities of determining the relationship between strip cultivation and early settlement, throwing light on the origin of open field elements.

For Parish Survey work in the upland areas of the region, aerial photographs are equally useful, although the oblique purpose-flown coverage is slight. More use here has been made of non-specialist vertical cover, especially the complete County survey carried out by Fairey Surveys in 1962, already mentioned. Unfortunately, although we have access to these for consultation purposes, cost prevents us from obtaining the full set of prints for our own collection. What use we have made of these prints shows that they are invaluable when studying the topographical history and development of a parish, providing a wealth of evidence from either soil or crop marks, according to the time of year; for picking up boundary features which one might have otherwise missed; and for providing a much easier correlation with cartographic evidence than can be provided by obliques. Within the Oxford region other sources of vertical cover have been profitably employed from time to time, notably by Rhodes in his surveys of the celtic field patterns on the Berkshire Downs, using RAF verticals (Rhodes, 1950), and by Sutton in his study of ridge and furrow in Berkshire and Oxfordshire (Sutton, 1965). However, no use of verticals in this way has been made recently. When one realizes that there is so much more information to be derived from available vertical sources, it is frustrating that there is not sufficient time or resources to extract data, especially at a time when so much of these large area patterns is being destroyed.

There are many other uses of aerial photographs in a single region which I have had no space to develop here. I would, however, like to point to the use of oblique and vertical photographs in interpreting the origin of, and developments within, towns and villages. Thanks to the work of Mick Aston and Trevor Rowley on this subject in the Oxford region, we have become increasingly conscious of the importance of the evidence contained within small town and village plans. This is an area where good oblique photography can stimulate ideas and understanding in a way that a map alone does not, bringing out relationships between amorphous growth and deliberately planted elements of whatever period, in a vivid and provocative way. Photography apart, a tremendous amount may be gained from undertaking our own reconnaissances. For those concerned with the whole historical development of the landscape, whether urban or rural, I am sure that the more we can exchange our view of the ground from the ground, for one from the air, the better will be our perspective.

REFERENCES

Benson, D. (1973). A Sites and Monuments Record for the Oxford Region. *Oxoniensia*, **37**, 226–38.

Benson, D., & Miles, D. (1974a). *The Upper Thames Valley: An Archaeological Survey of the River Gravels.* Oxford.

Benson, D., & Miles, D. (1974b). Cropmarks near the Sutton Courtenay Saxon Site. *Antiquity*, **48**, 223–26.

Rhodes, P. P. (1950). The Celtic Field-Systems on the Berkshire Downs. *Oxoniensia*, **15**, 1–28.

Sturdy, D. (1973). The Temple of Diana and the Devil's Quoits: Continuity, Persistence and Tradition, in Strong, D. E. (ed.), *Archaeological Theory and Practice*, 27–43. London.

Sutton, J. E. G. (1965). Ridge and Furrow in Berkshire and Oxfordshire. *Oxoniensia*, **29/30**, 19–115.

Aerial photography and the field archaeologist

C. C. Taylor

Synopsis

This paper examines the value of aerial photography for field archaeologists and especially their work on the reconstruction of past landscapes. It summarizes the impact of aerial photography on the changing ideas of landscape development and deals with its role in the present state of field archaeology. The paper concludes with a plea for more effort from and co-operation between aerial photographers and field archaeologists alike.

This paper is primarily concerned with the use of aerial photography as a tool for the field archaeologist. As there is much misuse of the term, it is perhaps as well to begin by defining field archaeology. Basically it is the discovery and recording of archaeological information without excavation. That is, it involves detailed field examination to discover sites and the careful study of the remains to interpret them, not only in terms of each individual site but, more important, in terms of the relationship of the site to others and to their contemporary environment. Such work means that, as well as field examination and survey, many other aspects of archaeology, including aerial photography, have to be used. Ultimately the field archaeologist's job should be the reconstruction and cartographic presentation of past landscapes to show the totality of land-use and occupation at any given period of the past. This is perhaps in contrast to the excavational archaeologist, who, in the first instance at least, is primarily concerned with the elucidation of the economic, social, and technological basis of individual sites.

If the field archaeologist is to be concerned with past landscapes and their total use, aerial photography must and does play an important role in the work. Yet aerial photographs have many serious limitations for field archaeology. It is too easy to accept air photographs as the answer to all our problems, and this includes not only the academic side of field archaeology, but also the more important aspects of preservation and destruction of archaeological remains of the past in the second half of the twentieth century. Too much reliance on aerial photographs can easily result in the establishment of a totally misleading picture of past landscapes. Field archaeologists need to use other methods of discovery and recording, even though these methods can be time-consuming and require specialized knowledge, as well as being less visually pleasing.

There can be no doubt that the development and use of aerial photography over the last fifty years has changed our ideas. Up until the 1920s, and even beyond, there was a generally deterministic view of habitation and land use in the pre-Saxon periods. The existence of the large numbers of upstanding archaeological sites on the generally lighter and upland soils of southern

The author is with the Royal Commission on Historical Monuments (England).

Britain led to the understandable concentration of archaeological work in such areas, notably Wessex. There was therefore much discussion of these light soils in relation to early occupation and the general assumption was made that all or most of the areas of heavier soils of the country were covered with impenetrable forest until at least the Roman period. The mass of archaeological material, usually in the form of chance finds, which had been discovered in the areas of heavy soils, as well as along the river valleys, was generally interpreted as 'trade routes' or 'lines of entry' (Bowen, 1936; Fox, 1932; Crawford, 1912). The work of the early air photographers tended, at first, to support these ideas when they produced evidence of other large areas of early occupation from these light upland soils (Crawford and Keiller, 1928). However, the continued air-photographic work, which led to the discovery of the thousands of crop-mark sites in the river gravel zones, changed archaeological thinking and this was aided by the recognition of other areas of lighter soils in lowland areas and their significance in terms of early settlement (Wooldridge and Linton, 1933). It became clear that these river valleys could no longer be regarded as trade or invasion routes but were part of the permanently settled areas throughout all periods of the past.

This new evidence did not, however, change the deterministic approach to archaeology. The new evidence was still interpreted in terms of light, well drained soils, ideal for so-called primitive societies with their limited technology. The general picture was still one of dense occupation on the easily cultivated soils, whether upland chalk or limestone, or valley-bottom gravels and loams. The claylands and heavy soils elsewhere were still regarded as largely unused and unusable, until the advanced technology of the Roman empire enabled a start to be made on clearing the forest. This process was then said to have been developed and extended by the Saxons and their successors. The result was that the late Roman and early medieval periods tended to be seen as 'one long assart'.

In some quarters this picture is still regarded as substantially correct. It is seemingly being given additional support by the continued development and the use of aerial photography on an ever-growing scale. Better cameras and films, more photographs and flying time have led to a constantly growing body of information which is enabling us to present in cartographic form the prehistoric and Roman pattern of occupation over large areas of the British countryside. Yet these areas are still mainly those of lighter soils for two basic reasons.

First, and obviously, crop and soil marks are visible at their best on light soils. Therefore the bulk of air-photographic evidence is likely to come from these areas. Secondly, understandable if somewhat regrettable, there is a marked tendency for aerial photographers to fly over areas where they know crop marks are going to be visible. There are, of course, notable exceptions to this, but in the writer's experience it is very difficult to persuade air photographers to carry out constant and long-term reconnaissance of regions of heavy soil usually unresponsive to air photography. This is because the rewards are inevitably poor when compared with chalk, limestone, or gravel areas and the results, when expressed in cost-benefit terms, very expensive. It may

be that new techniques may overcome this problem, but it is at the moment a serious one for field archaeologists.

As a result of this history of interest in the lighter soils and the continual air-photographic evidence, it remains increasingly difficult for field archaeologists and others to shake themselves free of the deterministic approach, long since abandoned by the geographers whose idea it originally was. The inevitable concentration of work on the areas of light soils leads to the falsification of the total picture of ancient settlement and occupation.

In passing, it may be said that it also distorts other aspects of archaeology, such as rescue excavation and preservation. Thus when major threats to whole areas of land appear, particularly urban expansion and new town development, aerial photography is usually, and too often, the main source of information on the archaeological sites there. Because the most obvious and impressive sites are those on soils most conducive to air photography, these are the ones which are inevitably regarded as the most important and in need of excavation or preservation. These sites are then dug or saved for posterity, while others which cannot be recognized by air photographs remain unknown and unexcavated, and are therefore destroyed. Even when these sites are known to exist from chance finds or from fieldwork they are often ignored in the process of selection for excavation or preservation. It is always much easier to be impressed by a remarkable and complex crop-mark site on a gravel terrace than by a collection of potsherds picked up from the adjacent clayland. Yet both types of sites are probably of equal complexity and importance.

Thus the old imbalance of evidence between that from the lighter soils when compared with that from the heavier soils remains and is being actually increased by the flood of new air-photographic material coming mainly from areas of lighter soils. The only difference is that the logical, if outdated, explanation of determinism has been replaced by the academically illogical explanation of the technical limitations of film emulsion and crop and soil response, which is not fully recognized.

Certainly some of these technical limitations will be overcome in the future, and indeed are already being so. Even so some imbalance will inevitably remain as long as air photography is allowed to be the only, or even the most important, method of discovering past land use. If we are to achieve our desired aim as field archaeologists to discover as much as we can of the past landscape, as well as to find the best sites for excavation or preservation, we must accept air photography as just one very useful part of a larger repertoire. Air-photographic evidence by itself gives only a distorted picture of the overall distribution and importance of archaeological sites, which is as lacking in meaning as the old diagrams of 'routes of entry', which we now rightly reject.

In fact, this imbalance of evidence is being rectified slowly. It is being achieved, not by academic archaeologists, but by an uncountable band of part-time field archaeologists, led by a few devoted professionals. Over the last ten to fifteen years these people have in fact revolutionized archaeology. This revolution has been largely ignored in the archaeological literature, probably because the evidence is of such proportions that it cannot be assimilated. The evidence has come and is coming from detailed field examination by local archaeological groups of large areas of the country. The main concern of these groups has been the discovery of sites from scatters of pottery and other small finds. They work both on special places which are threatened with immediate development, such as motorways, urban expansion, and extractive industry, and on large areas of countryside regardless of threats, known archaeological importance, or soil type. The amount of archaeological material coming from this work is truly remarkable even though most of the results are, as yet, preserved only on unpublished record cards or in ephemeral papers. Much of this new work is being carried out in areas which are almost totally unresponsive to normal air photography as it is now being used. Thus, on the M5 from north Gloucestershire to Somerset, systematic fieldwork by local archaeologists both before and during the road construction produced 130 sites, where less than ten were previously known. This is an average number of about two sites in every one mile (Fowler, 1972). In southern Northamptonshire and north Bedfordshire detailed fieldwork over the last four years by only three people has produced over 200 new sites of prehistoric or Roman date (Hall & Nickerson, 1966; Hall & Hutchins, 1972). Much of the land here is covered with heavy glacial clay and has produced few crop or soil marks, despite being one of the rare areas to have had regular reconnaissance from the air.

In eastern Northamptonshire, some 430 Roman settlement sites are now known to exist in an area where only 130 had been recorded up to 1956. Of these less than a quarter have been revealed by air photographs. The majority have been discovered by fieldwork on the Oxford Clay or glacial clay uplands. Even so, this area has not been examined at all systematically for a variety of reasons (Taylor, 1974). Certainly many more sites remain to be discovered. Elsewhere the amount of new material is equally impressive. In Cornwall the number of known round barrows, around 3,000, is nearly four times that which had previously been recorded before systematic work started only a few years ago (Thomas, 1972). Though much of this work is admirable, in general terms it still falls far below even a reasonable standard. Little of it has been carried out systematically and the results are often inadequately recorded. There has to be not only much more fieldwork but it must be of a much higher standard. While the greater part of this material has been discovered by the slow process of detailed field examination, such fieldwork is not the only way new archaeological sites have come to light. There is also a growing concentration on documentary research of a fairly simple kind which, when carried out by local WEA, extra-mural classes, or archaeological groups, has produced important results. This research falls into two categories. First there is the use of documents, mainly maps, to discover potential archaeological sites of all periods. Such work involves recording and mapping of field names and other place names which indicate possible sites. Names such as *Round Field*, especially in south–west England, *Black Lands, Long Walls, Stony Field, Chequer Field*, etc. are a few of the many which lead to the identification of sites. More specialized research on Saxon land charters and medieval and later surveys also produces evidence of

possible prehistoric and Roman sites. Such work has, when combined with field checking, already produced numerous archaeological remains of all periods.

The second aspect of this kind of documentary work is involved in the combing of local archaeological and non-archaeological literature such as parish magazines, newspapers, and local guides which, though a time-consuming process, can and does lead to unexpectedly useful results.

Other aspects of modern field archaeology in its widest sense involve the checking of all museum collections as well as the often remarkable groups of material in private hands, many of which remain largely unknown. All these methods are being used today to add to the ever-growing records of archaeological material all over the country. The implications of this flood of new evidence, which has been called the "quantitative explosion in archaeology", have as yet hardly been appreciated, probably because of our inability to assimilate it. Yet the results are spectacular, primarily because they are at last forcing us to abandon the deterministic approach imposed upon us by earlier generations of archaeologists and backed up by air-photographic evidence. It is now possible to see that prehistoric, Roman, and later peoples lived almost everywhere in Britain, the high mountains and marshlands excepted, in much greater numbers and using the land more intensively than we have hitherto conceived. Not only are our distribution maps being altered, but our ideas on the ability of early people to control and alter their environment, as well as on the population densities of the past, are also being radically changed.

The very amount of this new information, however, leads to serious problems of presentation which have not yet been dealt with. If we are to use all the new information, from air photographs and fieldwork combined, we must present it in such a form that it can be correctly interpreted. The obvious and apparently best way of doing this is, of course, to produce the information in the form of distribution maps. This has in fact been done by all archaeologists for at least the last seventy years, though usually with unfortunate results.

This is largely because of an inability to recognize the limitations of archaeological distribution maps. A map of, say, milk production in the British Isles, based as it is on the Ministry of Agriculture statistics, is a statement of the total evidence of the product, from which certain valid conclusions may be drawn. Any archaeological distribution map is of a very different and lower order, for it does not show the total evidence. In fact, we do not even know what proportion of the total evidence it does show. Most archaeological distribution maps illustrate only the distribution of archaeologists, or rather the areas in which they have worked. As such they can hardly be used to draw valid conclusions as to past occupation and land use, unless their limitations are either spelt out or visually illustrated very clearly indeed.

Generally speaking, when presenting cartographically the results of archaeological air photography and fieldwork, a simple distribution map is of very limited value. Any map should have other information on it as well as the purely archaeological evidence or the geographical background. For example, the map should indicate areas in which, after concentrated air photography and fieldwork have been carried out, no

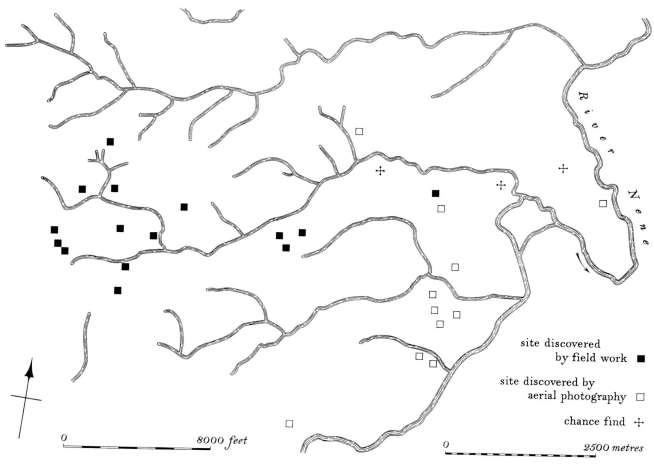

Fig. 1   Roman settlements near Oundle (Northants): basic distribution of archaeological evidence

archaeological material or evidence whatsoever has been discovered. That is, it should, if possible, indicate regions not occupied or used by man at any given period. Such places are, in terms of landscape history, as important in the evaluation of that landscape as those which have archaeological sites on them.

The depiction of those areas is, at the moment, almost impossible, for the work has not yet been done, but it should be contemplated. In addition the maps ought, and can even now be made, to indicate those districts which are archaeologically empty because either detailed fieldwork or aerial photography has not been carried out, or because the present land use, such as the existence of built-up areas, permanent pasture, and woodland, prevents it. Only in this way can we make any useful statements about what the existing pattern of distribution might mean. In Figs. 1 and 2 an attempt has been made to show this for a small area of eastern Northamptonshire. From Fig. 1 the interpretation of the Roman occupation of the area could easily be related to the initial occupation of the lighter soils and subsequent expansion of settlement into one part of the clay area, perhaps the result of one active overlord or maybe unknown but favourable physical conditions. However, Fig. 2 shows that this distribution is entirely related to the amount and methods of recent archaeological fieldwork and aerial photography, when combined with present land use. In fact the most important reason for the present distribution on Fig. 2

is the amount of permanent arable land which enables fieldwork and aerial photography to take place. This in turn is related partly to the considerable amount of woodland there, but mainly to the present land ownership of the area and in particular the existence of a large estate which, using modern methods of agriculture, is almost entirely arable, and which is surrounded by small farms whose methods involve large areas of permanent pasture. As such, the archaeological pattern thus revealed tells little about the Roman occupation of the area, though it indicates clearly what needs to be done, and where, before a clear picture can emerge. It is the construction of maps such as Fig. 2 that indicates how much more, as field archaeologists and air photographers, we need to do. These needs come under four main headings.

Firstly we want more air photographs. However, it is the type of air photograph that is important, not just quantity. There is at the moment, from the point of view of field archaeologists, a superfluity of photographs of well known sites. These are naturally very useful for detailed interpretation and for excavation, but what the field archaeologist wants is evidence of new sites from areas at the moment devoid of any known remains. Such work requires good weather, good crop and soil conditions, and, most of all, good luck. It involves long hours of unproductive flying with probably very few photographs at the end of it. Yet a single photograph of a new site, however indistinct,

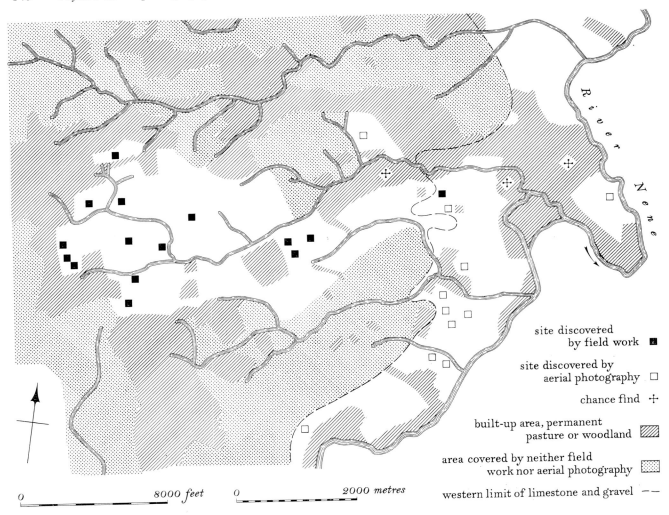

site discovered
by field work ■

site discovered by
aerial photography □

chance find +

built-up area, permanent
pasture or woodland ▨

area covered by neither field
work nor aerial photography ▦

western limit of limestone and gravel — —

0 _____ 8000 feet   0 _____ 2000 metres

Fig. 2   Roman settlements near Oundle (Northants), showing the relationship between the archaeological evidence, the present land use, and the limited nature of fieldwork from aerial photography

is of more value to the field archaeologist than ten superb photographs of a well known one. Continuous reconnaissance, using new techniques, over areas normally regarded as poor or unrewarding is a basic need for future field archaeology. For, except in a few places, our existing cover is hopelessly defective both at local and national level. The local gaps are illustrated in Fig. 2. At the national level it has been well illustrated by the published map of the distribution of air photographs held by the National Monuments Record in 1972 (Hampton, 1972). The NMR, as a national archive, has over 100,000 photographs, taken by a variety of individuals and organizations, and it is therefore reasonably representative of the areas covered by available air photographs at the moment. Yet, as the map shows, the great majority of these photographs are of sites in the chalklands of Wessex and Eastern England and on the gravels of the major river valleys. Most of the country has no overall archaeological air-photographic cover at all.

The second need, to put alongside more air photographs, is more and better fieldwork. This must be carried out on a much wider scale and in more detail than at present. It may be that we cannot think of systematically combing every available field in this country, but samples of small areas, or spot checks, could and should be undertaken. At the moment any map showing areas where detailed fieldwork has been carried out would show many more empty spaces than does the NMR air-photographic map. Even then the 'filled' spaces are not accurate enough in detail to make any sensible statement of previous land use.

The third need is much more careful presentation of the results, both of air-photography and of fieldwork, on the lines discussed above. Simple distribution maps are of a limited value and we must learn, develop, and expand the many cartographic techniques long known to geographers, so that the evidence is presented in such a form that not only the limitations of the material and its distribution are obvious, but also inaccurate interpretations may be avoided. Such maps will also show which areas remain to be examined. Finally, but perhaps most important, there is a continuing and growing need for closer co-operation between aerial photographers and field archaeologists to ensure that the material from all the various sources is brought together and made easily available. It can then be interpreted and assessed quickly and easily not only to advance our knowledge of past landscapes, which is our long-term aim, but ensure judgments on the importance of sites which have to be made for planning and development purposes. This latter need is, at the moment, the prime one. We as archaeologists cannot expect co-operation and sympathy from planners and fund-providing organizations if we do not ourselves have any overall idea of what we want to be preserved or excavated. The archaeologists, of whatever variety, whether flyers or walkers, must work harder, faster, and together if the necessary information on the heritage of the past is to be provided for the decisions on its future.

BIBLIOGRAPHY

Bowen, E. G. (1936). Prehistoric South Britain, in Darby, H. C. (ed.) *An Historical Geography of England before 1800.* Cambridge.

Crawford, O. G. S., & Keiller, A. (1928). *Wessex from the Air.* Oxford.

Crawford, O. G. S. (1912). The Distribution of Early Bronze Age Settlements in Britain. *Geogr. J.,* **40,** 184–96.

Fowler, P. J. (1972). Field Archaeology in Future, in Fowler, P. J. (ed.) *Archaeology and the Landscape.* London.

Fox, C. (1932). *The Personality of Britain.* Cardiff.

Hall, D. N., & Hutchins, J. B. (1972). The Distribution of Archaeological Sites between the Nene and Ouse Valleys. *Bedfordshire Archaeol. J.,* **7,** 1–16.

Hall, D. N., & Nickerson, N. (1966). Sites on the North Bedfordshire and South Northamptonshire Border. *Bedfordshire Archaeol. J.,* **3,** 1–6.

Hampton, J. (1972). RCHM (Eng.), NMR: The Air Photographic Unit. *Antiquity,* **46,** 59–61.

Taylor, C. C. (1974). Roman Settlement in the Nene Valley, in Fowler, P. J. (ed.) *Recent Work in Rural Archaeology.* London.

Thomas, C. (1972). The Present Significance of Field Work in the light of the Cornish Parochial Check-List Survey, in Fowler, P. J. (ed.) *Archaeology and the Landscape.* London.

Wooldridge, S. W., & Linton, D. L. (1933). The Loam Terrains of South-Eastern England and their Relation to its Early History. *Antiquity,* **7,** 297–301.

Air, ground, document

Harry Thorpe

Synopsis

An important branch of research in the field of historical geography is concerned with the nature of man–land relationships in times past, and with the contribution that such interaction has made to the complex landscapes of the present. In attempting reconstructions of former environments, the historical geographer makes detailed analyses of remnant features seen on the ground today with the aid of aerial photography and field surveys, and uses excavation techniques and documentary material to provide clues to date, form, and function. In this paper the approach of historical geography is applied to an investigation of 'the past in the present' within the Warwickshire parish of Wormleighton, whose settlement and land-use patterns have undergone several dramatic changes since Domesday times.

Historical geography studies man's impress on a once natural landscape, and the latter's conversion slowly and subtly into the complex cultural landscape of today. It makes use of both archaeology and history in order to examine the geography of former ages, and sees landscapes, past and present, as a subtle reflection of the man–land relationship through time. In reconstructing former landscapes, appropriate use is made of relict features seen on the ground today or identifiable from the air, of data revealed by remote sensing and by the spade, and, by no means least, of documentary and cartographic sources. The present paper illustrates the use of such material in a reconstruction of the changing landscape of a single south Warwickshire parish, Wormleighton, from late

Saxon times to the present day. Parts of the story have already been told elsewhere (Thorpe, 1965), but here the presentation is quite different, being moulded to the particular objectives of this Symposium.

As Fig. 1 shows, the parish of Wormleighton (OS 1 : 50000 Sheet 151, SP 448539) covering some 2451 acres, lies on the borders of south–east Warwickshire, its boundaries abutting both Oxfordshire and Northamptonshire to the east. From the Cotswold Fringe, forming the south–eastern upland half of the parish, the land drops gently north–westward to embrace part of the broad Feldon Plain, whose solid geology of heavy, impervious, grey-brown Lower Lias Clay contrasts markedly with the hard, russet-brown Middle Lias Marlstone of the Cotswold scarp. Our first simple appraisal from the air, using stereo-pairs or single vertical photographs (Fig. 2), shows the sinuous course of the Oxford Canal (AD 1769–1789) worming its way along the 400ft (122m) contour, amid an intricate pattern of fields, some large and irregular in shape, others small and rectilinear. Across many, the distinctive corrugations of former ridge-and-furrow can be seen, with old clusters of selions revealing earlier patterns which, however, are by no means always co-terminous with the later enclosure overlays, though some of the latter clearly disclose aratral determination. Apart from a thin stipple of scattered farmsteads, the major settlement feature is the nucleated village of Wormleighton, **T**-shaped in form, with its longer axis thrust along a spur whose gentle extension northward explains the proboscis-like deviation of the canal. The wooded tip of the spur

The author is Professor of Geography and Head of Department in the University of Birmingham.

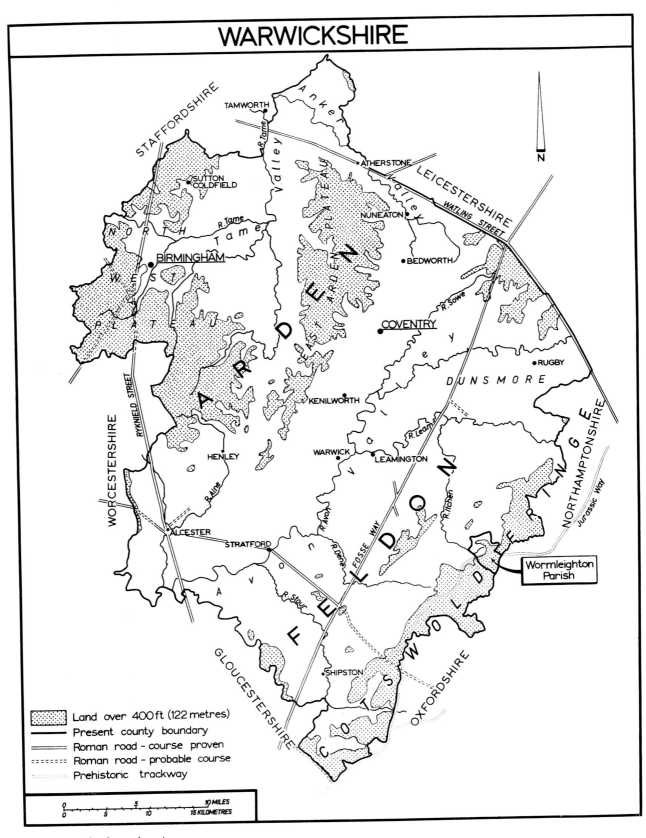

Fig. 1   Wormleighton: location

Fig. 2   Part of the vertical aerial photograph (ref. 0161/V58RAF/8420 of 15 November 1967, north-east at the top) showing the village of Wormleighton which occupies a small hill-top within a loop of the Oxford Canal

Photo: Crown Copyright

overlooks a three-sided enclosure (is a fourth side weakly discernible?) beyond which a number of strongly rectilinear earthworks extend as far as the canal, with trackways apparently continuing beyond. What, one may ask, is the relationship, if any, between this earthwork complex and the present village? Has the village perhaps shrunk, or changed its site; if so, when and for what reason?

Examining, with the aid of an oblique aerial photograph (Fig. 3), the morphology of the existing settlement, one identifies a very orderly, **T**-shaped, estate village, whose major axial road flanked by a narrow green leads towards a square-towered church at one end (just discernible on the extreme left of Fig. 3). On its way to the church the axial road passes

through a gatehouse, associated with a complex of large old buildings, some of Tudor date. The presence of a loop road skirting the gatehouse well to the left makes one ponder whether this block of buildings was once much larger and more extensive, thereby compelling traffic that did not seek or gain entry to the main complex to run around it on the way towards the church and beyond.

Ground investigation confirms that the two blocks of homesteads near the **T**-junction are indeed estate cottages of stout and regular construction, the easternmost block (bearing the date 1848) being facetiously called 'The Ten Commandments' by their occupants who are tenants of one of the leading noble families of England. Walking down the axial street

Fig. 3   Oblique aerial photograph (13 April 1953) of the modern estate village of Wormleighton looking north–east and showing the T-pattern of roads flanked by the remnants of the village green; the orderly rows of estate cottages with their large gardens; farmsteads with their outbuildings; the old gatehouse with the remains of the manor house beyond; the church, with its square tower, on the extreme left of the photograph; old ridge-and-furrow patterns of former arable land-use beyond the great hedges that sharply define the rectangular limits of the village

Photo: University of Cambridge; Crown Copyright reserved

towards the church, one finds that the gatehouse, which bears the date 1631, leads to the remains of a fine red-brick Tudor mansion (Fig. 5) and beyond that to a well maintained, though rather austere, church, with early 12th century work in the squat tower and in the nave. As the Domesday Book entry (Page, 1908, 316) mentions a priest in Wormleighton, dare we assume that a church then stood on this spot? Recalling the Tudor mansion, the estate cottages, and the strong association of Wormleighton with a famous titled family, it is with a feeling of eager anticipation that one enters the interior of the church, only to emerge puzzled by its plain interior and by the complete absence of a family chapel with fine tombs and effigies. Thus, seen both from the air and on the ground, the present fabric of Wormleighton raises important questions, answers to which must be sought as much in patterns of earthworks as in existing buildings, using documentary and cartographic evidence wherever one can to provide or to corroborate facts, as well as to test theory.

A more detailed examination of the earthworks in the valley bottom is now necessary, first with the aid of

oblique aerial photographs and then by means of ground investigation. In a preliminary analysis of the many features to be seen on the oblique aerial photograph (Fig. 6) attention is focused on the following:

(1)   The long ribbon of an easily datable feature, the Oxford Canal (of which the section between Coventry and Banbury was opened by March 1778), closely following the 400ft (122m) contour. At first this cuts transversely from right to left across the cultural 'grain' of the site, then turns sharply to truncate one end of a prominent, rectangular banked and ditched enclosure, after which it follows part of the ditch itself before disappearing from view on the left of the photograph. So the past continues to function in the present, though in a rather different way!

(2)   This moated site has a small circular grassy tump at its south–western end, fronting the canal, which quite early attracted the attention of some of my students until it was discovered

Fig. 4 Wormleighton House from the magnificent Sheldon tapestry map bearing the date 1588. The fine Tudor building and the strong gatehouse are depicted from the south with the square tower of the church rising behind. The original gatehouse was clearly more impressive than that shown in Fig. 5. The tapestry map is on display in the County of Warwick Museum, Warwick

that it was neither a corner tower, a dovecote, nor a windmill but merely a Home Guard post from the Second World War!

(3) The fact that the hedged banks of the large rectangular enclosure (with straight ridge-and-furrow in the bottom) are here shown complete along four sides indicates that this oblique was flown at an earlier date than the vertical of 1967 (Fig. 2). I often use this point to demonstrate to students in a simple, jocular way that one must not fall into the trap of considering that most or all relict features on aerial photographs of DMV sites are necessarily legacies of immediately pre-depopulation patterns. I also use it to impress on my students the necessity for courtesy, diplomacy, and sound psychology in their dealings with land-owners, for the intrepid Warwickshire farmer who owns *Old Town,* as this site is called, was suddenly given official notice several years ago that his site had been Scheduled, in consequence of which he should not plough it or damage it in any way. He thereupon lost no time in fulfilling a long-suppressed desire to effect easier access to this

enclosure by bulldozing out one of the four sides, effectively demonstrating at the same time the rapid and dramatic changes that modern technology can make to our landscapes. But I am very pleased to say that both he and his wife have since taken very great interest in our work on this site, and my students and I are most grateful for the ready access that they have given us (and so many other scholars) to 'Old Town'.

(4) The central part of the site carries a chain of very interesting features, beginning with four small, long rectangular depressions. If these are fish stews, do they pre-date or post-date the large Fish Pond described under (3) above? Beyond the stews runs a broad village street (perhaps incorporating a green), with tofts and crofts regularly disposed on each side, the street itself continuing well beyond the canal.

(5) Open-field remnants, heavily ridged and furrowed, border the occupation site, but how should one interpret the capillary pattern of sunken features? Are any or all of them roads or trackways? Would roads be likely to run to the middle of fish stews?

Fig. 5   These drawings of the north side of Wormleighton House made in 1877 show (above) *the principal remnant of the fine red-brick Tudor mansion now used as a farmstead, with a barn hoist clumsily set in the wall. Water for the pump in the yard was derived from glacial sands and gravels capping the hill.* (below) *The remains of the two-storied stone-built gatehouse, bearing the date 1631 on the two Spencer shields*
From W. Niven, Illustrations of Old Warwickshire Houses *(1878)*

Fig. 6 *Oblique aerial photograph (3 May 1953) looking north–west, showing the old church of Wormleighton and a cluster of cottages on the hill-top (bottom left); earthworks of the deserted medieval village and rectangular moated homestead near the canal; outlines of a secondary cluster of deserted dwellings on the hill flank below the church; a great square fish pond with four small fish-breeding tanks (now drained); old water channels leading from the fish ponds into the valley below; remains of the great double hedgerows set up soon after 1499; ridge-and-furrow patterns of former arable land-use in the fields around the past and present settlements (cf. Fig. 9)*

(6) Many of the field boundaries are seen to comprise twin banks and ditches, sometimes carrying double hedges. For example, such features are clearly seen running from the edge of the wood, in the bottom right of the photograph, towards and beyond the canal, 'balanced' by a second line to the left of the large Fish Pond extending from the moated site to skirt what seems to be a second fossilized toft and croft pattern in the bottom left of the photograph.

(7) What was the water-supply for the fish-pond system, and why is the system dry today?

(8) Did the present church, seen in the bottom left of Fig. 6, serve the former settlement in the valley bottom, for they appear to be linked by two prominent trackways? Was there perhaps a separate cluster of earlier homesteads around the church, as the tofts and crofts referred to in (6) might suggest?

(9) That the valley bottom site is fairly dry is suggested by the presence of sheep, the great depopulators of the 15th century, in Fig. 6 seen grazing happily on former arable selions and completely oblivious of an implied land-use incongruity between past and present. In the course of field work, during winter and summer alike, we have never found the site waterlogged, despite the fact that it occupies Lower Lias Clay with only a thin drift cover in places. Would it be reasonable to conclude, therefore, that the settlement in the valley bottom was not destroyed or abandoned because of any dissatisfaction with its physical setting? But did local conditions remain unchanged during previous centuries, particularly during the more inclement phases of the 14th and 15th centuries (Flohn, 1949; Utterström, 1955; Le Roy Ladurie, 1973)?

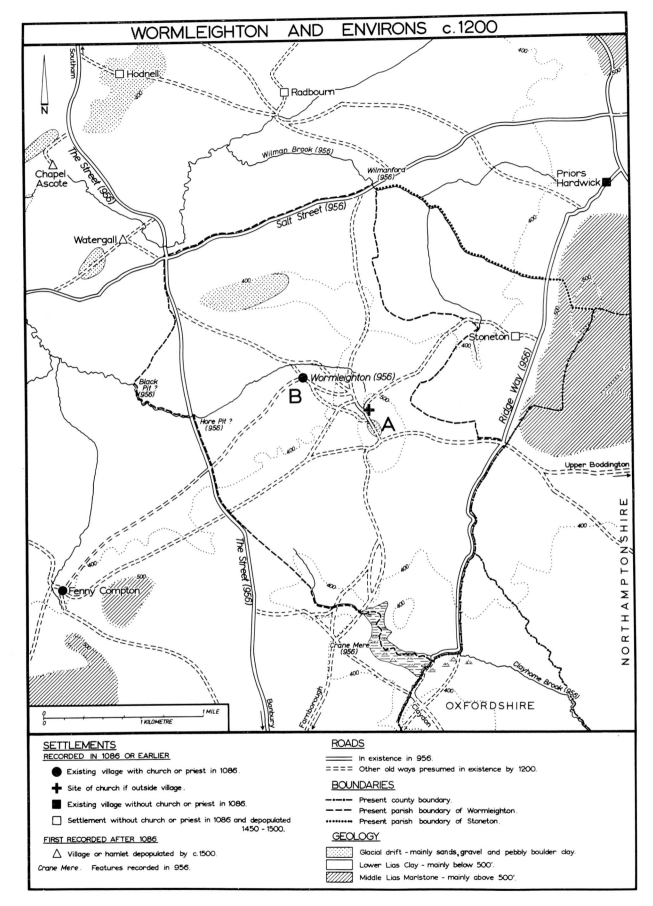

Fig. 7   Wormleighton and environs c. 1200

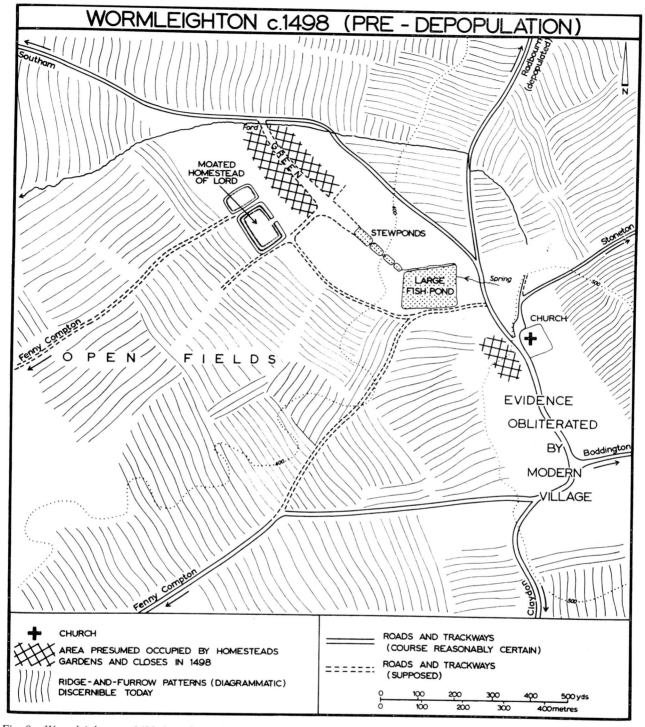

WORMLEIGHTON c.1498 (PRE - DEPOPULATION)

CHURCH

AREA PRESUMED OCCUPIED BY HOMESTEADS GARDENS AND CLOSES IN 1498

RIDGE - AND - FURROW PATTERNS (DIAGRAMMATIC) DISCERNIBLE TODAY

ROADS AND TRACKWAYS (COURSE REASONABLY CERTAIN)

ROADS AND TRACKWAYS (SUPPOSED)

Fig. 8   Wormleighton c. 1498 (pre-depopulation)

Enough has been said thus far in this short paper to establish a framework for the detailed analysis of existing patterns recognized both from the air and on the ground. A synthesis is now attempted, using the combined evidence of air, ground, and document, in the course of which the results of detailed investigations using all three approaches will be introduced. Although there is plentiful evidence for pre-Roman occupation and clearing along the Cotswold Fringe, and of Roman settlement along the Fosse, settlement in the Wormleighton area would appear to date

primarily from Anglo-Saxon times (Thorpe, 1950 and 1971). The name is first recorded in AD 956 as *Wilman lehttune* (Wilma's kitchen-garden), *Wilma* apparently being one of a small group of Anglo-Saxon colonists who entered this area. The place-name appears in a charter (Birch, 1885, 946) of King Eadwy, granting an estate to Earl Ælfhere, and the description of the estate boundaries is so detailed and complete that one can easily perambulate the township on the ground today. Figure 7 shows that the boundary ran from Crane Mere along The Street (i.e. the Southam to Banbury road) via a Hore Pit and a Black Pit to swing east along the Salt Street to Wilmanford, where it crossed Wilman Brook. Thence it turned south to join the Ridge Way as far as Clayhome Brook, which carried the effluent from Crane Mere. It is interesting to find that the boundaries of AD 956 were almost co-terminous with those of the present parish! Unfortunately, the charter tells us nothing about the location of Wormleighton, but, after a careful study of the entire area using aerial photographs and the ground, it would seem that the major settlement probably lay on the dry site in the valley bottom (B in Fig. 7) with potable water obtainable from a spring emerging at the point where fluvio-glacial sands and gravels met the underlying Lower Lias Clay at the foot of Church Hill. It has earlier been conjectured that a second and smaller cluster of homesteads may have sprung up on the hill either before, or at the time when, a church was established there (shown as *A* in Fig. 7).

Domesday Book (Page, 1908, 316, 324, 335) records that there were three manors in Wormleighton in AD 1086, with a total recorded population of fifty families representing about 250 persons. The presence of 23 ploughteams (7 belonging to the three demesnes and 16 to the ordinary folk) suggests intensive arable land use in a township probably largely cleared of woodland, for none was recorded. It is rather surprising, however, that no mill is mentioned. Although, apart from ploughteams, livestock are not specifically mentioned, some measure of their likely number and importance may be gained from the reference to 45 acres of meadow providing the valuable hay crop on which cattle and sheep depended for supplementary feed to carry them through the harsh winter months following Martinmas. The principal meadows no doubt bordered the brooks and the Crane Mere. Of the two manors mentioned earlier, two were in Norman hands, while the third and largest was still held (though not for long) by an Anglo-Saxon lord, Turchil of Warwick. The likelihood that the priest to whom Domesday Book refers had a simple church, perhaps then merely one of wood, on the hill has been discussed earlier. In Warwickshire, it is by no means exceptional to find a church standing some little distance from its main settlement, so Wormleighton should not be considered unusual in this respect (Fig. 7). From a variety of evidence (Thorpe, 1965, 46; Harley, 1958, 12), it would seem that by the mid-13th century the total population in Wormleighton had failed to grow beyond the Domesday figure, suggesting perhaps that a fine point of balance both here and elsewhere in Warwickshire had now been reached between natural resources and the carrying capacity of land in terms of man and animals.

At this time, and indeed in Domesday times and earlier, livestock were a most important element in rural economy, providing not only meat and dairy produce but also hides, skins, and wool for local rural and urban industries. With increasing emphasis during the 14th century on the 'Golden Fleece', both for export and to supply the thriving broadcloth industry in Coventry and elsewhere, flexibility of land use became a distinctive feature on the heavy Lower Lias Clays of south Warwickshire which were eminently suitable for either grain or grass. Land use (in general essentially mixed-farming in character) in south Warwickshire could, therefore, react promptly and positively to changes in either physical conditions, such

as successions of bad winters and wet summers (Flohn, 1949; Utterström, 1955; Le Roy Ladurie, 1973), or social and economic circumstances. For example, judging by the rapid succession of priests in many local parishes, Wormleighton would seem to have been hard hit by the Black Death of 1348/9, leaving perhaps a severely depleted, half-starved, and understocked labour force to cope with neglected fields, large tracts of which by now carried grass atop their former arable selions. It appears, too, that almost four decades later the principal manor in Wormleighton came into the hands of distant absentee landlords, who probably relied on a bailiff to handle local affairs (Leadam, 1897, 485; Finch, 1956, xii–xiii; Thorpe, 1965, 50). The result was a general and successive rundown in population, farming intensity and prosperity, though it was not until as late as 1499 that final depopulation occurred.

Using a variety of ground and documentary evidence an attempt has been made in Fig. 8 to reconstruct the essential character of the site before depopulation struck. From this it will be seen that the spring issuing from the base of the drift-covered Church Hill fed the large Fish Pond, the overflow from the latter emerging close by on the upslope side thereafter forming a leat which ran parallel to the northernmost of the longer sides to feed the four stewponds. In addition to the large moated homestead lying immediately south–west of the valley village, we have since located a minor moated site (shown on Fig. 9) which possibly served as the principal dwelling of one of the two minor manors referred to earlier. A slight circular swell of ground nearby, clearly reflected in a darker coloration of grass, was also probed with the aid of soil augers and deemed to be a dovecote!

By 1495 the main manor of Wormleighton had fallen into the hands of the Crown, and in 1498 the King granted it to William Cope, Cofferer of the Royal Household, who promptly bought up the minor manors and finally depopulated the site in 1499 putting it down to grass and livestock (Thorpe, 1965, 55). At this stage we first make the acquaintance of a prosperous freeman farmer and butcher-grazier by the name of John Spencer, whose family was associated with the depopulated parishes of Hodnell and Radbourn, both of which adjoin Wormleighton. Although not a depopulator himself, John Spencer had nonetheless been quick to seize opportunities of renting local depopulated manors and stocking them with sheep, cattle, and horses. After first renting the abandoned acres of Wormleighton, he eventually bought the entire manor from William Cope for no less than £1900 in 1506, and followed this in 1508 by acquiring another large empty parish just over the county boundary in Northamptonshire. It was here at Althorp that John Spencer established what was to become a great family seat, forerunner of the magnificent mansion that stands there today. So increasingly prosperous and successful were the Spencers that John Spencer was knighted shortly before his death in 1522; by 1603 there was a Baron Spencer, soon succeeded by an Earl Spencer in 1643. Thus, within the short space of just over a century the Spencers had risen from butcher-graziers to one of the most influential titled families in England!

From a wide range of documentary and cartographic sources (Thorpe, 1965; Finch, 1956) which I have been privileged to consult in Earl Spencer's muniment room

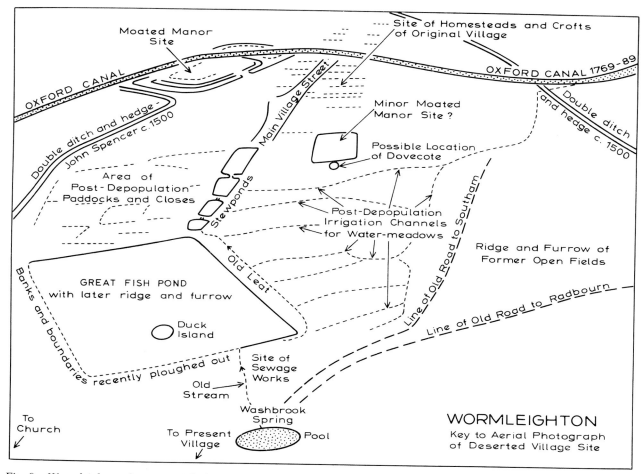

Fig. 9   Wormleighton: key to aerial photograph (Fig. 6)

at Althorp, I have been fortunate in obtaining a wealth of information concerning John Spencer's activities at Wormleighton which are of value in attempting to interpret relict features seen on the ground and on the aerial photographs of the deserted village site. One must bear in mind, however, that ground patterns may incorporate relics not only of the pre-depopulation landscape but also of what William Cope, John Spencer and even recent farmers have done to that landscape since depopulation occurred. Some of these features (such as the missing side to the large Fish Pond!) we can date accurately, but others we cannot, though we may know much concerning their purpose. For example, we know the following:

(1) By 1522 John Spencer had, at least partly, rebuilt a settlement (possibly almost an early 'model village') on the spur-top not far from the church with some twelve homesteads to house his shepherds, cowherds, drovers and general labourers, as well as great barns for the storage of wool and hay (Leadam, 1897, 485–7, 658).

(2) He had also repaired the church, which 'he found greatly in decay', and had furnished it with a 'cross, books, cope, vestments, chalices and censers' (Leadam, 1897, 486). Moreover, he had re-established regular choral services, remembering that before the depopulation the local congregation "were so poor and lived so poorly that they had no books to sing service

on in the Church" (Leadam, 1897, 486). He was also proposing to provide more than one priest.

(3) John Spencer was not impressed by 'the sorry thatched house' (Leadam, 1897, 486, 489) with its large moat in the valley bottom and so between 1516 and 1519 had built for himself a fine red-brick house on the hill (Figs. 4 and 5). This fine Tudor house is clearly recognizable in the magnificent multi-coloured Sheldon Tapestry Map of Warwickshire bearing the date 1588 and, at a scale of $4\frac{1}{2}$ in = 1 mile, being the largest extant single map and also the largest-scale map of the county before the Ordnance Survey 6 in = 1 mile sheets were produced from 1883 onward (Harvey and Thorpe, 1959, 5). The stately gatewayed house, with buildings extending well to the left of the gateway, and the square church tower beyond are clearly seen in Fig. 4. It is apparent, too, that at this time the gateway boasted two towers, rather than the one which remains today (see Fig. 5).

(4) In bringing block enclosure to the depopulated site and its former open fields John Spencer worked at two scales. On the large scale, he fashioned great enclosures in which flocks and herds could be carefully segregated, and clearly described the strong field boundaries 'double ditched and double hedged' that were required

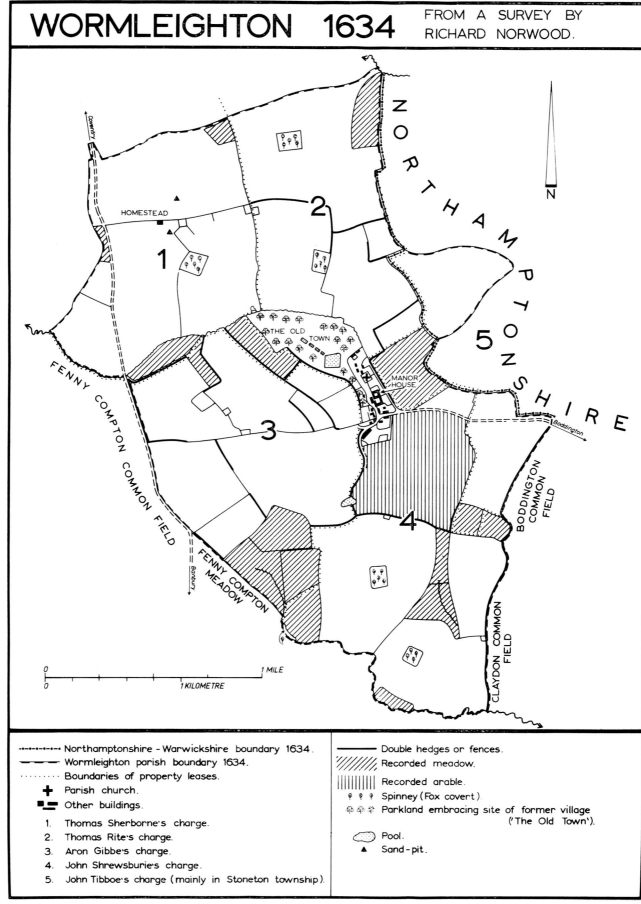

WORMLEIGHTON 1634
FROM A SURVEY BY RICHARD NORWOOD.

N

NORTHAMPTONSHIRE

HOMESTEAD

Coventry

1

2

5

THE OLD TOWN

MANOR HOUSE

FENNY COMPTON COMMON FIELD

3

Boddington

BODDINGTON COMMON FIELD

Barbury

FENNY COMPTON MEADOW

4

CLAYDON COMMON FIELD

0 _____ 1 MILE
0 _____ 1 KILOMETRE

— · — · — · — Northamptonshire - Warwickshire boundary 1634.
————— Wormleighton parish boundary 1634.
·········· Boundaries of property leases.
✝ Parish church.
▪▬ Other buildings.

1. Thomas Sherborne's charge.
2. Thomas Rite's charge.
3. Aron Gibbe's charge.
4. John Shrewsburie's charge.
5. John Tibboe's charge (mainly in Stoneton township).

————— Double hedges or fences.
▨▨▨▨ Recorded meadow.
||||||| Recorded arable.
♀ ♀ ♀ Spinney (Fox covert).
🌳🌳🌳 Parkland embracing site of former village ('The Old Town').
⬭ Pool.
▲ Sand-pit.

Fig. 10   Wormleighton 1634, following block enclosure

(Leadam, 1897, 486–488; Thorpe, 1965, 62). The latter features are clearly shown in Figs. 6, 9, and 10. Emphasizing that there was 'no wood nor timber growing within 12 or 14 mile', so that poor folk had to "burn the straw that their cattle should live by", he became one of our earliest conservationists, setting acorns 'both in the hedgerows and also betwixt the hedges adjoining to the old hedges that William Cope made before' (Leadam, 1897, 486). The rotten boles of the very oak trees planted by John Spencer over four hundred years ago are still to be seen in the ancient hedgerows. On the smaller scale, a draughtboard pattern of small pens, paddocks, and closes seems to have been established for breeding ewes, rams, calves, bulls, and stallions west of the stewponds (Fig. 9).

The purpose of the dendritic or tributary-like pattern of sunken features shown in the oblique aerial photograph (Fig. 6) gave us initially much food for thought. They were clearly not roadways or trackways, for their heads stopped short at either the central point of the smaller fish breeding tanks or at the leat which by-passed the large fish pond (Fig. 9). Feeling that this might offer a clue to their purpose, we ran a series of levels along each sunken feature and found, as we had suspected, that there was a steady, unbroken fall throughout the dendritic pattern whose several branches eventually coalesced to form one major 'channel'. It now seemed clear that these were part of an irrigation system, presumably of post-depopulation date, designed to take water from the ponds and main leat for use in the controlled floating of meadows to yield the extremely valuable hay crop on which the large numbers of livestock depended for supplementary winter feed (Thorpe, 1965, 62). Recalling the dryness of the site, to which reference has been made earlier, such irrigation would be a considerable asset during parched springs and summers; every means had to be taken to ensure not only a large harvest of hay, but also a strong bite of grass during the aftermath if the large number of stock was to be kept in good condition. As Fig. 9 shows, at the foot of Church Hill a steady flow of spring water was collected in a circular pool, the effluent from which fed a sunken sheep-dip from which the Washbrook, as the outgoing stream was called, ran into the large Fish Pond (Thorpe, 1965, 62). Within the pond stood a small island, a convenient home for ducks, geese, and swans, and its distinctive outlines can be seen as a tump-like swell on the oblique aerial photograph (Fig. 6). The straight ridge-and-furrow found on the dry bed of the pond today would appear to be the result of an attempt to cultivate the fertile silts some time after 1734 when the water was deflected into the Oxford Canal. The line of the underground pipe can be faintly discerned on Fig. 6, running transversely and centrally across the straight ridge-and-furrow, the spade incisions being clearly seen on the ground.

The block enclosure patterns inscribed in the period from 1499 to 1522 on the former open-field landscape are clearly seen on a Spencer plan of 1634 (Fig. 10) which shows the emergence of four composite holdings, later to be leased by the Spencers to other graziers and cultivators, so paving the way for the springing up of individual farmsteads outside the reconstructed village such as that shown in Block 1 on Fig. 10 (Thorpe, 1965, 67). One may well ask why the descendants of

John Spencer were prepared in later centuries to lease Wormleighton land to upstarts. The answer, which is more fully discussed elsewhere (Thorpe, 1965, 71), lies partly in the fact that the main family residence of the Spencers lay at Althorp, so that crenellated Wormleighton House was often occupied by one of the sons, the Old Town becoming emparked as an attractive landscape feature once the stock boom had passed away. But there was another reason, of at least equal importance, for at one stage during the Civil War there was imminent danger of Wormleighton House falling into the hands of the Parliamentarians. An entry for 7 January 1646 in the diary of Sir William Dugdale, the great Warwickshire antiquary, tersely records its fate: "Wormleighton House, in Warwickshire, was burnt by his Majesty's forces of Banbury, to prevent the Rebels making it a Garrison" (Hamper, 1827, 83). So a substantial part of the fine structure was destroyed, leaving a mutilated stone gatehouse and the Great Hall of Tudor red brick as shown in the etchings of 1877 (Fig. 5). Since 1646 further enclosure has taken place, and several farmsteads can today be identified within the village, as well as outside (Fig. 2). Seen from the air, therefore, the parish appears at first glance to reflect traditional Feldon patterns, but a close scrutiny of intricate earthworks set within a puzzling void, together with a critical look at an unpretentious church and mutilated great house, provide an eloquent reminder of the importance of time in the understanding of place.

REFERENCES

Birch, W. de G. (1885–1893). *Cartularium Saxonicum,* 946–7. London.

Finch, M. E. (1956). The Wealth of Five Northamptonshire Families, 1540–1640. *Northamptonshire Record Society,* **19**, ch. 3.

Flohn, H. (1949/50). Klimaschwankungen im Mittelalter und ihre historisch-geographische Bedeutung. *Berichte zur deutschen Landeskunde,* **7**.

Hamper, W. (1827). *The Life, Diary and Correspondence of Sir William Dugdale.* London.

Harley, J. B. (1958). Population Trends and Agricultural Developments from the Warwickshire Hundred Rolls of 1279. *Econ. Hist. Rev.,* **11** (no. 1), 8–18.

Harvey, P. D. A., & Thorpe, H. (1959). *The Printed Maps of Warwickshire, 1576–1900.* Warwick.

Leadam, I. S. (1897). *The Domesday of Inclosures. 1517–1518.* 2 vols. London.

Le Roy Ladurie, E. (1973). *Times of Feast, Times of Famine: A History of Climate since the Year 1000.* London.

Page, W. (Ed.) (1908). *The Victoria County History of Warwickshire,* **1**, 316, 324, 335. London.

Thorpe, H. (1950). The Growth of Settlement before the Norman Conquest, in Wise, M. J. (ed.), *Birmingham and its Regional Setting* (British Association Handbook), 87–112. Birmingham.

Thorpe, H. (1965). The Lord and the Landscape, illustrated through the Changing Fortunes of a Warwickshire Parish, Wormleighton. *Trans. Birmingham Warwickshire Archaeol. Soc.,* **80**, 38–77.

Thorpe, H. (1971). The Evolution of Settlement and Land Use in Warwickshire, in Cadbury, D. A., Hawkes, J. G., & Readett, R. C. (eds.), *A Computer-Mapped Flora: A study of the County of Warwickshire,* 20–44. London.

Utterström, G. (1955). Climatic Variations and Population Problems in Early Modern History. *Scandinavian Econ. Hist. Rev.,* **3**, 3–47.

The distant view

P. J. Fowler

In a few years we shall doubtless fly from hill to hill and, apart from the attractive directness of this mode of travel, aviation will undoubtedly do much for the study of earthworks (Williams-Freeman, 1915, xx–xxi).

At the present moment the problem before us is to devise a system by which the pictures may become generally accessible to archaeologists for purposes of study (Crawford & Keiller, 1928, 6, from which page the title of the present paper is also a quotation).

INTRODUCTION

One of the main impressions to come through very clearly from the *Symposium* was that, although technically and perhaps organizationally air photography is on the brink of a break-through, most of the photography that matters archaeologically, in Britain and abroad, is still being taken by amateurs in the proper sense of that word. Individuals dedicated to their largely self-appointed tasks are trying, by experiment and discipline, to bring about some realization of the potential of their craft, not only in academic fields but in the all-important councils of the land users. Such a vast amount of illustrative material was displayed and so many good things were said, however, that any summary must perforce be both inadequate and repetitive; however, even without slides (or here, plates), some points are so important at the current stage of development in air-photographic studies that they cannot be made too often.

THE EXPANSION OF AIR-PHOTOGRAPHIC STUDIES

Though we record and present our perceived evidence as photographs taken from an aerial viewpoint, it is perhaps worth reminding ourselves that it is the aerial viewpoint and not photography which, in so simple a way, enables us to see features and patterns of features not as visible or so well appreciated at ground level. The camera enables us to record, more or less, that which is visible to the human eye and makes permanent the fleeting image, but, certainly for the topographer, the student of landscape, flying time spent other than in exposing emulsion can be time well spent in studying *three-dimensionally* the palimpsest of varied evidence (most of it not 'archaeological sites' in the conventional sense) displayed below. It needs the trained eye to recognize (and point the unselective camera lens at) the modern field shape betraying 13th century assart or Tudor enclosure just as much as it does to appreciate the markings of a Mucking for what they are (Jones *et al.*, 1968). The landscape is there to be read like a symphonic score rather than plucked as discrete chords.

Though the best air photography—which is tantamount to saying the best of St Joseph—demonstrates an art which is probably unteachable, the techniques of air photography for archaeological purposes certainly are teachable. Indeed, the qualities required

The author is Reader in Archaeology, University of Bristol.

of the individual photographer—and here I am obviously thinking more of the selective approach to archaeological features through oblique photography rather than saturation, vertical cover—are as much personal ones of local knowledge, assiduity, and patience as a practical knowledge of flying and camera technique. Nevertheless, it would be possible with relatively little outlay to encourage the emergence of competent air photographers in those areas where regular and systematic local surveillance is not yet in being.

The training need, however, is not so much for more takers of air photographs but for more interpreters of air photographs. The archaeological content—Clark, Daniel, Grinsell, Piggott *et al.*—among RAF Air Photographic Intelligence personnel in World War II is well known, but there seems to have been virtually no conscious attempt to develop an archaeological expertise on a group basis since the demobilization of that elite caucus. Of course, varying amounts of air-photographic interpretation are taught both internally and extra-murally at British universities, and the staffs of the Royal Commission and the Ordnance Survey Archaeology Division interpret air photographs as a matter of routine in carrying out their official duties, but there is no 'think-tank' study group, like the Medieval Village Research Group in another field, setting up ideas and guiding archaeological thinking into a specifically archaeological interpretative expertise equivalent to, for example, that dedicated to La Tène decorated metalwork. The absence of a standard textbook on the archaeological interpretation of air photographs and the elementary treatment accorded to the topic in field archaeology books are indeed sufficient comment on the point. Archaeology lacks the manual equivalent of the War Office's *Air Photo Reading* (War Office, 1958), the academic equivalent of geography's *Maps and Air Photographs* (Dickinson, 1969), and the educational equivalent of *Human Geography from the Air* (Minshull, 1968). It is surely symptomatic of archaeologists' failings in this respect that among the most influential and percipient interpretative studies of 'landscape air photographs' since Crawford and Keiller's (1928) pioneer work are those by an economic historian (Beresford and St Joseph, 1958).

What is needed is a national training scheme, feeding successful trainees into a career structure related to a national interpretative centre. Such a centre is necessary to provide the continuity in the development of the corporate archaeological expertise and to supply the rest of the archaeological and related fields with information abstracted from air photographs. Whether such a centre developed from a Civil Service or university basis is not my concern here: the fact is that, for practical, training, and research purposes, such a centre is already an urgent requirement.

The key problem in all this, however, is that of communication. This has to be viewed in the light of, firstly, the sheer magnitude of the amount of information now available on air photographs and,

154

secondly, the revolutionary importance of this material. Perhaps the significance of both these points has not yet been appreciated by those whose work does not make it necessary for them to consult air photographs continually. The sheer number of these photographs and the significance of the information they contain now represent one of the biggest problems and challenges in British archaeology.

Communication between the photographers themselves must first be improved. At the moment different individuals are using different techniques for different purposes and much will be gained by establishing formal and improved contact between them. Much more important, however, is the problem of improving communications from photographers to archaeologists. At the moment a vast store of information is filed away in various repositories and the great bulk of that information is not readily available as a 'communication flow' to the people not only having to do the work on the ground but increasingly having to take decisions with political and financial implications on the basis of what they clearly know to be inadequate information. This problem also applies to the third area in which communications have to be improved, and that is from the air-photographers and archaeologists to other, and probably non-academic, land users—those who increasingly manage our landscape in the interests of the public good. I am thinking here in particular of those concerned with town and country planning, the historic environment, the National Parks, Nature Conservancy and so on. Their need for archaeological information is increasing and most of that information is not on maps, as they believe, but on air photographs.

We clearly need a national data bank into which information (i.e. air photographs) is fed, at which it is interpreted, and from which the information flows out to all legitimate users. The essence of such a scheme must be its *national* basis, though it would have to be organized regionally so that information was also available locally. Within the foreseeable future, however, this is not a major difficulty since computers, provided that there were adequate outlets regionally distributed, could easily make the information locally available. The essential point is that the information should be stored and processed centrally to common standards. Such a centre must obviously be adequately staffed and, in political terms, it seems to me in the light of recent experience that unless we ask for that right from the beginning we will simply continue to perpetuate the existing inadequacies, with all due respect to that organization, in the National Monuments Record. Clearly such a bank, which could easily be linked to the training centre (see above p. 154), would have a huge cataloguing task, but equally important would be the establishment of regular and recognizable channels of communication to the people on the ground. We must recognize now that to talk in these terms is no slight to any individuals or existing organizations: it is simply that, with the best will in the world, the situation now is not only different in order but is also considerably worse than it was ten years ago, despite the fact that the NMR and several more individuals are now engaged in this field full-time.

The reason for this is the point already stressed: the sheer magnitude of the amount of information now available, but in practice only potentially available, despite its physical existence in the form of air photographs. Those air photographs must be accessible and they must be interpreted before the already existing bank of information is usable. The NMR has in fact already represented the essence of this idea for a decade: as usual in British archaeology, it simply needs to be expanded so that its resources are appropriate to the task which it is expected to do. At the moment it and other parts of the existing establishment structure represent *in organizational terms* a political and administrative reluctance to face up to the implications of air photography.

MAPS AND AIR PHOTOGRAPHY

Much was said during the *Symposium* about maps, and clearly they provide one of the most important means of communication, in particular from a specialist user of air photography to the non-specialist. In archaeological terms, we must recognize that there are at least two levels at which air-photographic information needs to be presented. In the first place we have a need for our own detailed and accurate maps for academic research. Equally we must recognize that we have increasingly a large amount of information relevant to planners. For their purposes, they do not need the detail. Their prime concern is with area, and it is therefore one of our jobs to prepare archaeological maps with zones blocked out in various ways to indicate an archaeological assessment of the archaeological importance of whole stretches of countryside.

In other words, it is our duty, increasingly using air photographs, to identify and grade for the benefit of others the horizontal archaeological dimension in the study of present land uses. The significance of the horizontal and not the vertical dimension is something that needs to be stressed in landscape studies because archaeologists, by their very training, have been taught to think vertically in terms of stratigraphy. The recent publication on the Upper Thames Gravels (Benson and Miles, 1974) is a good example of the sort of publication I have in mind, though perhaps even that goes into too much detail for planners' purposes. It could indeed be argued that the publication falls between two stools since, on the other hand, its authors will be the first to admit that the accuracy of their published maps is not sufficient for them to be used in making academic assessments of settlement detail. Nevertheless, it provides a basis for field research while, at the same time, demonstrating the extent and nature of the problem for planners and developers. Such a publication becomes an important interim statement in its own right and clearly points to the need for detailed vertical study, including excavation, to exploit the potential of the evidence displayed in historical, cultural, and chronological terms.

Such maps, whatever their purpose, must be directly related to the quality of the air photographs available, and the quality of the air photographs themselves is directly related to their envisaged function. Most of the air photographs with which we are familiar display to a lesser or greater extent the art of the air photographer, but in fact many poor air photographs contain pieces of valuable archaeological evidence. It is perfectly possible to have a poor air photograph which is archaeologically crucial. This is not the place to discuss the limitations of air photographic technique and their dependence upon as yet little understood vegetational and soil difference, but it must be re-emphasized that, whatever sort of air photograph is used for whatever sort of mapping purpose, the evidence being used is by its very nature extremely fragmentary. As takers and users of air photographs, as students of the landscape for whatever purpose, we are always dealing with minima. Whenever we are studying woodlands, blanket peat bogs, or areas of pastoral farming, we will have air photographic blanks, at least in terms of subterranean features. We must recognize this limitation on the use of our marvellous technique and recognize, for example that, impressive though our individual air photographs may be, there are whole areas both of landscape and of types of evidence which air photography cannot touch. Palaeo-environmental evidence, for example, arguably the most important type of evidence in relation to questions currently being asked, is not susceptible to air photography at all.

SOME IMPLICATIONS OF AIR PHOTOGRAPHY

Among the implications of the present air-photographic situation, one thing is quite clear: we can never, even if it were desirable, excavate all the evidence on and in the ground that we already know about. It therefore follows that over 95% of our knowledge is going to be based on fieldwork and air photography rather than upon the results of excavation. This is going to lead to a reappraisal of the nature of archaeology itself and will certainly affect the future direction of research. At the moment, despite the efforts of various individuals, archaeology as taught is to a very large extent based upon a relatively small number of, on the whole, inadequately executed excavations carried out for a large number of diverse reasons. In addition, it leans heavily upon numerous typological studies. As archaeology adjusts to a situation in which increasingly our understanding of the past adjusts itself to the availability of palaeo-environmental evidence, so simultaneously we will have to fit this understanding into a framework deriving from non-excavational sources, e.g. air photographs.

The sheer quantity of evidence raises a further point: not only must we accept that we can never excavate anything but a small fraction of that which has been located, but we must also ask ourselves whether we can even hope to record everything. Once we ask such a question, not only are we toying with the limitations of the discipline itself but we are verging on archaeologico-political questions relating to Ancient Monuments legislation and the functions of the Ordnance Survey and the Royal Commissions. Since in a sense the Ordnance Survey is *sub judice* from the archaeological point of view at the moment, I will forebear to comment except to say that, sadly, current indications are that it has given up attempting to cope with what have hitherto been regarded as its archaeological obligations. The question is extremely relevant, however, to the functions and indeed the very existence of the Royal Commissions on Historical and/or Ancient Monuments. These were originally set up in 1908–10 "to make an Inventory of the Ancient and Historical Monuments and Constructions connected with or illustrative of the contemporary culture, civilisation, and conditions of life of the people in England [Scotland, Wales and Monmouthshire] from the earliest times [to the year 1714], and to specify those which seem most worthy of preservation". This was based on the belief, existing up to the present, that the attainment of a complete national record of monuments on a County basis is not only desirable but is also achievable. This fundamental point must

now be questioned: is it really possible to achieve a comprehensive national record? It is no criticism of RCHM to ask this question but it does seem to me realistic to ask it at a time when we are very carefully considering our national archaeological resources as a whole in relation to the major challenges which we must meet in the last quarter of this century. My own view is that, far from this line of argument even hinting that the Royal Commissions should be disbanded, there should actually be more Salisbury/York/Cambridge-type offices regionally situated throughout the country so that field recording to the accustomed Commission standards may be speeded up and more evenly displayed across the face of our landscape.

Furthermore such a move would restore to the Commissions an up-dated version of the social function in the minds of their Edwardian promoters (Earthworks Committee Reports, 1901 onwards). In practice it would lead to the development of more fieldworkers and the more widespread diffusion of their influence in parts of the country where a tradition of and skills in field archaeology have not developed. Clearly any such expansion poses problems of finance and personnel, but my belief is that if we get our organization right the rest, and the results, will follow.

One other political implication relates to the Ancient Monuments Acts, like the OS also under active consideration. Out of some 10,000 monuments Scheduled under existing legislation, about 250 are flat sites revealed by air photography. In other words, the most powerful tool that this century has produced for the exploration and elucidation of the archaeology in our landscape has so far been responsible for something like 5% of the officially existing (for that is what Scheduling means) archaeological sites in this country. Clearly there is an imbalance here, a failure of official provision to march with new circumstances, and new legislation must take into account the fact that the archaeological best in 1975 is not what our Victorian predecessors conceived it to be in drafting their first and admirable Act nearly a century ago (Kains-Jackson, 1880). There ought also to be some serious discussion, in the light of modern air-photographic results, of the *desiderata* for permanent preservation, that is for a site acquiring the status of a Guardianship monument under present legislation.

By and large, this accolade has so far been accorded to visible and monumental sites in stone, often with an aesthetic and/or historical significance. An archaeologically important site can, of course, have all of those four qualities, but essentially they are irrelevant to its archaeological significance in the sense of being a source of cultural information. Many of Major Allen's and Professor St Joseph's best crop-mark photographs illustrate the point exactly: a complex like that near Yelford or south–east of Langford, Oxon. (Benson & Miles, 1974, Maps 4, 19, and Pls. 1, 2, and 4), is not visible to the visitor at ground-level and is distinctly lacking in monumental characteristics for the tourist and the teacher, nor is the place it occupies particularly satisfying to the senses, aesthetic or historical. Yet both areas, and many another like them, are clearly of archaeological interest just as they appear and, beyond that, are of a high but unknown potential as a reservoir of knowledge. The permanent preservation of such sites, by public purchase and the cessation of cultivation, is as important a part of an informed preservation policy as the acquisition of more abbeys and priories. Indeed, it could be argued to be more important in the sense that we know less about what such sites represent than we do about medieval religious life. While it would be appropriate to see a practical lead in such matters coming from central government, developing the splendid initiative demonstrated by the 1973 purchase of the many 'blank' fields containing buried *Viroconium*, the preservation of such site-complexes could well be a major contribution to the historic environment to be made by the new (1974) local authorities. Once they appreciate the wealth of archaeology in the landscape, surely they can be persuaded that there is no difference in principle between setting aside an apparently flat field known to contain stone walls and one containing the much subtler evidence of timber structures. There would also seem to be here an opportunity for a positive and enlightened purchasing policy by the National Trust, which must already be the largest archaeological landowner in the country if we are reading the implications of air photography aright.

THE FUTURE OF AERIAL ARCHAEOLOGY

Air photography is so important for the future of archaeology that a conscious and planned national and international programme must be formulated and carried out over the next decade. With the cost of flying escalating to give a very practical urgency for rationalization and research to replace much that is inadequate in the present situation, the case for co-ordination, communication, and experiment is considerably strengthened. On the technical side, question-orientated photographic studies exploring the practical values of infra-red, thermal, satellite, and other remote-sensing recording processes should be undertaken systematically, together with projects to assess a whole range of variables from camera/subject relationships to image enhancement. As has been acutely remarked by Pickering (1974), "Interest in the information [air photographs] provided has preceded an understanding of the processes that produce the evidence": so much more field study on the ground is also needed.

Carefully controlled land/air research and experiment investigating the soil, weather, and crop conditions, as well as the archaeological nature of features recorded, need to be developed in differing localities as part of a national, broad-based scientific enquiry into the little-understood phenomena of crop marks. The deliberate planting of selected crops on known archaeological features is a necessity rather than an ideal in these circumstances, and certainly the deliberate execution of archaeological excavations to examine features on air photographs (rather than air photographs merely being an aid to excavation) should become a standard practice. Forty years ago, one of the reasons for excavating Little Woodbury was precisely to see what was producing the features on the air photograph, and before that, Woodhenge itself emerged for a similar reason (Bersu, 1938; Cunnington, 1929). Now that our view is of the landscape and its relationships rather than of single sites, and now that our air-photographic record is so infinitely more complex, the deliberate pursuance of such an excavation policy is essential to build up the experience on which to base the interpretations of so much of the primary data in British archaeology. For it is the photographs themselves which in a very real sense, certainly as far as crop marks are concerned, often are the primary evidence. Anyone who has made a return

sortie for a better view of a previously recorded site only to find that it has disappeared will appreciate that, as presumably will the excavator who finds 'nothing' where a feature shows on the photograph (cf. Bowen above, p. 110). On the other hand, investigations are also needed to demonstrate which features do not show up in various circumstances, and, if possible, why, especially on complex air-photographic sites which prove on excavation, as at Mucking, to be even more complex than the camera has recorded (Jones *et al.*, 1968).

Another relationship worth investigating, bringing a third element into the assessment, is the correlation between artefact distribution on the ground, the air photographic features, and the excavated structures. It is often assumed that constant cultivation spreads artefact concentrations but this needs testing rigorously since, if it is not so, surface material can be more reliably used in interpreting crop-mark features—an important point since it will never be possible to excavate every known 'site' (see above, p. 156). Meanwhile, scarce resources have to be applied in the field and laboratory in rescuing evidence constantly under threat. It is impossible to see how the right decisions can be made at the moment except by chance, even though the decision-makers are acting on the best available information. 'Twas ever thus, but significantly different now is the fact that we can not only guess that there is a lot more information to be brought to bear but, gallingly, we also know that much of it has already been obtained. It cannot, however, be processed for use, for want of a few thousand pounds per annum. Yet never has archaeology and, as important, a range of other land-based responsibilities to which archaeology is contributory—never has it been so important to circulate that information. The air-photographic results of the last two decades are a direct function of modern society's use of its own environment; those results should be informing management now as well as the long-term planning which will determine the nature and interpretation of the historic environment bequeathed to the twenty-first century. How frustrating, and silly, it will be if we arrive at AD 2000 with all that information still carefully preserved but unused, an archive of a lost opportunity.

REFERENCES

Benson, D., & Miles, D. (1974). *The Upper Thames Valley: an archaeological survey of the river gravels* (Oxfordshire Archaeological Unit). Oxford.

Beresford, M. W., & St Joseph, J. K. S. (1958). *Medieval England: an aerial survey*. Cambridge.

Bersu, G. (1938). The Excavations at Woodbury, Wiltshire, during 1938. *Proc. Prehist. Soc.*, **4**, 308–313.

Crawford, O. G. S., & Keiller, A. (1928). *Wessex from the Air*. Oxford.

Cunnington, M. E. (1929). *Woodhenge*. Devizes.

Dickinson, G. C. (1969). *Maps and Air Photographs*. London.

Earthworks Committee (1901–). *Annual Reports* of the Committee on Ancient Earthworks and Fortified Enclosures (Congress of Archaeological Societies).

War Office (1958). *Manual of Map Reading, Air Photo Reading and Field Sketching*: part II, *Air Photo Reading*. HMSO, London.

Jones, M. U., *et al.* (1968). Crop-mark Sites at Mucking, Essex. *Antiq. J.*, **48**, 210–30.

Kains-Jackson, C. P. (1880). *Our Ancient Monuments and the Land Around Them.* London.

Minshull, R. (1968). *Human Geography from the Air.* London.

Pickering, J. (1974). Aerial Reconnaissances 1974, Rpt. No. 7 (privately circulated).

Williams-Freeman, J. P. (1915). *An Introduction to Field Archaeology as illustrated by Hampshire.* London.